Women Education, Employment and Gender Discrimination

Women Education, Employment and Gender Discrimination

Pragya Singh

MOHIT PUBLICATIONS
New Delhi - 110002 (India)

First Published : 2010

ISBN : 978-81-7445-523-9

Published by :
MOHIT PUBLICATIONS
4675/21, Ansari Road, Daryaganj-110002
Phone : 23255141; Fax. : 23284126

PRINTED IN INDIA

Published by Sangita Goel for Mohit Publications, New Delhi-02, Typeset by Abhijeet Typesetters and Printed at Nav Prabhat Printing Press Delhi.

Preface

The main purpose of this book is to review the evidence available from countries as well as other studies at the regional and global level on women and their involvement in the so called informal sector, and the implications for poverty. There is indeed a vast literature pertaining to women and the informal sector. This review draws upon this literature as well as other published and unpublished empirical research and data sources from countries, covering the period after 1970 but mostly the 1980s and early 1990s. The quality and coverage of data on which this review is based vary considerably, which implies that the conclusions emerging from the review needs to be interpreted with caution. Some of the data are not comparable over time, even for the same country because of differences in coverage, concepts and measurement. These pitfalls in data also indicate the areas where the data base could be further strengthened to improve the analyses, and our understanding of the issues pertaining to gender, informality, education, employment and poverty. The analysis presented here, though extensive, should be considered as exploratory, since the knowledge on the subject is still in a process of evolution. As the work on this review proceeded it became clear that the analytical framework underlying it may have broader relevance to the broader issue of women and development. The scope of the review is however limited owing to time and resource constraints. The conclusions presented here should be considered as interim, pending further research based on more reliable data. Thus it would appear that there is scope for further improvement. The conclusions are mainly in the form of issues, intended to stimulate further thinking.

This review does not go into the question of interventions that are currently being undertaken worldwide on behalf of women. Nor does it go into related issues such as women's organisations and their role in the informal sector. But the review however does raise a number of questions for further research. In this sense the review should be viewed as contributing to the debate on gender, informality and poverty in developing countries.

—*Author*

Contents

1

Gender Inequality in Education and Employment

This chapter will focus on how and why education is the key to gender equality and to larger employment opportunities for women. The paper will take a look at education opportunities for women and the reasons for the inherent gender bias in many societies. It will explore links between lack of education and its impact on women's employment avenues. Taking a look at some of the trends, and more relevantly at some success stories, it will explore options that could provide women better avenues for education and employment.

"Importantly, the session would be a debate and discussion from a civil society/NGO and development perspective.

"Discussion points have been woven into each section of the paper as suggested points for group discussions in the session

INTRODUCTION

There is little denying the fact that investing in human capital is one of the most effective means of reducing poverty and encouraging sustainable development. Yet, women in developing countries usually receive less education than men. More so, women in general enjoy far less employment opportunities than men the world over.

Any claims and efforts then, to remove poverty, can show results only if they address the issue of gender inequality. In recent decades, there have been large gains, no doubt on comparable levels, in basic rights and opportunities, in life expectancy and enrolment ratios for women. But despite these gains, the stark reality has not changed. There still are large gender disparities in basic human rights, resources, and economic opportunity, and in political rights- the world over.

In South Asia, women have only half as many years of schooling as men. In much of Sub-Saharan Africa women obtain land rights, chiefly through their husbands as long as the marriage endures and women account for only ten percent of seats in Parliaments worldwide.

So until nations are able to address this issue of gender inequality and resolve it, the vicious cycle of poverty will continue to pervade. This is because poverty leads to and aggravates gender discrimination - it is in the poorer sections and nations that instances of gender biases and inequality are more evident.

Women and girls who are at the bottom of the social, economic and political ladder in these societies, get even lesser opportunities to have a command over productive resources such as land or credit. Access to the means to influence the development process is a rare and difficult possibility.

And yet, by the same logic, gender discrimination hinders development. So while denial of basic rights (be it education, employment or health care for women) is detrimental to women, this denial, ultimately also harms the society, the nations at large too, by hampering development.

There are several social and economic indicators to support this point. For instance, reports say that if girls and boys in Sub-Saharan Africa get equal schooling, child mortality could be lowered by as much as 25 per cent.

Clearly, then gender gaps that are widespread in access to basic rights, access to and control of resources, in economic opportunities and also in power and political voice are an impediment to development. The only solution to this is gender equality, which strengthens a country's ability to grow, to reduce poverty and provide its people - men, women and children - a better life. The issue of gender equality then, needs to be at the core of development policies- both in national and international arenas.

Just because gender inequality is inextricably linked to societal norms, religion or cultural traditions, it should not be either a deterrent or an excuse to gender sensitive development planning.

GENDER BIAS IN EDUCATION

Education is widely recognized as the gateway to economic security and opportunity- particularly for girls and women.

World figures in literacy relate a sorry tale. Of the 130 million 6-11 year-old children not in school - a majority - 60 percent are girls. The figures only go to show how in most regions of the world, specially the developing societies, gender bias impinges on girls' education.

The foremost factor limiting female education is poverty. Economics plays a key role when it comes to coping with directs costs such as tuition fees, cost of textbooks, uniforms, transportation and other expenses. Wherever, especially in families with many children, these costs exceed the income of the family, girls are the first to be denied schooling.

All this despite the fact that educating girls is one of the best investments a society can make. An educated woman has the skills, the self-confidence and the information she needs to become a better parent, worker and citizen.

Girls' lack of access to education isn't always related to scarcity of places in schools. It also emerges from expectations, attitudes and biases in communities and families. Economic costs, social traditions, and religious and cultural beliefs limit girls' educational opportunities.

Whatever the underlying reason(s), having large number of girls outside the formal schooling system brings developmental challenges to both current and future generations. Individuals, families, communities and nations are affected. Inability to read, write and calculate complicates a girl's efforts to engage in both market-focused production and household activities as effectively and efficiently possible. This affects her family's welfare and diminishes her potential contribution to the development of the household, local and national economy.

Despite reported progress, there is still a persistent gap between women and men's access to education. Combating the high rate of illiteracy among women and girls remains an urgent global need. According to the UNESCO Institute of Statistics, it is now estimated that two-thirds of the world's 875 million illiterate adults are women.

In Southern Asia, nearly three in five women are illiterate and it is estimated that half of all women in Africa and in the Arab region are still illiterate. However, gender disparities and literacy rates are less marked among young adults. There is now, little or no gender difference in the literacy rates of 15-24 year olds in several regions of the world including Europe, North America, Latin America and the Caribbean and the Eastern Asia and Oceania. Over the past 20 years, significant progress has been made with regard to higher education. It is of particular interest that in countries where tertiary education has expanded significantly, women's school enrolment has increased more than men's.

According to a fact Sheet on Review and Appraisal of the Implementation of the Beijing Platform for Action - report of the secretary general, in Namibia, 50 per cent more women are enrolled in higher education than men; Libya reports that more women go abroad for higher education than men; in Canada, New Zealand, the United States, and many European as well as some Latin American and Caribbean countries, women's enrolment in tertiary education has reached more than 50 per cent. But this is not all and enough to ensure that women get equal employment opportunities.

IMPACT OF EDUCATION ON EMPLOYMENT OPPORTUNITIES

Thanks to the fight for women's rights, increasing participation of women in the job market and to the right to vote, women have emerged from the strictly private sphere to which they were formerly restricted. Women have broken the implicit social contract that for more than hundreds of years confined them to home, child rearing, household tasks and fieldwork, while men worked outside the home.

In Asia, more and more young women have been joining the official workforce in recent years and are experiencing some of the benefits - financial independence, higher status and lower fertility rate through delaying the age of marriage. Children also benefit because women usually devote more of their income to the family's welfare compared to men.

However, in the context of the developing world, lack of education has forced many women into the risky "informal" economy as street traders, domestic servants, home workers and seasonal laborers.

This in turn reflects a continuing belief that there is little benefit in educating a girl when she could be working in the market place or fields. Boys are affected by this thinking, too, though not to the same extent.Although economically productive to society, once again, women's work, if they get the opportunity at all, is rarely recognized in official statistics and the women often get no protection from unions or employment legislation Just as women's domestic work is undervalued, so are their skills in the world of employment.

Most are concentrated in the poorly-paid, low-skilled "women's" sectors of the economy like Free Trade Zones set up in many developing countries to attract foreign companies. Exhausting 18-hour days in unsafe and unhealthy conditions are the norm, along with sexual harassment and lack of job security.

Gender Stereotyping

This stereotyping continues to prevail in technical and professional fields. Even where women have open access to all professions, they overwhelmingly opt for traditionally female occupations.The gap separating men and women in the job market remains wide in many countries, whether in the North or the

South. With marginal variables between most countries, women have a lower employment rate, are unemployed longer, are paid less and have less secure jobs. Young women, particularly pay the price of job market flexibility. They suffer double discrimination.

First for being young, in the difficult phase of transition between training and working life, in an age group that has, on an average, twice the jobless rate or older workers and are at the mercy of employers who exploit them under the pretext of enabling them to acquire professional experience.

Secondly they are discriminated against for being women and are more likely to be offered low paying or low status jobs. Discrimination is still very much in evidence and education and training policies specially targeting young women are needed to restore a balance.

Although young women are increasingly choosing typically 'male' professions, they remain over-represented in traditionally female jobs, such as secretaries, nurses, and under represented in jobs with responsibility and the professions.

In the new and upcoming sectors too, there is an imbalance in the representation of men and women. An instance is ICTs where, despite their rapid growth, where women generally occupy positions towards the bottom of hierarchy. And even in female dominated sectors like health, women work as nurses, but a large majority of hospital directors and department heads are men.

The Indian Experience

India represents a picture of contrasts when it comes to education and employment opportunities for girls. Cultural, social and economic factors still prevent girls from getting education opportunities so the question of equality is still a mirage.

However, the rural and the urban areas present a contrast. In the rural areas the girl child is made to perform household and agricultural chores. This is one of the many factors limiting girls' education. Cleaning the house, preparing the food, looking after their siblings, the elderly and the sick, grazing the cattle and collecting firewood are some of the key tasks they have to perform.

Households are therefore reluctant to spare them for schooling. Physical safety of the girls, especially when they have to travel a long distance to school and fear of sexual harassment are other reasons that impede girls' education.

In the urban areas, however, there is a discernible difference in the opportunities that girls get for education and employment. Though the figures for girls would still be low as compared to boys, what is heartening to see is that whenever given the opportunity, girls have excelled more than boys.

For instance, in the Central Board of Secondary Examinations for grades 10 and 12, which are at an All India level, girls have for over a decade now, bagged all the top positions and secured a higher over all percentage compared to boys. In employment opportunities too, women in India today have stormed all male bastions.

Be it piloting aircraft, heading multi-national corporations, holding top bureaucratic positions, leading industrial houses, making a mark as photographers, filmmakers, chefs, engineers and even as train and lorry drivers, women have made it to all hitherto considered male bastions in India.

However, this is not reason enough for cheer. For the number of girls and women who have been left out of education and employment opportunities, still far outweighs those who have got them. And what needs to change this scenario, is not just governmental efforts but a change in societal norms, in cultural and traditional biases and in general mindsets of people. And in this the media, the civil society, and the youth, the women and girls have a lot to contribute.

Need to Break the Mould

What we need today are trends where girls are able not only to break out of the culturally determined patterns of employment but also to offer advise about career possibilities that look beyond the traditional pale of jobs.

In many countries, special initiatives have been taken to direct girls to non-traditional fields of study. In Austria, special computer and Internet courses have been offered to increase the number of girls enrolled in technical courses. In India can such efforts be initiated for the girls and women? Perhaps yes. And here I would like to point attention to some efforts where women are being trained for IT jobs.

I would like to mention here briefly some projects that have shown that women too can harness the potential of the ICTs.

The M. S. Swaminathan Research Foundation, MSSRF, in Chennai, India has piloted a path-breaking project, in the tiny coastal state of Pondicherry. The project, being run by the foundations Rural Technology Centre, has helped local women become computer-literate and in the process, empowered them. The programme has taught them how to download the latest weather reports from the US Oceanographic department on the Net. The women broadcast these reports on the public address system - information that is often crucial to their husbands out fishing on the high seas. They have earned respect from the community that once looked down upon them. Encouraged by this, the women have also started accessing information on issues crucial to them - reproductive health, basic education and so on. And this is just the beginning.

In another effort, Nari Raksha Samiti (NRS), an Indian social welfare organisation devoted to improving the lives of poor and destitute women. Founded fifty years ago to help women in distress, NRS focuses on promoting the safety and security of women, family welfare, employment, health, and training in job-oriented professions. The Samiti has twenty centres headed by volunteers.

Under the leadership of Vandana Sharma, NRS has begun using twenty-first century technology to address the wrongs that result from the age-old traditions associated with the dowry system. Vandana recognized the impact that computers are having on the changing Indian economy and established a small computer education centre in the NRS building.

Vandana and the NRS volunteers are now training 250 young women -- sixty of whom are dowry victims and have a history of harassment and exploitation -- in basic computer literacy as well as office software such as MS Excel, Word, and Power Point. This IT training program joins training programs in tailoring, interior decoration, cooking, food preservation, and weaving in providing needy women with the job skills necessary to break out of the cycle of poverty and abuse which affects so many women in India.

The NRS computer centres not only provide job training, but have also allowed NRS to establish an online complaint system for solving dowry and family dispute issues. Women can confidentially lodge complaints through the system and receive assistance from NRS and police and government authorities. NRS has been successful in training more than four hundred dowry victims and poor women in the community.

2

Strategies to Meet Women's Needs

Women confront many obstacles to better lives. Women need change in many areas simultaneously. Thus the agenda for policies to give women more opportunities must be broad. In addition to assuring women's ability to control their own fertility, important elements include efforts to:

Improve Health: In the nations with the best health care, the life expectancy of women is 10% longer than that of men. In developing countries, however, women's life expectancy is closer to or shorter than men's. This occurs because women receive less than their fair share of health care and food, often beginning in childhood. As adults, many women do not get the food and health care needed for healthy childbearing.

Encourage Education: Over the last 20 years more and more girls have been going to school, but boys still get more education than girls. An estimated two-thirds of the 300 million children without access to education are girls. Two-thirds of the 960 million nonliterate adults are women.

Ensure Job Opportunities and Fair Pay: Most women work long and hard, and they earn less for it than men do. Even in developed countries, for example, women earn 75% or less of what men earn. Much of women's work is unpaid. Women's unpaid household labor accounts for about one-third of the world's economic production. When unpaid agricultural work and housework are considered along with wage labor, women work more hours than men.

Guarantee Legal Protection: Legal codes often sanction inequality between husband and wife. They may allow marriage of very young women, marriage without the woman's consent, unequal ownership and control over family assets including land and other property, unequal inheritance rights, and unequal access to divorce and to support after divorce. In many cases the law does not recognize women as adults with the same capacities and right to make decisions as their husbands. Laws that do protect women's rights often are not enforced.

Permit access to reproductive health care. The International Planned Parenthood Federation (IPPF) has reported that 46 of 94 surveyed countries require spousal consent for contraception, abortion, or voluntary sterilization-services used primarily or exclusively by women. Worldwide, 54 countries require a woman to obtain her husband's approval before voluntary sterilization, but only 20 of these countries also require a man to have his wife's approval. Young women and unmarried women often have little or no access to reproductive health services. Yet surveys in eight sub-Saharan countries, for example, find that 20% to 47% of adolescent women become pregnant before marriage. Prevent violence against women. Many women live every day in fear of violence, often from their husbands. In surveys in Chile, Colombia, Kenya, India, Mexico, Pakistan, Papua New Guinea, San Salvador, South Korea, and Thailand, 40% to 99% of women reported physical abuse by their husbands. Most of these women have no choice but to live with this abuse and fear. Leaving the marriage is often not a realistic option when women, denied education, jobs, and inheritance rights, are economically dependent on their husbands.

Unwanted sexual intercourse is a major form of violence against women. In a US national sample survey, 13% of women reported that they had been raped at some time in their lives, not counting marital rape. This amounts to one woman raped every minute. Half of these women were under age 18 when raped, and 75% knew the man who raped them. Detailed data on rape are not available from developing countries.

Fear of desertion or violence prevents women from acting in their own best interests. For example, in Egypt many women do not seek care for gynecological problems such as vaginal discharge or fistula because they fear that their husbands will divorce them for spending time and money on their own health. Threats of violence prevent some women even from participating in development projects.

Increase respect for women. Since most societies value females less than males, many women grow up believing that they are inferior to males. Such perceptions are difficult to change. For example, China has promoted equal roles and rights for women for 40 years. Still, 30% of Chinese women surveyed in 1990 thought that men are born to be more important than women, and 33% agreed that women should hold back so that they are not more successful than their husbands.

PROGRAMS TO IMPROVE WOMEN'S LIVES

Programs to help women often focus on their economic or legal position. Women themselves have started many of these programs. For example, women in India formed the Self-Employed Women's Association (SEWA) in 1972 and the Working Women's Forum (WWF) in 1977 to change local ordinances that interfered with their ability to work as market traders. Both groups broadened their agendas as members began to request help with health, education, and other needs. In Tunisia in the 1970s President Habib Bourguiba led the government to legislate better legal protection of women. In Bangladesh university professor Mohammed Yunus convinced the Grameen Bank, a private bank, to give poor women small loans.

Development planners have developed two broad approaches to assessing women's needs and designing programs to address them:

- The status of women approach compares the positions of women and men in a society or cross-nationally. After identifying the areas in which women are disadvantaged, planners design programs to address the problems.
- The empowerment of women approach aims to help women gain more control of their lives. This approach often begins with women identifying and prioritizing their own needs. Program organizers then help women to design programs that meet those needs.

Both approaches have advantages. Focusing on objective measures of women's status documents the problem for top-level policy-makers and helps motivate their support for policy changes. The United Nations has based its efforts to eliminate discrimination against women on status measures such as years of education and hourly wages. The empowerment approach may bring faster results for individual women, although usually on a smaller scale. Involving women in solving their own problems builds their skills and self-confidence and finds solutions that are locally appropriate.

Using both approaches could speed improvements for women, and in practice the two approaches are not always distinct. Program organizers can use the status-of-women approach to influence policy nationally and to evaluate its impact and at the same time can use community-based empowerment programs to begin change locally. Some of the most successful community programs at first address a need that women clearly recognize, such as the need for income, and then build skills that women can use in many areas of life.

Women's advocates are asking that development plans pay more attention to the effects of planned changes on women's lives. Some development plans have required, for example, male labor migration or female volunteer labor, which place additional burdens on women. "Gender planning," as the approach is called, considers the impact of a proposed program on women, men, and their relationship. Its goals are to ensure that development programs do not inadvertently harm the lives of men or women and to see that women's situation is improved.

A BETTER LIFE

"The main thing that makes the times different, I think, is the control women have over the number of children in a family. A family can be planned now; it can live a better life. Women have more facilities for everything because of this. I began to take contraceptives when the last child was eight months old. I take the pill."

> "...we were very poor when I was a child. We were six children, and my father didn't earn much. That is why I want just two or three children. I don't want my children

[two daughters] to grow up like me-without an education. I feel very ashamed and bad about not having any education. I want my children to go to school and learn many, many things.... I want them to be independent and proud of themselves." -19-year-old Mexican woman using contraception without her husband's knowledge.

SON PREFERENCE, DAUGHTER NEGLECT

In some countries parents tend to prefer sons and to treat them better than daughters. Boys sometimes get more to eat and more medical care, while girls are slighted in education and jobs and in some cases are neglected, abused, and even killed. While the majority of studies on son preference come from countries in South Asia and North Africa, where son preference is believed to be strongest, son preference appears to exist to some degree in other regions of the world as well. The preference for sons is both a symptom and a cause of limited opportunities for women.

Extent of Son Preference

A common index of preference for sons comes from survey responses: the ratio of the number of parents who say that they prefer their next child to be male to the number who prefer their next child to be female. A ratio also can be derived from survey responses about desire for additional children among women with different numbers of living daughters and sons. Among countries surveyed, those with strong preference for sons-indices of 1.6 or above-are Bangladesh, Jordan, Nepal, Pakistan, South Korea, and Syria. Moderate preference for sons (indices of 1.2 to 1.5) has been documented in many other countries, including the Dominican Republic, Egypt, Mexico, Senegal, Sudan, Turkey, Nigeria, Tunisia, and Yemen. Some countries, such as Colombia, Ghana, and Indonesia, show no preference, and two-Jamaica and Venezuela-show a slight preference for daughters. In most countries parents desire at least one daughter as well as sons.

Reasons for Son Preference

Why do many parents favor boys? Often the reasons are both economic and cultural.

Economic Security: In many developing countries sons are their parents' only source of security in old age. Particularly where women have little economic independence or cannot inherit property, sons are insurance for a mother against the loss of her husband's support due to death or desertion. Where women have few opportunities to earn income, investing household resources in female children, who will marry and leave the family, is likely to have little pay-off, and so poor families tend to invest what little they have in sons. In cultures with dowry systems, such as India's, daughters are more expensive to marry off than sons.

Cultural Factors: In many countries kinship systems, tradition, and religion value males over females. In parts of Bangladesh, China, Egypt, India, and Tanzania, for example, traditional patrilineal kinship systems require women to marry out of their families of origin and then not to provide financial or even emotional support to their own parents.

In both Hindu and Confucian traditions, practiced throughout Asia, only sons can pray for and release the souls of dead parents, and only males can perform birth, death, and marriage rituals.

Effects of Son Preference on Female Children

Although females are thought to be genetically more resistant to respiratory and other infectious diseases than males and more likely to survive infancy, in some developing countries this advantage rapidly disappears as female babies grow up. Females are more likely than males to die in early childhood (ages 1 to 4), particularly in South Asia, the Near East, and North Africa. Poorer nutrition and health care are important reasons.

Nutrition: In some places boys get more and better food than girls. Breast-feeding and weaning practices also seem to favor boys in some countries. In the Indian state of Punjab, for example, boys from both wealthy and poor households are better nourished than girls. An analysis of DHS data from 18 countries, however, found few significant differences in the nutritional status of boys and girls.

Medical Care: Girls are sick as often as boys, but boys sometimes receive more treatment and more medicine. For example, boys were seen 66% more often than girls at a diarrhea treatment center in Bangladesh even though the center provided free ambulance transport and treatment.

Parents bought drugs and sought medical care three times more often for boys than for girls. Girls often receive less preventive health care, as well. Studies in Latin America and India show that girls often are immunized later than boys or not at all.

Female Infanticide: Some unwanted female children are killed or abandoned soon after birth. It is not clear how common or widespread the practice is, but some demographers have long suspected its existence. They base their conclusions largely on reported sex ratios at birth. Others argue that underreporting explains the discrepancy. In China, where sex ratios show that 5% of all infant girls born are unaccounted for, some observers suspect that female infanticide accounts for at least some of these missing girls, although informal adoptions, sending girls to faraway relatives, or raising the girls covertly probably explain most of the cases.

Abortion of female fetuses. Selective abortion of female fetuses reportedly is widespread in such Asian countries as China, India, and South Korea. Increasing use of prenatal ultrasound and amniocentesis procedures, which make selective abortion possible by revealing the sex of a fetus, may be contributing to a growing gap in the number of males and females born in some countries. Although governments in China, South Korea, and three Indian states have banned prenatal gender tests to prevent selective abortions, illegal tests are available, and females are more often aborted than males.

Son Preference, Fertility, and Contraceptive Use

Does a preference for sons result in higher fertility? Do more couples adopt family planning after having a son than after having a daughter? The answers may depend on current fertility levels. In general, where most couples have large families, son preference has little impact on fertility levels because most couples will have at least one son by biological chance. As contraceptive use becomes more widespread and average family size decreases, however, in some countries the desire to have at least one son begins to affect fertility decisions: Trying for a son, many couples have more children than they would otherwise.

A recent study in Matlab, Bangladesh, indicates that son preference can have a strong effect on contraceptive use and fertility. In Matlab, where intensive family planning services are available, contraceptive prevalence now tops 50%, and couples average four children, researchers calculated that eliminating preference for sons would increase contraceptive use by 10% and continuation rates by 15%. These increases would avert nearly one birth for every two couples.

What can be Done?

Attempts to improve the position of girls in society often focus on economics. Increasing economic opportunities for women and raising the value of women's labor increases the likelihood that parents will see daughters as economic assets and not as liabilities. Also, increasing girls' education may increase their income-earning potential and, thus, their economic value to their parents. Other recommendations include better access to food and medical care so that parents will not have to choose between male and female children in allocating household resources.

Also, better access to pension plans and other forms of old-age security that do not depend on children would relieve some of the pressure to have sons. While specific measures can help, some researchers insist that only far-reaching improvements in the cultural, social, legal, and economic position of women will improve the well-being of female children.

CHANGES IN WOMEN'S LIVES

How do women's lives differ between countries where contraceptive use is common and countries where it is rare? The Demographic and Health Surveys (DHS) are one source of information. Contraceptive prevalence varies widely among surveyed countries, from over 60% in 4 of 30 countries to 5% or lower in 3 countries. The surveys reveal that in countries where contraceptive use is widespread, women:

- Are older when they have their first child,

- Complete their childbearing earlier,
- Spend fewer years pregnant, and
- Spend fewer years with young children in the household.

Age at First and Last Births

Where total contraceptive use is above 40% (the average for use of modern methods in developing countries), women ages 25 to 29 at the time of the surveys first gave birth on average about three years later than in countries where contraceptive use is below the average. Median age at first birth in the 30 countries from about 18 years in Niger and Uganda to close to 25 years in Morocco, Sri Lanka, and Tunisia.

First births come soon after marriage in most countries. Still, on average women in the countries with higher contraceptive prevalence first give birth more than two years after marriage, while women in countries with lower than average prevalence give birth about a year and a half after marriage.

Last births come sooner in countries where contraceptive use is above average levels. Where contraceptive use exceeds 40%, most women had their last births in their early thirties, while in countries with lower levels of contraceptive use, women last gave birth in their late thirties. Age at last birth for women ages 40 to 49 at the time of the survey, the age group most likely to have completed childbearing. This analysis may underestimate the impact of contraceptive use on average age at last birth, because women in this age group are the least likely to have been affected by recent rises in the use of contraception in many countries.

The median age at last birth ranges from 31 years in a few Caribbean countries where contraceptive use is widespread to 38 or 39 years in several African countries where there is little use of contraception. Of course, other factors besides contraceptive use help to determine the age at last birth, including age-related sterility, divorce, widowhood, and reduced coital frequency at older ages.

The number of years that women can expect to live after the birth of their last child varies tremendously. This difference reflects both a woman's age at the birth of her last child and her life expectancy. Life expectancy tends to be longer in the more developed countries, where also age at last birth is lower. In all surveyed countries where contraceptive prevalence is above 40% except Peru, a woman still has more than half of her life ahead of her when she last gives birth. In contrast, in most countries where contraceptive prevalence is below 40%, women average fewer years of life after their last birth than before it.

Duration of the Childbearing Years

Where the level of contraceptive use is above average, women devote less of their lives to childbearing and child-raising. Also, within countries the length of the childbearing period has decreased as contraceptive use has spread.

Differences Across Countries: The interval between average ages at first and last births among women ages 40 to 49 ranges from just 11 years in Trinidad and Tobago and in Thailand, where contraception is widely used, to nearly twice as long in Zambia and Senegal, where contraception is little used. In Trinidad and Tobago women ages 40 to 49 averaged four children.

The first child was born when the mother was 20 years old, and the last, when she was 31. In contrast, in Zambia women ages 40 to 49 had given birth to an average of seven children. The first was born when the mother was 18, and the last, when she was 38. Because contraceptive use is increasing in nearly every country, the childbearing years probably will be shorter for women who are now in their 20s or 30s.

By comparison, US women have fewer children over a shorter period of time. In the US, where about three-quarters of married women use contraception, those born between 1940 and 1949-and thus about the same age as women ages 40 to 49 in DHS surveys-married at a median age of 20.5 years. They first gave birth a little over a year after marriage and had their last child at age 30. They gave birth to an average of 2.8 children over the course of approximately eight years, and their life expectancy at the time of their last birth was 47.5 more years.

Both the number of children that women have and the spacing of their births influence the number of years that mothers spend with young children. In countries where use of contraception is widespread, women spend an average of 14 years with at least one of their children under the age of six. Where contraceptive prevalence is low, women have young children for an average of 20 years.

Changes over time. Women's childbearing patterns have changed as contraceptive prevalence has risen. In 16 countries at least two comparable surveys have been conducted since the 1970s.

Where contraceptive use has increased most, the childbearing period has decreased most. Also, in all 16 countries the time that women had a child under age six in the household decreased, but in some countries the decline was small.

The changes are most obvious in the five countries where three surveys have been taken. For example, in Morocco, where the level of contraceptive use more than doubled between 1979-80 and 1992, women's average childbearing period decreased by almost two years.

The number of years spent with a child under age six fell by almost three years. In the Java-Bali region of Indonesia, contraceptive prevalence rose from 26% to 53% between 1976 and 1991. Over the same period the childbearing period decreased by 3.5 years, and the amount of time spent with at least one young child at home declined by five years. Age at last birth declined substantially in Colombia, the Dominican Republic, and Peru, and so did the length of the childbearing period.

Because the DHS are internationally comparable surveys, they offer a unique comparison of women's lives across a large number of countries with varying levels of contraceptive use. But they cannot tell the whole story. Cross-sectional surveys such as the DHS cannot explain much of how contraceptive use affects individual women. This is because surveys usually have not recorded the sequence of events such as the timing of contraceptive use, births, and employment. Also, surveys can reveal full childbearing patterns only for women whose reproductive years have ended. As noted, these women's experience is least likely to reflect recent changes in contraceptive use.

FAMILY PLANNING AND WOMEN'S LIVES

Not enough is known about the way contraceptive use affects women's lives. Researchers know that women's education, economic position, household characteristics, and social status influence use of contraception and thus fertility. In contrast, little is known about the opposite perspective-how changes in contraceptive use and thus in fertility affect other aspects of women's lives, particularly the ability to take on new roles.

The Rockefeller Foundation funded early research on the relationship between the status of women and fertility. Findings indicated that the status of women is defined differently in different cultures and that multiple factors affect both fertility and women's status. The researchers did not find any universal relationship between the status of women and fertility. Assessing current understanding of this issue, Sawon Hong and Judith Seltzer observed, "(1) good data and rigorous analysis are scarce; (2) the relationship is complex and varies by social, cultural, and economic setting; and (3) no simple conceptual model has yet been set forth."

To improve understanding of how contraceptive use affects women's lives, the United States Agency for International Development has funded a 5-year, US$8.6 million research project, begun in late 1993 by Family Health International. Its purposes are (1) to support social and behavioral research on the immediate and long-term consequences for women of both family planning programs and contraceptive methods and (2) to help improve family planning and related reproductive health policies and programs through increased knowledge of the needs and perspectives of women. The project will support qualitative and quantitative research in six to eight countries. In-country advisory committees will help establish the research agenda. Based on its findings, the project will recommend improvements in program design and implementation from the perspective of women's interests and needs.

WHO MAKES REPRODUCTIVE DECISIONS?

Who makes reproductive decisions? How and why are these decisions made? Family planning programs can better serve their clients, both male and female, if they can answer these questions. They also can better find ways to help women express their needs and to help men understand and respect women's concerns.

Complex Situations, Complex Decisions

The reproductive decision-making process reflects tradition, religious belief, community norms, family structure, household economics and the value of children, and access to new ideas and innovations, all expressed in peoples' attitudes and opinions. Research on the reproductive decision-making process is limited and scattered, but a study in areas of North and South India illustrates the complexity of the process. Women in southern India are valued agricultural workers, marry later than women in the North, have more contact with and support from their parents and families, and are closer emotionally to their husbands. Their daughters are less likely to die in infancy.

Women in southern India are better treated because they marry within their own extended families-groups of people who depend upon each other for continuing support. In contrast, women in northern India marry out of their extended families into families that have no on-going relationship with the women's parents and other relatives and that permit married women little contact with their own families. Meanwhile, men's families form close, mutually supportive groups. Most men are not close to their wives. In the northern system women have little value to their own parents and are valued by their husbands' families chiefly when they produce sons. Women in the southern kinship system are better able to make reproductive choices such as using contraception because they are more valued, less isolated, and more autonomous. They also are under less pressure to produce sons.

As this example illustrates, the extended family or the community is often the ultimate decision-maker in matters of reproduction, even in countries as diverse as China, India, and Mexico. Such influence can extend even to decisions about what contraceptive method to use.

While the web of influences on decision-making is complex, people nonetheless have perceptions of who actually makes decisions in the household or who has the most say. Here and there surveys and focus-group research have asked people who makes household decisions including decisions about reproduction.

When Men Decide

Within marriage, in many cultures men typically have more say than women in the decision to use contraception and in the number of children that the couple will have. In Ghana, for example, both Demographic and Health Survey (DHS) data and focus-group research reveal that the husband is usually the effective decision-maker about fertility. Furthermore, husbands' family planning attitudes and fertility goals usually are not influenced by those of their wives. When partners disagree on whether to use family planning, the man's preference usually dominates. In South Korea researchers found that 71% of women whose husbands approved of family planning had used contraception at some time compared with 23% of women whose husbands did not approve.

When Women Decide

Within marriage some women make the decision to use family planning. In the few studies comparing various household decisions, women seem to have more say about using contraception than about most other important decisions. In Turkey, for example, 62% of the semi-urban wives surveyed made their own decisions about contraceptive use. In general, better educated women have more decision-making power within marriage, including more influence over decisions about reproduction and family planning.

Some women decide to use contraception without telling their husbands. In DHS in African countries, a small minority of women report doing so because they think that their husbands would disapprove. In rural Nigeria, as elsewhere around the world, some women secretly use contraceptives, use patent medicines as abortifacients, or make secret trips for abortions even though they risk eviction from their homes if found out.

Many unmarried women make reproductive decisions by themselves, of course. These decisions add up; in many countries women spend much of their lives outside marriage. For example, in Botswana women older than age 20 spend an average of 46% of their remaining reproductive years unmarried. In Colombia women spend an average of 40% of their entire reproductive lives unmarried.

Discussion Between Partners and Joint Decision-Making

Married couples together sometimes make household decisions of various kinds, including the decision to use contraception. Whether a couple discusses family planning can affect the decision to use contraception.

In many places such communication is the exception rather than the rule, however. In Kenya, for example, lack of communication between spouses proved to be a more common obstacle to contraceptive use than male opposition. In a study of monogamous couples in Ghana, 35% of the wives and 39% of the husbands reported discussing family planning during the previous year. Even among women who said that they had discussed family planning with their husbands, however, 39% reported their husbands' attitudes to be different from what their husbands independently told interviewers. Still, contraceptive use was higher among the couples who had discussed the subject.

Focus-group discussions in Tanzania found that different people had different reasons for not discussing contraception. Older people did not discuss using contraceptives because they believed that God determined the number of their children or because they used abstinence or herbal medicines to space pregnancies. Women did not discuss the topic because they thought that their husbands did not approve of contraception. Married men said that discussion was unnecessary because the women decided on their own the number and timing of pregnancies. Young people did not talk about contraceptives for fear of being considered promiscuous.

Program managers need to be aware of the variety of ways that individuals and couples make decisions about contraception-a variety that reflects not only the social position of women relative to men but also the different types of sexual relationships, from long-term monogamous marriages to one-time contacts between strangers. Communication campaigns and counseling are most likely to be effective when they recognize existing patterns of communication and decision-making. In some cases that means reaching out to couples. At the same time, communication needs to address men and women as individuals. In many cases communication programs may seek to influence men's and women's roles in the decision-making process as well as its outcome.

EFFORTS FOR LEGAL CHANGE

What can be done to eliminate the inequities that women face? While laws alone are seldom enough to change women's lives, legal change can be crucial. Change can start at every level, from international organizations to local women's groups.

INTERNATIONAL LEADERSHIP

The United Nations has advocated equality between men and women since its start in 1945. The UN Charter affirms the equal rights of men and women and prohibits discrimination based on sex. The United Nations considers reproductive choice a basic human right.

In 1979 the UN General Assembly adopted the Convention on the Elimination of All Forms of Discrimination Against Women. The Convention specifies steps to prevent discrimination against women in education, employment, public life, health, family planning, and other areas. It also suggests actions to change laws and attitudes. As of June 1993, 116 countries had ratified or acceded to the Convention. Many nations attached reservations to their acceptance, however. For example, Austria, Brazil, Ireland, Jordan, Libya, Malta, Thailand, Tunisia, Turkey, and the United Kingdom attached reservations to Article 15, which gives women full legal capacity. Some 52 countries have not yet signed the Convention, including India, Pakistan, South Africa, and the United States.

The UN called attention to the need to improve women's lives by declaring 1976 1985 the Decade of Women. The 1985 World Conference on Women set forth strategy to achieve equality between men and women by 2000, and the UN General Assembly endorsed the plan. This endorsement obligates all UN members to implement measures ending discrimination against women in such areas as access to education, rural development resources, legal protection, marriage, and access to health and family planning services. In 1995 the UN will convene the Fourth World Conference on Women, in Beijing.

National Initiatives

National efforts to improve the status of women are organized in various ways. Among 50 countries answering a 1989 questionnaire from the UN Commission on the Status of Women, some had set up separate bureaus or offices for women's affairs while others gave the ministry for social welfare authority over programs for women. Eleven of 14 industrialized countries and 22 of 36 developing countries reported programs to make people aware of gender inequality. All 50 countries said that they were promoting economic equality for women. In addition, developing countries sought to improve women's access to education, health services, family planning services, and child care. Most countries identified public attitudes favoring the subordination of women as the greatest problem facing their efforts.

Specific efforts vary widely. Recently, for example, Barbados gave priority to reducing violence against women; China reported programs to involve men in family planning; and Guatemala adopted a policy to incorporate women into development efforts through specific projects.

Of course, such policies make a difference only when government leaders have the political will to carry them out. Some national leaders have championed legal reforms on behalf of women. In Tunisia President Habib Bourguiba issued a new Personal Status Code in 1956 requiring that a bride consent to her marriage, abolishing polygamy, giving women the right to divorce while limiting men's ability to divorce at will, setting minimum ages for marriage, and establishing equal rights to custody of children. Bourguiba's government also provided family planning services for men and women. In Zimbabwe the courts have enforced the 1982 Legal Age of Majority Act, which asserts equality between men and women even in matters covered by customary law.

Often policy-makers' opinions are divided, however, and inaction results. In Kenya the constitution asserts equality between men and women but at the same time allows customary law to take precedence in cases of alleged discrimination. Revisions to the Marriage Act proposed in 1979 would have required a first wife's permission for her husband to take a second wife, given women a share of the couple's property at divorce, and recognized the possibility of a woman's having custody of her children after divorce.

Heated debate arose, and the bill has never passed. As a result, customary law, which grants women few rights, takes precedence in these matters. In some cases legal advances have even been reversed. Laws giving Egyptian women the right to seek divorce within a year after her husband's taking a second wife were passed in 1979 but repealed in 1985.

Women have few opportunities to change laws and policies because their political influence is limited. So is their direct participation in policy-making. In 1987 women comprised no more than 35% of members of parliament and government ministers in any country. In fact, women rarely made up even 25% of parliamentary representation.

WOMEN'S ORGANIZATIONS

Women's organizations have been powerful agents for change. They were early advocates for reproductive choice. Women's welfare organizations in Bangladesh, Egypt, and Pakistan were pioneers in supporting reproductive health services for women. In Thailand and Ecuador in the early 1970s women's medical and nursing organizations were among the first to provide family planning services.

Around the world women (sometimes joined by men who believe in equal rights) have formed groups to see that women receive fair treatment under the law. For example, in Brazil women's rights advocates began a campaign in 1985 to influence legislators writing the new constitution. They organized vigils, sent letters to newspapers, and aired television spot announcements. As a result the new constitution gives women equal rights and protection from domestic violence. Women's advocates in Brazil, Malaysia, and Zimbabwe have helped to train police to handle domestic violence and to involve police in drawing up laws to prohibit domestic violence.

FAMILY PLANNING FIELD WORKER HELPS CREATE NEW ROLES FOR WOMEN

"Because I have that job, our family is better off, and we are able to raise our children in a better way," says Zanati Begum. Zanati is an especially effective and articulate family planning field worker in rural Bangladesh. "And given the situation [of large families and poverty] prevalent in the society, it is our duty and responsibility as conscientious people to help solve the problem." Zanati's example is helping to change attitudes toward women's roles among men and women in her community.

THE ROUTE TO A NEW ROLE

Zanati believed in the importance of family planning before she became a field worker. After the birth of their first child, a daughter, in 1984, Zanati and her husband Sarkee decided to delay the birth of their second child. Zanati took oral contraceptives for four years before the couple decided to have their second child. Both Zanati and Sarkee thought that many of their neighbors had more children than they could afford to raise. The poverty of some large families saddened the couple. When they saw a newspaper announcement in 1988 asking for family planning field workers, they agreed that Zanati should apply. "At the beginning some of my neighbors and relatives were against my work," Zanati recalls. "They felt working as a family planning worker, going house to house and talking to people about it, was degrading. They also didn't think it was right for a wife to earn for the family. A wife's taking up a job was a sign that her husband wasn't capable of supporting his family, they thought."

But now the neighbors' attitudes are changing. "Now people realize that women, too, can take up jobs and help their communities and families," Zanati says.

Sarkee has become increasingly committed to his wife's work. At first he thought only that her small income as a field worker would benefit their family. He also knew that his friendly and energetic wife would get satisfaction from working with others. But after Zanati began discussing her work with him, he became interested in the problems of her clients. Now he feels that she should be a field worker even if she were not paid. In fact, he tells her that, if a household task would keep her from her work, he will do that task for her. Her work, he says, will prevent hunger and hardship in the community.

Sarkee is not troubled that some might criticize him. "If my wife...can do good for the society, I will allow her [to work]. No matter what obstacles come, I will overcome them. And if anyone comes and asks me directly, 'Hey, how come you allowed your wife to go outside the house?'...I will explain to them why I allowed her to do that." Besides, Sarkee says, men now recognize that small families are necessary. "Even in the men's circle...everyone says the same thing, 'We have no choice but to adopt this.'"

Learning New Skills

Zanati has learned new skills from her job. She works with the Jiggasha program of the Bangladesh government and Johns Hopkins Population Communication Services. She meets with groups of women, who listen to tape recordings of songs and dramas and discuss family planning and other maternal and child health issues. The women enjoy this rare entertainment, and they become less timid about talking about their needs and desires. Zanati also notes, "If people know that their neighbors practice [family planning], then they are more ready to adopt. That's why the Jiggasha idea works so well."

Zanati uses her new skills in other areas of her life. "...There are things which I'd never done before, for example, going house to house, holding meetings, keeping records of each day's work.... I do try to use these skills in my personal life and even to teach them to my neighbors."

As a result of her training in counseling, Zanati encourages women to talk and ask questions. "There are certain techniques we learn in counseling.... We learn that during counseling we must give the client greater opportunity to speak.... I should help a client to select a method according to her taste--according to her likes and dislikes." Zanati feels that she has done a good job when the women whom she counsels are willing to tell their friends openly that they use family planning.

Changing Attitudes Toward Women

Zanati says that her work is helping to change community attitudes toward women. "I've set an example in the community, by taking up a job in the family planning office. In the past it was hard to imagine women coming out of their homes to work. Now many of them realize that a girl's place in the family is just as important as a boy's," she says. "That's why they've begun to send their daughters to school as well."

"Society's attitudes toward women going to work have also changed. After I've taken up a job, people have begun to realize that there is nothing wrong with women going to work and that, like men, they can contribute to their societies, localities, and families...."

Many women have become interested in Zanati's work. Some have asked her advice about working. "Two of them are now teachers at the BRAC [Bangladesh Rural Advancement Committee] semi-formal education center," Zanati observes. "Women are no longer working only at home, as they have been doing for a very long time. The reason is an increasing awareness of their place in society and the family. For example, there are women in my family who say with regret, 'If we could only take up a job like you, we would have greater value in the family and society. Most of us who look after our families don't have any authority. Our opinions are never heeded.'"

Men's attitudes are changing, too. "After I began working in the field, the men have also given up their age-old ideas about women and their place in society. For example, they used to think that women should only look after the household affairs and their children, husbands, and mothers-and fathers-in-law. But now many of them realize that women should also be educated and allowed to work outside the home and that their work can bring prosperity to the family."

Zanati and Sarkee have two daughters. They do not plan to have more children. In Bangladesh most couples wish to have sons for support in old age. But Zanati and Sarkee say that, if parents can give daughters a good education, daughters can do just as much for their parents in their old age. Zanati says that her mother-in-law used to advise her to have a son, but no longer. "I explain to my mother-in-law that since my parents educated me and since I have a job, I can give my mother two saris every year if I want. I can take all the burden."

TEN PROGRAM STRATEGIES TO MEET WOMEN'S NEEDS

How can family planning programs improve their response to women's reproductive health needs? Ten possible strategies include:

1. Meeting unmet need by identifying and overcoming the institutional, cultural, and personal barriers to family planning that women face.
2. Widening the clientele to serve neglected groups such as young people, unmarried people, and men.
3. Training personnel to respect and communicate with clients, provide good technical care, and ensure informed choice.
4. Offering more services to meet a broader range of reproductive health needs.
5. Seeking women's opinions, including involving women in program planning.
6. Helping men and women to communicate, cooperate, and share responsibility by informing and educating men as well as women about men's and women's reproductive health and by providing convenient services.
7. Presenting new images in the mass media of competent women and caring men communicating and collaborating.
8. Adding criteria for evaluation of programs and personnel to assess how well clients' needs are met.
9. Promoting capable women employed in family planning programs.
10. Speaking out on behalf of women and in favor of policies that support women's rights to personal autonomy and more opportunities.

3

A Matter of Global Realm

DEBATE OVER POLICY

Many people involved in family planning policy and programs seek to balance a variety of concerns. Most agree that couples and individuals should be able to plan the number of their children and the timing of their births.

They do not always agree, however, on how to prioritize the goals of family planning programs. Some focus primarily on reducing the rate of population growth; others, on the reproductive health needs of couples and individuals; and still others, on adhering to ethical or religious beliefs. In preparation for the International Conference on Population and Development (ICPD) in Cairo, September 1994, many voices have spoken up, advocating differing, but not always mutually exclusive, priorities.

Population Growth: Those concerned about rapid population growth emphasize that:

- Rapid population growth threatens the progress of all other efforts to improve the standard of living.
- Environmental resources are threatened by increasingly large populations.
- Family planning programs should provide services to as many people as possible as soon as possible.
- Family planning programs should focus first and foremost on providing contraceptive supplies and services.

Needs of couples and individuals. Those concerned about the needs of couples and individuals emphasize that:

- The preferences, satisfaction, and safety of current family planning clients should receive higher priority than increasing the number of contraceptive users.
- Family planning services should be part of programs that help women and men not only with avoiding pregnancy but also with a range of other reproductive health needs.
- Reproductive health care programs should devote more attention to improving the quality of care that they offer.
- Family planning programs should help women to achieve equity in society as well as to meet their reproductive goals and health needs.
- Environmental degradation and resource conservation should not be addressed primarily by emphasizing limitation of childbearing in developing countries.

Strongly felt ethical and religious beliefs underlie many people's differing positions on population and family planning issues, including the positions of people concerned about population growth or about the needs of couples and individuals. Some advocates, however, particularly identify themselves as speaking from an ethical or religious point of view.

Ethical Considerations: Those concerned primarily about ethical considerations emphasize that:

- All individuals and couples should have the right to make their own decisions about their fertility, free of coercion or pressure.
- Family planning programs should not set targets for numbers of new contraceptive users, incentives for contraceptive use, or field workers' quotas that might result in pressure on people to use contraceptive methods.
- Clients should be given an informed choice of contraceptive methods.

Religious beliefs. Some, but not all, who express a religious viewpoint emphasize their contentions that:

- Abortion is not acceptable.
- Only married couples should have access to contraceptive methods because sexual activity outside marriage is immoral.

Alone among major religions, the leadership of the Catholic Church objects to all contraceptive methods other than periodic abstinence. This position seems to have had more impact on policy-makers and the availability of services in some countries than on the attitudes of individual Catholics.

Labels Polarize Positions

Most policy-makers and advocates recognize that many of these viewpoints are legitimate and yet prioritizing program goals is necessary. In the public debate, however, labels are often used-sometimes unfairly and inaccurately-to imply that individuals and groups advocate extreme positions, ignore other points of view, or have malicious intentions.

For example, those who focus on rapid population growth are sometimes labeled "population controllers" who disregard women, and those concerned with reproductive rights are sometimes portrayed as "radical feminists" who ignore the consequences of rapid population growth. As a result, positions have sometimes become polarized, focusing on disagreement rather than on the broader areas of accord.

Seeking Common Ground

In reality the serious debate concerns allocating scarce resources to achieve the multiple goals of meeting clients' needs, slowing population growth, and protecting the environment in ways that respect individuals' religious, ethical, and cultural beliefs.

Can population policies both satisfy demographic goals and advance individual rights? A growing number of experts and policy-makers argue that conflicts, although they cannot be completely resolved, need not be as great as they sometimes appear. Suggested approaches include:

- Base national population policy on human rights as well as economic concerns. Policy often focuses on the economic benefit to all citizens of slower population growth. Policy-makers can emphasize more strongly, at the same time, that control over one's own fertility is a human right and that providing services that satisfy clients is as important a program goal as reducing total fertility rates.

- Focus on unmet need. Millions of women do not want more children, want to delay their first or next pregnancy, or need better reproductive health services. High-quality services that meet these people's existing needs would increase use of contraception, lengthen continuation, and in the process often reach demographic goals.
- Support public policies that indirectly reduce population growth. If policies support roles for women other than childrearing and make these roles socially acceptable and economically independent, some women may choose to have fewer children. Also, women who can provide for themselves and their children can better protect themselves from coerced sex and unwanted pregnancy. Changes that support more options for women include ending policies that encourage parents to favor sons over daughters, eliminating arranged marriages of young girls, enacting and enforcing minimum marriage ages, eliminating policies or tax provisions that favor large families, and assuring equitable male financial responsibility for women and children during marriage and after divorce.

FAMILY PLANNING-AN ASSET FOR WOMEN

Women want better lives for themselves, their children, their families, and their communities. They want to do their best in their current roles as mothers, wives, workers, and community members. Many women also want new opportunities in life-chances to learn, to make their own decisions, to have more say in the course of their own lives. Women want to have choices. Family planning is one important way that women can take control of their own lives and make more choices possible. Choices are essential to human dignity. Without choices and without opportunities, a person cannot hope for a better future. Without choices, a person can have little self-respect. A person imprisoned is punished by being denied choices; a person denied choices is punished even without being imprisoned.

Although poverty and lack of education often limit choices and opportunities for both men and women in the developing world, in general women's choices are especially limited. Social norms, often embodied in a husband, parent, or mother-in-law, prevent many women from having much say in their own lives or much autonomy to choose their own paths. Even if women were allowed to make choices, social and economic options and opportunities are often beyond women's reach. As a result, compared with men, women have less health care, less education, fewer choices of jobs, poorer pay, and less legal protection.

Family Planning Can Help

Family planning can help women meet their needs-both their practical need to perform conventional roles more effectively and their strategic need to find new roles and opportunities. By enabling a woman to control her own fertility, contraceptive use can help meet a woman's practical needs in several ways. Safe contraception contributes to good health: when women avoid unwanted pregnancy, they avoid the risks of childbearing or abortion. In the developing countries one woman in every 50 or so dies from causes related to childbearing. Also, birth spacing helps her children survive. In addition, contraceptive use may give a woman more choice in the use of her time by helping her avoid unwanted pregnancy, childbearing, and childcare. With better health and more control over her time, a woman may be able to do more in her customary roles for herself, for the children she chooses to have, and for her community.

Beyond meeting these practical needs, contraceptive use can help to meet women's strategic needs. Women who are healthier and have more control over their time are in a better position to take advantage of education, employment, or other opportunities if they are available. Also, by planning their pregnancies, women may find that they can plan more of other aspects of their lives.

Contraceptive use is often necessary but seldom sufficient to change a woman's situation in life. When a woman controls her own fertility, she may have more choice about the course of her life. Whether she can make changes in her life, however, depends on her personal circumstances, social norms, economic development, and law, among other factors. Changes in many households and throughout society will be needed before women can realize their full potential.

Family planning programs also can help meet women's needs, both practical and strategic. Of course, they do so chiefly because they provide contraceptive methods. In addition, programs can design high-quality services so that to some degree they may help women meet strategic needs. For example:

- Family planning programs can demonstrate to the community that women have a right to be informed and to have their decisions respected.
- Programs can help women recognize the value of their own opinions by seeking and heeding women's views and advice.
- Programs can help women practice making decisions in new areas and learn interpersonal skills needed to pursue their own interests.
- Programs can expand services to meet a broader range of women's reproductive health needs.
- Programs can help men both to play their part in contraception and to understand and appreciate women's new roles.
- Programs can provide women with income and skills by hiring, training, and promoting women and by offering them opportunities for leadership.

In these ways family planning programs help prepare women to make decisions and choices that formerly were not available to them. Of course, family planning programs cannot singlehandedly solve all the problems confronting women, but they can seek ways to help.

FAMILY PLANNING SAVES LIVES

Each year an estimated 500,000 women die of complications due to pregnancy, childbearing, or unsafe abortion. All but about 6,000 of these deaths occur in developing countries. Where poor health, frequent childbearing, and little access to good medical care are a way of life, an early death is too often a woman's fate. Contraceptive use can help protect women's lives and health by avoiding pregnancies. It is one of three crucial measures to improve maternal health: (1) reducing the number of pregnancies,

(2) reducing the likelihood of complications during pregnancy, and (3) improving outcomes for pregnant women with complications. Reducing complications and improving outcomes require access to better obstetric care, more health care for poor and rural women, and improvements in women's living standards. Currently, emergency care often is unavailable.

Women who do not want to become pregnant can reduce their exposure to the risks of pregnancy and childbirth by using effective contraception. In this sense, using contraception is a strategy that women themselves can adopt to protect their health. Family planning and concern about maternal health have long been linked. The hope to relieve women's suffering and save lives inspired early advocates of contraception in both developed and developing countries. Now, worldwide, policy-makers recognize the importance of contraceptive use to women's health. The Draft Program of Action of the International Conference on Population and Development asserts that countries "should seek...reductions in maternal mortality through measures to reduce high-risk births, including births to adolescents, eliminate all unwanted births and all unsafe abortion, [and] expand cost-effective obstetrical and gynaecological care...". Answering a 1989 UN questionnaire, 62 of 67 countries wishing to modify fertility levels cited improving family well-being as a rationale.

Causes of Maternal Deaths

Pregnancy is the main reason that women of reproductive age die at higher rates than men. In Matlab, Bangladesh, the mortality rate for women ages 15 to 44 was 26% greater than for men in this age range. Some 30% of all women's deaths between ages 15 and 44 were related to childbearing. This study, conducted between 1976 and 1985, is one of the few long-term, detailed examinations of maternal mortality rates and causes.

The World Health Organization (WHO) defines a maternal death as "the death of a woman while pregnant or within 42 days of termination of pregnancy, irrespective of the duration and the site of the pregnancy, from any cause related to or aggravated by the pregnancy or its management but not from accidental or incidental causes." Behind the direct causes of maternal mortality-obstetric complications and unsafe abortions-lie the conditions of women's lives: inadequate care during delivery, chronic disease and malnutrition, poverty, isolation, and unwanted pregnancies.

Better care at childbirth and more access to that care would substantially reduce maternal mortality rates. Most maternal deaths occur among poor women who live in remote areas. Studies in Cuba, Egypt, Indonesia, Jamaica, Tanzania, and Turkey have demonstrated that maternal mortality is higher where access to a hospital is more difficult. When access improves, death rates drop. For example, in Oran, Algeria, the maternal mortality ratio fell 42% between 1971-75 and 1976-80 after fees for public hospital services were waived, a policy that greatly reduced the number of home deliveries.

Yet many women give birth without any trained help. For example, in 12 of 26 countries surveyed by the Demographic and Health Surveys (DHS) between 1986 and 1989, women had received no trained assistance in half or more of all births in the five years before the survey.

Chronic diseases and malnutrition leave many women unable to meet the physical demands of pregnancy. For example, anemia, often a result of poor nutrition, affects about 40% to 60% of pregnant women in developing countries excluding China-more than twice the percentage in developed countries. (By comparison, about 20% of men have anemia.) Malaria, sexually transmitted diseases, and infectious hepatitis also cause serious problems for many pregnant women and, unless treated, may kill them or their infants.

A woman's age and parity affect her chances of dying in childbirth. Health risks related to age and parity have been summarized as "the four too's"-too young, too old, too many, too close together. First births and births after the fourth are more dangerous than the second through fourth births. Women under age 18 and, more dramatically, those over age 35 face greater risk than women between these ages. Of course, age and parity are not risks in themselves; they stand in for the higher likelihood of specific risks associated with age and parity. For example, pregnancy can be dangerous to very young women because their pelvises are not yet large enough to accommodate birth. Many of these specific conditions can be managed if high-quality delivery care is available. Some family planning programs have emphasized serving women in these high-risk age and parity categories, particularly older, high-parity women. The Mexican social security system found that this emphasis interested more doctors in family planning and thus helped expand contraceptive services. Still, the "four too's" do not justify overriding women's own informed decisions about whether and when to have children or to pressure them to use a contraceptive method that is not their preference.

Deaths from unsafe abortion. Many women resort to abortion to prevent unintended births. Because abortions are illegal in most developing countries, many women seek them clandestinely and undergo unsafe procedures. Even in some places where abortion is legal, poor-quality services put women at risk.

An estimated 10 to 20 million illegal abortions are performed worldwide annually, and an estimated 100,000 to 200,000 women die as a result-about one in every 100. These deaths account for 20% to 40% of all maternal deaths. In some Latin American cities abortions account for over half of maternal deaths. In Romania unsafe, illegal abortions were responsible for 86% of maternal deaths. After the procedure was legalized in 1992, the overall maternal mortality ratio fell in the first year to 40% of the 1989 level. Women who survive an unsafe abortion may suffer chronic pelvic pain, chronic pelvic inflammatory disease, and/or infertility. They face a greater risk of ectopic pregnancy, premature delivery, and other adverse health consequences in the future. The majority of deaths due to abortion can be prevented. Access to effective contraceptive methods reduces unwanted pregnancies. The procedure itself is safe if the practitioner uses safe techniques.

While contraceptive use can greatly reduce unwanted pregnancies, it cannot eliminate them. An estimated 25 million women become pregnant each year due to failure of their contraceptive method. Many women, especially young women, become pregnant as the result of forced sexual intercourse. A smaller number of women develop health conditions that make continued pregnancy unsafe. Many of these women will choose an unsafe abortion if they do not have access to a safe procedure.

Incidence of Maternal Deaths and Illnesses

While the number of maternal deaths is often estimated at 500,000 per year, the true number may be even larger. In many developing countries official statistics underreport maternal deaths, perhaps by one-fourth to one-half. Many maternal deaths go unreported. Others are attributed to other causes. Often deaths are reported but causes are not.

Even less is known about the extent of maternal illnesses in developing countries. A frequently cited estimate is 16 illnesses for each maternal death-a figure based on a 1980 study of one village in India. Applying this ratio to the entire developing world yields an estimate of eight million cases of nonfatal maternal complications every year. Such complications are often chronic and debilitating.

Maternal mortality is usually expressed as the maternal mortality ratio-the number of maternal deaths per 100,000 live births. The maternal mortality ratio measures the risk of dying that a woman faces each time that she becomes pregnant. This ratio is often mistakenly called the maternal mortality rate. (A ratio compares the numbers of two differing events; a rate compares a part to the whole.)

Maternal mortality ratios range widely, from an estimated 12 maternal deaths per 100,000 live births in North America to more than 700 per 100,000 in some parts of sub-Saharan Africa. For the developing world as a whole, maternal mortality is estimated at more than 400 deaths per 100,000 live births, while the ratio is below 30 per 100,000 in the developed world.

Due to poor health and poor health care, many women in developing countries face much greater risk in each pregnancy than most women in developed countries. They also face this risk more often because, on the average, they have more pregnancies. Thus the lifetime risk of maternal death-a statistic that reflects both the risk per pregnancy and the number of pregnancies-is far greater in most developing countries than in developed countries. Between one-fourth and one-third of all deaths among women in their reproductive years in developing countries are related to maternity compared with only one-half of 1% in the US.

In the developing world as a whole, any one pregnancy is, on average, about 16 times more likely to kill than in the developed world. And the higher fertility levels in developing countries double that relative risk over a woman's lifetime. Thus the average woman in developing countries is about 30 times more likely to die from pregnancy- elated causes than the average woman in a developed country.

Contraception can Safeguard Women's Health

While family planning programs should not be treated as a substitute for urgently needed improvements in delivery care, reducing the number of pregnancies that women have in their lifetimes also substantially reduces the risk of maternal mortality and morbidity, particularly where fertility rates are high and health facilities are poor or unavailable. The study in Matlab, Bangladesh, illustrates how fewer pregnancies results in fewer maternal deaths. In 1977 more intensive family planning services, including home visits by trained female family planning workers, were introduced in selected Matlab villages. In these test villages the percentage of married women using contraception rose from 8% in 1976 to almost 40% by the end of the study in 1985. In comparison areas, where services were not expanded, the rate rose much less, from 5% to 17%. By the end of the study, maternal mortality in the test villages had fallen to less than half of that in the comparison villages-even though there was no change in the risk of dying from any one pregnancy. Contraception and psychosocial stress. Lack of control over one's own life is a major cause of stress. Thus the use of contraception can improve women's emotional health by providing more reproductive control and greater choice about childbearing. Also, because using contraception, like other preventive health practices, reflects an orientation to the future, it can be an important step toward overcoming fatalism and lack of self-worth.

In some circumstances, however, obtaining and using contraception can itself be stressful, especially where modern contraceptives are not yet widely accepted. A woman may worry about visiting a family planning clinic and undergoing questioning or a physical examination. She may fear disrespectful treatment or negligent care. She may also fear that visiting a clinic or using contraception will provoke her husband's anger or will bring criticism from her family, her in-laws, or others. She may experience painful or worrying side effects from using a contraceptive method. She may hear frightening false rumors about the dangers of contraceptive methods. Family planning managers must recognize these possible stresses and develop strategies to relieve them. As contraceptive use becomes the community norm and as services improve, using contraception may become less stressful.

Spacing Pregnancies Improves Children's Health

A child's serious illness or death is a common event in many places and a cause of great stress and grief. Couples can reduce their children's health risks by spacing births. Children who are born within 17 months after the preceding birth are about twice as likely to die before age 5 as those born 24 to 47 months after the preceding child. Even children born after an interval of 18 to 23 months are about one-third more likely to die than children born 24 to 47 months after the preceding child. In Brazil and Egypt the child mortality rate could be cut by up to one-third if all births were spaced more than two years apart.

Many women are having their children closer together than they wish. The World Fertility Survey (WFS) and Demographic and Health Surveys (DHS) indicate that 90% of women who plan to become pregnant would like to space their children at intervals longer than 24 months. More than one-third, however, have a second birth within 24 months.

Research also shows that children are more likely to die if their mothers are younger than age 18. According to the WFS and DHS, delaying the first birth until the mother is at least 18 years old reduces the risk of the first child's death by an average of 20%. In the Dominican Republic, Egypt, Mexico, and Peru, delaying childbearing at least until the age of 18 would reduce the risk of the first child's death by 30%.

CONTRACEPTION USE HELPS WOMEN PLAN

Women who can decide if and when they will become pregnant are better able to plan other aspects of their lives. In the short term women who use contraception effectively may have more choice about the use of their time because they have fewer children. Women may be better able to make plans to take new educational, economic, and other opportunities. Also, in the long term society in general and women themselves may change their expectations of how women lead their lives. Young women probably benefit most from being able to control their own fertility.

THE CHANGING NEEDS OF YOUNG WOMEN

Young women's lives are changing. Almost everywhere in the developing world, more women are delaying marriage. In 29 of 36 countries that have conducted Demographic and Health Surveys, the percentage of women who had married by age 20 was at least 10% lower among women ages 20 to 24 than among the oldest women interviewed, usually those ages 45 to 49. As women delay marriage, they have more opportunity to complete their education, to develop remunerable skills, and to choose their husbands or to choose not to marry at all.

Avoiding unintended pregnancies is critically important to allow women to make these choices, especially in cultures where unplanned pregnancy precipitates marriage or where premarital births have particularly disastrous social or economic consequences. In Latin America and the Caribbean, the Young Adult Reproductive Health Surveys (YARHS) document that many women are sexually active before marriage but are not consistently using contraception. For example, in a 1985 survey in Mexico City, 13% of women age 15 to 19 and 44% of men reported premarital intercourse. Only 22% of the women and 31% of the men used contraception at their first sexual experience, however. Among unmarried women ages 15 to 24, half of all first pregnancies were unintended. Among married women in this same age group, 11% of first births were conceived before marriage.

Nevertheless, offering contraceptives to unmarried adolescents and young adults remains controversial. Some parents and policy-makers assume that the availability of contraception will lead adolescents to have sexual relations before marriage. This assumption is one reason that, formally or informally, many family planning programs refuse to serve unmarried young people.

In fact, data do not suggest that the availability of contraceptives encourages early sex. Most research on the subject comes from the US and other developed countries. For example, an international comparison found that sex education and contraceptive services were more available in Europe than in the US. Sexual activity among adolescents, however, was about as prevalent in the UK, France, and the Netherlands as in the US, while the US teenage pregnancy rate was much higher. Another US study found that teens who had a sexual education program in their school delayed intercourse and were less likely to become pregnant. Still other studies have found no link between the presence of contraceptive clinics in the schools and levels of sexual activity among students.

Contraception and Education

For many young women the most important fork in life's path is the divide between education and early pregnancy. It is true that many barriers stand between young women and an education. Some parents think that it is wiser to educate sons because there are more and better-paying jobs for men than for women. Also, some girls are taken out of school to work at home. Some families are not willing to educate girls if the school is distant or the teachers are male.

Still, once girls reach puberty, the greatest threat to their staying in school may be pregnancy. Students who become pregnant often drop out of school, or they are expelled by school authorities-a fate that does not befall male students who father children. In many African countries pregnancy is the most common reason that girls leave school and the main reason that the school-leaving rate is higher for girls than for boys.

To ensure that girls are not forced to leave school due to unwanted pregnancy, girls need to be able to refuse unwanted sexual intercourse and to have access to contraceptives, information, and counseling if they choose to be sexually active. Also, schools should help young women continue in school, not expel them, even if they are pregnant or have a child.

Policies that help young women avoid pregnancy and stay in school could help change attitudes in the long run. Parents and communities might be more willing to invest in girls' education if they had more confidence that their daughters would not become pregnant and leave school. Also, as more women complete an education, and as more women hold paying jobs, the perception of women's potential is likely to change, helping to break the vicious cycle that holds women back.

Some young women recognize that avoiding pregnancy protects their futures. For example, in a Kenyan study female students of high socioeconomic status viewed contraception favorably. Those who ranked in the top quarter of their class were nearly four times more likely than other female students to have used contraception at their most recent act of intercourse. These young women could afford contraceptives and recognized that an early pregnancy would endanger their chances for academic success and economic security.

Children benefit in various ways from their parents' use of contraception. Education appears to be one area in which women pass on the benefit to their daughters: Both sons and daughters from small families have better educational opportunities than children from large families. In a Thai community, in families with three or fewer children, 44% of the children went to lower secondary school, and 31% went to upper secondary school. By comparison, in families with four or more children, 24% went to lower secondary school, and 14% went to upper secondary school. In this study couples with small and large families were matched for wealth, religion, residence, parents' educational attainment, and parents' ambitions for their children's education. All couples had had access to modern contraceptive methods throughout their reproductive years. Similarly, in Matlab, Bangladesh, children in small families stayed in school longer because they did not need to care for younger siblings at home. Still, in both Thailand and Bangladesh parents provided more education for their sons than for their daughters.

Contraception and Employment

The relationships among women's status, employment, and childbearing are complex. Some statistical studies find lower fertility associated with more female participation in the labor force, while others find the opposite. Such inconsistency is not surprising, given the variety of jobs and occupations, demographic and household characteristics, cultural forces, and socioeconomic circumstances around the world.

While statistical research into women's labor-force participation and women's use of contraception has not produced clear findings, the conceptual links are clear. With effective contraception, women are better able to work when they need to without the interruption of unplanned childbearing. Women also may find the burden of household work somewhat lightened. In addition to caring for children, women nurse the sick. Women in developing countries raise 50% to 90% of their families' food. In most rural areas women spend long hours carrying water, gathering fuel, and preparing and cooking food. How spacing and limiting births influence the daily lives of women working in the home also deserves research.

Wherever unplanned pregnancy would limit the types of work available to women, effective contraceptive use may help provide women with broader opportunities to obtain the economic security of a job. When a woman cannot be sure of avoiding pregnancy, her occupational choices often are limited. She may have to find employment that can be combined with childcare, that permits flexible hours, and that is easy to enter and leave frequently. Such jobs typically earn low, static wages. Most such jobs are in the informal sector of developing economies--for example, agriculture and petty trade. Even in the formal sector of developed countries, such jobs as nursing and teaching have been held mostly by women since employers did not care if pregnancy forced teachers or nurses to leave after a few years on the job. Seen as jobs that young women held until they had a family, these professions have commonly been paid less and offered less opportunity for advancement and less status.

More detailed studies, rather than large-scale statistical analyses of fertility levels and labor force participation, may offer a clearer view of how contraceptive use and employment are linked. For example, in Nigeria researchers found that young unmarried women out of school were using contraception in order to work longer before marriage. In one area studied, 75% of single women ages 18 to 25 were using contraception, more than five times the contraceptive prevalence of married women in the same age group.

Of course, many factors other than contraception affect women's employment. Women's autonomy within the family is one such factor. In some countries cultural norms call for women to remain at home no matter what their own preferences are. Also, some employers discriminate against women, partly because employers assume that women's commitment to their jobs is weaker than men's. Nevertheless, in modernizing economies women are an increasingly important part of the labor force. Where contraception is widely available and its use is accepted, employers can be more confident that female workers will not be forced to leave because of unplanned pregnancies. At the same time, however, the possibility that a woman may become pregnant is not legitimate grounds for denying her a job.

When women have access to contraception and new economic opportunities, many take advantage of both. In Bangladesh the Grameen Bank offers poor women small loans for income-generating projects. The women attend regular meetings at which they receive advice on their projects. They also learn the "Sixteen Decisions"-resolutions to make changes in their lives including planting vegetables, educating their children, and having small families. Women who have taken advantage of this new economic opportunity are more likely to be using contraception than women who are not receiving loans.

HOW CAN FAMILY PLANNING PROGRAMS BENEFIT WOMEN?

Contraceptive use protects women from the health risks of unwanted pregnancy and gives women more control over their own lives. Family planning programs help women primarily by providing contraceptive methods. What more can family planning programs do to meet women's needs? Women interact with family planning programs only briefly and infrequently. Still, in addition to providing contraception, those brief contacts can be designed to strengthen women's abilities to fulfill current roles and take on new ones. Program managers can seek to:

- Encourage respect for women,
- Provide a range of reproductive health care, and
- Design program activities to strengthen the skills that enable women to take new opportunities.

Encouraging Respect for All Women

By showing respect for women, family planning programs help women build self-confidence and self-esteem and thus strengthen their ability to make their own decisions and to act in their own interests. Also, showing respect for women as clients sets a good example for the community.

Family planning programs have an excellent opportunity to promote respect for women. Unfortunately, some programs have missed that opportunity-perhaps because program personnel share widespread social attitudes that denigrate women, because a program focuses on enrolling more clients rather than meeting clients' needs, because personnel are simply not aware that courtesy is important, or because service providers have too little time for each client. Program managers can encourage respect for clients in several ways:

- Ensure informed choice. Programs that help women make their own informed choices about their fertility show respect for their clients' right and ability to make decisions. To ensure informed choice, managers can see that clients are (1) offered a choice of methods, (2) given the information they want about each method, and (3) allowed to choose the method that they want, provided there is no medical reason to withhold it.
- Communicate respectfully. All personnel, no matter what their function, can act politely and in a respectful, friendly manner with all clients at all times. Program personnel demonstrate their respect for clients by paying attention to what clients say, answering their questions fully, never belittling their concerns and questions, and understanding and honoring their clients wishes. Also, programs must be sensitive to clients' modesty and preserve client-provider confidentiality.

- Train staff. Program managers can train staff to think of clients' needs and to communicate with clients. Staff also can learn how to communicate respect.
- Reward respect. Managers can reward personnel who treat female clients respectfully. They can measure the success of programs and providers by client satisfaction rather than just by numbers of clients. To measure client satisfaction, managers can survey clients about the care that they received. Whether clients return for further services when needed also indicates whether they are satisfied.
- Improve staff morale. Family planning personnel may treat clients poorly if personnel themselves have to work with insufficient time, supplies, space, or pay. If so, managers can acknowledge the problems, remedy them if possible, and at the same time make clear that the staff's frustrations are not an excuse for treating clients disrespectfully. Also, public promotion that enhances the image of providers, along with training, improves morale and inspires staff to live up to their new image.
- Set an example. Managers are role-models for other program personnel. If they do not treat clients and staff with respect, they cannot expect their staff to do so.

Clients know when they are treated with respect. Among Chilean women interviewed at a family planning clinic run by the Instituto Chileno de Medicina Reproductiva (ICMER), "being treated like a human being" was the most frequently identified element in high-quality care. In a clinic run by the Bangladesh Women's Health Coalition, a woman commented on the care that she had received: "I'd heard about family planning before, but not this way. This is the only clinic where I was asked to sit down and where I was treated as an equal. If I knew about it in this way, do you think I'd have six children?"

People who are treated with respect develop self-respect. Brief contacts with a family planning program are not likely to revolutionize women's lives. Still, for some women, contact with high-quality family planning services can be a start; for others, a step forward; and perhaps for a few, a big step. A young mother in Chile credited a family planning service with improving her self-esteem: "I am valuing myself more. I am realizing that I am really worth something. I am a person, and I should take care of myself..."

OFFERING OTHER REPRODUCTIVE HEALTH CARE

A reproductive health approach to family planning services can improve women's health and therefore women's choices. Judith Bruce and Anrudh Jain define a reproductive health care approach as one that helps clients reach their fertility goals in a healthful manner. This approach focuses first on ensuring that clients receive high-quality family planning services and then on offering additional services to help women meet multiple health needs at the same time and place.

To attain high quality, family planning services require two components: respectful, helpful interaction between provider and client and technically skilled personnel. To assure high quality, family planning programs can (1) determine the services that they can offer, (2) develop locally defined standards of care, and (3) establish quality-monitoring procedures. For example, those who counsel clients about contraceptive use must be trained to explain whichever methods are offered, to understand clients' needs, and to help them consider their options. Those who perform medical procedures need technical training. All training should raise providers' skills to a demonstrated standard of competence. Monitoring and supervision reinforce quality standards to assure that programs offer an informed choice of methods, hygienic care, and safe medical procedures. AVSC International has developed the COPE technique and the Population Council has developed the Situational Analysis approach to evaluate the quality of both client-provider interaction and providers' technical skills.

Many medical professionals favor a reproductive health approach because they see a visit to a family planning clinic as a rare opportunity to inform, screen, and treat women for a variety of reproductive health conditions, such as certain common sexually transmitted diseases (STDs) and conditions of pregnancy. Also, girls and adolescent women can be counseled about nutrition, anemia, and general health to help prevent later pregnancy-related morbidity and mortality. Some programs, too, may want the convenience of dealing with multiple health needs on one clinic visit.

Women often see little distinction among family planning, other reproductive health needs, and still other health needs, including their children's. When family planning personnel cannot help, some women feel that program personnel are not really interested in their health. In the ICMER clinic in Peru, women wanted a clinic visit to be an opportunity to learn more about their reproductive health and how to protect it. They preferred to discuss all their health problems with one provider.

Meeting a variety of needs encourages women to use services. For example, in Tunisia a family planning program recognized that new mothers have multiple concerns-about their new infants' health, their own health, and their ability to breast-feed. Therefore a clinic in Sfax began to offer neonatal, postpartum, and family planning services on one visit. Women are encouraged to come to the clinic on the fortieth day after giving birth, the traditional day on which a new mother first leaves the house. In 1987, 83% of postpartum women came for this visit, and 56% of these women adopted a family planning method. The approach is now being applied nationwide.

Not all women want all services, however. For example, some women may want a contraceptive method but not a pelvic exam or Papanicolaou smear. Requiring clients to accept services that they do not want could discourage them from getting any services at all.

In counseling women, programs also might broaden their focus beyond preventing pregnancy and disease. For example, women have a right to refuse unwanted sexual intercourse but often cannot do so. Helping women with such matters requires learning more about their private lives. Ruth Dixon-Mueller argues that providers cannot truly meet women's needs for contraception, disease prevention, or safety from violence without knowing something about how each client is sexually active. Providers may need to find out, for example, if a client has multiple sexual partners or is forced into unwanted sexual acts. Few family planning providers are prepared to elicit such information, which must be discussed in a sympathetic and reassuring manner. Training and a new way of thinking about the providers' role will be required. Of course, clients should not be required to disclose intimate information if they choose not to.

Weighing program options. Each program must determine its own ability to offer new services. Some programs may be strained to capacity, already serving as many clients as possible. For such programs, the scarcity of resources limits how much more they can offer. Other programs may want to attract more clients. For these programs, broadening services-and improving quality-may help. In choosing which services to add, each program has to assess clients' needs as well as program resources.

Still, some general principles apply to making these decisions. Elizabeth Maguire, Acting Director of the Office of Population, United States Agency for International Development, urges that family planning programs consider adding other reproductive health services "that will benefit the most women at an affordable cost and have the highest public health impact". Under these criteria a common, serious condition that is easily treated or prevented would have highest priority. Providers and other public health experts should involve clients in deciding which conditions are deemed serious, but without abandoning their professional judgement.

Many family planning managers are considering whether to offer services for sexually transmitted diseases. Adding STD services to family planning services can be appropriate because (1) many people need care, (2) combined services would be convenient for clients, (3) most STDs can be treated, (4) counseling could help women avoid STDs, and (5) most family planning programs offer condoms in any case.

Also, STDs are spreading and have serious health consequences. It is now known that infection with the AIDS-causing human immunodeficiency virus (HIV) is more likely in those with other STDs. Some family planning programs may find it difficult, however, to add STD services. Of course, family planning program managers can choose among several different levels of STD services: (1) prevention-information, counseling, and providing condoms and spermicides; or (2) in addition, initial screening and referral of suspected STD cases for diagnosis and treatment elsewhere; or (3) diagnosis and treatment as well as prevention and initial screening. The potential for impact and costs differs at each level.

Treatment after a septic abortion is also a serious need because so many women die from unsafe procedures. At the 1984 International Conference on Population in Mexico City, delegates urged governments to help women avoid abortion and to treat them humanely if they have had an abortion. Policy-makers can reduce the number of abortion deaths by improving treatment for septic abortion and by linking post-abortion care with contraceptive counseling and services. While offering contraception to all who want it, family planning programs can reduce abortion by reaching out especially to women at high risk of unwanted pregnancy, including adolescents, and by providing post-abortion counseling and family planning services in hospitals where women receive post-abortion treatment.

Around the world a variety of reproductive health programs are developing. For example, some affiliates of the International Planned Parenthood Federation (IPPF) in Africa and Latin America provide counseling and referrals for clients with STD symptoms. In Colombia the Asociación Pro-Bienestar de la Familia (Profamilia) offers contraceptive methods, screening for sexually transmitted diseases, sex counseling, clinics for men, AIDS prevention, and even legal services to low-income men and women.

In Bolivia a coalition of 18 public and private health institutions recently launched a national campaign to promote reproductive health services. The Bolivian National Reproductive Health Program encourages couples to use services that will improve family health including reducing the high maternal mortality rate.

These services include family planning, prenatal care, safe delivery and post-delivery care, breastfeeding promotion, and abortion prevention. To inform people about these services, the organizations, with technical assistance from Johns Hopkins Population Communication Services (JHU/PCS), have developed a campaign logo, clinic signs, posters, radio and television spots, in-clinic videos, client-provider materials, and audio cassettes for play on buses. The campaign tells couples that they have the right and responsibility to protect the health of women and children.

Strengthening Women's Skills

Women often need to build skills and self-confidence before they can take on new opportunities. Family planning program activities that strengthen women's assertiveness, communication, and decision-making skills can help prepare women to obtain fair treatment and to take new opportunities. In the process of delivering health services, high-quality family planning programs can help to build such skills by:

- Helping women learn to make informed choices in new areas of their lives,
- Supporting women's choices,
- Encouraging women to recognize their strengths and to build on them,
- Improving women's skills at communicating with their husbands and with people outside their families, and
- Creating new images and models of competent women and caring men.

These skill-building efforts do not necessarily require major new training, large new expenditures, or more staff. Much can be done in the everyday process of serving clients. A change of attitude and a change of emphasis can make a lot of difference.

Self-awareness can be the first step. Whether services meet women's needs can depend on providers' most basic assumptions about women and men. For example, if providers assume that women are solely responsible for contraceptive use, they may design services that make it difficult for men to obtain information and services. If, instead, providers assume that both men and women need services, they are more likely to design services that both men and women can use easily.

Making informed choices. Women make many decisions throughout their lives, but they may need to gain confidence in making new kinds of decisions, such as decisions to control their fertility or to seek new social roles. In a Mexican study young women with unplanned pregnancies seemed to be women with little awareness that they could make decisions for themselves. They were less likely than nonpregnant young women to know about contraceptives, to have discussed sex with their girlfriends, and to have aspirations and plans for the future. Women surveyed in parts of such countries as Bangladesh, Ghana, Jordan, Mali, Nigeria, Pakistan, and Tanzania say that they do not participate in decisions about having children. Many say that they obey their husbands' wishes or the will of God.

Reproductive health programs can help women make wider choices. By discussing reproductive needs and goals with clients, providers can give women practice in assessing a situation and making thoughtful decisions. Since making fertility decisions may be unfamiliar to some clients, the process requires skill and patience on the part of the provider. Ideally, the provider imparts information, listens attentively, encourages discussion, helps clients recognize their own needs, and answers clients' questions. The clients themselves make the decisions about whether and when to have children and how to carry out their plans.

Supporting women's choices. Respecting clients' wishes builds women's confidence in their own decision-making and their right to make decisions. For example, many women already know what contraceptive methods they want before they come to a family planning provider. Honoring a woman's preference is important to her satisfaction with family planning. In Indonesia, for example, 91% of women who were given the method that they chose were still using that contraceptive method after one year compared with only 28% of women who were given a method that was not their first choice. A 6-country IPPF study also found that women were more likely to continue contraceptive use when they received the method that they wanted.

Women's choices reflect their own needs. Providers cannot assume what women need or want. For example, in Peru some women in focus groups said that they preferred the rhythm method because it gave them the right to make choices about when to have sex. Also, its use implied the intelligence to take charge of one's life. Women chose this method because it requires cooperation between sexual partners, and that cooperation enhanced the relationship.

Therefore, to create the best services, managers can ask clients what they want and design programs and train staff accordingly. Even better, they can directly involve female clients and community members and groups in planning and monitoring services. Such a client-oriented approach is rare. Indeed, providers' biases often block access to contraception and to a choice of methods. Often because of misinformation about methods, providers may favor one method over all others or shun certain methods. Because of negative assumptions about clients, particularly about women, providers may deny clients a choice of methods or discourage use of methods that require clients to act-for example, using barrier methods at each act of coitus or taking an oral contraceptive tablet daily.

Recognizing women's strengths. Successful counseling helps women identify their strengths and build upon them in planning their lives. In India group leaders from the Institute of Health Management ask groups of women who is the most important person in their homes. At first, the women never mention themselves. Then the group leaders recite a list of household chores and ask the women who does each chore in their homes. The women repeatedly answer that they do the chores. When the leaders ask again who is the most important person in their house, the women laughingly answer that they are most important. Good counseling can help women recognize that they already plan their time, save money or grain, and care for their families and homes. Building on these skills, women may learn to plan other aspects of their lives, including their reproductive lives, in which they may have depended previously on others.

Recognizing their own managerial role in the home, women can have more confidence applying these skills elsewhere. A manual prepared by the United Nations Educational, Scientific, and Cultural Organization (UNESCO) suggests an exercise to help women build their self-esteem: Women list their skills, such as planning their time and organizing their families. Then they say how those skills would help them in a business situation.

Improving communication skills. Family planning programs can help women speak up on matters that concern them. In particular, programs can encourage and enable women, and men, to talk about contraceptive use and reproductive health. Women's discussion groups have been the approach most widely used to help women bring up and discuss these issues.

To help women learn to talk about family planning, a program in rural Bangladesh designed with assistance from JHU/PCS organizes volunteer discussion groups. The program was set up to reach more people than family planning field workers could reach in home visits and because women were isolated and unaccustomed to discussing family planning with each other or with their husbands. The discussion groups, called Jiggasha ("to enquire" in Bangla), are formed for men and women separately. Leaders and meeting places are chosen to take advantage of the existing networks of communication in the community. The Jiggasha meetings have encouraged women to discuss and use family planning. About 65% of participants report that, after attending several meetings, they have discussed family planning with their husbands or with other women in the group, and about 50% report talking to people outside the group or to a family planning field worker. Some 30% of the women began to use a modern contraceptive method, and 20% visited a health clinic.

In Bolivia in the early 1990s client-provider materials produced to improve the quality of reproductive health services and counseling contributed to communication between spouses. Before-and-after surveys found that significantly more clients had talked with their spouses about family planning after seeing and receiving the materials--95% compared with 84% before they had seen the materials in clinics. By comparison, the increase among those who had not seen the materials-from 83% to 88%-was not statistically significant. Later a video drama entitled Hablemos en Pareja (Let's Talk Together) was produced and shown in clinic waiting areas to help clients overcome barriers to communication between spouses.

Couples may find talking about family planning and reproductive health easier if they have discussed the subject first with someone of their own sex. Programs such as Jiggasha can help. For example, women in a rural area of northern India could not talk to their husbands about sexually transmitted diseases, even though they feared that their husbands might infect them. Health advisors organized the women into groups that discussed the problem and decided how to approach their husbands. After practicing the conversation in groups, the women were better able to talk with their husbands.

Family planning providers can help couples communicate better if they are aware of social conventions. For example, in Mexico a survey revealed that couples thought it immodest for the wife to start a discussion of family planning. These couples said that husbands should start such discussions and decide whether the couple uses a family planning method. In response, family planning providers designed counseling services for men and women advocating that women start discussion and that the couple make a decision together.

Strengthening communication skills is important to women and men who want their partners' support and cooperation in planning their families and protecting their reproductive health. For some, discussion may be a necessary step to taking an action they desire. For example, according to DHS data from six African countries, women who approved of family planning were more likely to use a modern contraceptive method if they had discussed family planning with their husbands in the year before the interview than were women who approved of family planning but had not discussed it. Studies in Java and South Korea have found that the more often couples discuss family planning, the more likely they are to use a contraceptive method. Discussion between partners may make continued contraceptive use easier, too. In the IPPF 6-country study, women who thought that their partners agreed with their use of a family planning method were significantly more likely to continue using that method than women who did not know that their partners approved. Although studies link spousal communication with contraceptive use, the nature of the link is not obvious. It is not always clear whether more communication leads to more contraceptive use or, instead, couples talk more about contraception because they already use or plan to use a method. Also, some couples may not have an immediate reason to discuss family planning-for example, the woman is pregnant, the couple wants a child, or they have no access to contraceptives. New images of women and men. It will be easier for women to take new opportunities when society respects them as strong and competent. Men will find it easier to help women when they see positive images of men who support those qualities in women. Family planning communication can provide these images by portraying competent women and caring men in radio drama, videos, films, advertisements, and users' testimonials.

ENCOURAGING MEN'S COOPERATION

Women's situation will improve faster if men help. Protecting reproductive health particularly requires commitment from both men and women. While a woman can control her fertility without a man's cooperation-and many do-men's understanding and help make contraception and family planning easier and widen the choice of methods that a couple can use. Also, to prevent sexually transmitted disease, a woman must have the cooperation of her male sexual partner, who must remain faithful to her or use condoms. What can family planning and reproductive health programs do to encourage men's cooperation?

CHANGING TIMES AND CHANGING ATTITUDES

Encouraging men's cooperation can start with understanding men's points of view. Many men approve of family planning and contraception. Even where few people use contraceptives, such as Burundi, Ghana, Kenya, Mali, and Pakistan, at least half of men surveyed approved of contraception.

Still, many men have negative attitudes about women choosing and using contraception. Some men fear that contraceptive use will make their wives independent of their control. They fear that their wives will have sex with other men if they no longer risk pregnancy. Some men may be unwilling to have their wives adopt family planning because they themselves know little about it. Some do not want their wives talking with strangers about sex and reproduction. Some worry that contraceptive use will harm their wives' health or their own . Some oppose contraceptive use for religious reasons. Some men think that large families reflect their masculinity or their wives' faithfulness in serving them.

These male attitudes about contraceptive use are part of some men's broader fears. Traditional social norms often have required men to maintain the honor and position of their extended family, village, religious group, or other social organization. Therefore men feel responsible for the behavior of their wives and children and think that women have no right to make decisions for themselves.

Men are not alone in imposing limits on women. Many mothers, even wealthier, better educated women, prefer sons and take better care of them (1, 374). In some places women dominate their sons' wives, pressure them to have many children, and even physically abuse them.

Paternalistic traditional norms are no excuse for the mistreatment of women, however. Violence against women, including violence from their husbands and other family members, can be condemned by religious and political leaders and prohibited by law, and the law, enforced. Also, legal changes in a variety of areas affecting women's well-being can be the catalyst to changing community norms.

Economic and social changes, too, are requiring couples to be more flexible about gender roles. More and more, both partners must produce income to support the family. As a result, men are finding that a wife with many skills can help support the family. In 1990 women made up 42% of the paid labor force in the developed world and 33% in the developing world. The need for women to earn income has changed gender roles. In the US some husbands and wives are arranging to work different hours, and more men are caring for the children. In 1991, 20% of children under age five were cared for by their fathers at home while their mothers went to work.

Some men find that they have gained through improvements in their wives' status. For example, in Colombia the Instituto Colombiano Agropecurio provides poor women with small loans and on-going help with planning and decision-making. The women and their husbands have worked together to make their enterprises succeed and to take care of their homes. Both husbands and wives said that they benefited from the project. The women became more self-confident and knowledgeable about dealing with local institutions such as schools and markets. Their new confidence made them better advocates for the family. In Zimbabwe and other areas of Africa, husbands report that their wives' employment as family planning field workers enhanced the prestige of their family. These men support their wives in their new positions even if the women do not bring in additional income.

ENCOURAGING MALE RESPONSIBILITY

Reproductive health programs can help men cooperate with their sexual partners to avoid unwanted pregnancies and to prevent sexually transmitted diseases. Specifically, programs can:

- Inform men about family planning, reproductive health, and contraceptive methods,
- Encourage and improve communication between spouses,
- Design convenient services for men,
- Provide contraceptive choices for men, and
- Promote images of male role-models who cooperate with women both in the family and in the community and who share the burden of ensuring reproductive health.

Informing Men: Many men want to know more about contraception and family planning and to be more involved. For example, in Malaysia, Nigeria, and Turkey, most men surveyed wanted to learn more about family planning. In Peru men in focus groups complained that false stereotypes of dominating men (machismo) limited their opportunities to obtain information about sexuality and family planning. In Tunisia men often accompanied their wives to the family planning clinic but then waited outside, talking among themselves. When asked, some said that they would like to be more involved. Men commented, "We are made to feel like strangers." "We are pushed aside...," and "From the way we are treated, one would think that this doesn't concern us."

Women, too, want men to have information. In Chile women asked that men be allowed to come to the classes at the clinic. One woman said that her husband did not always believe her and that she would "love to have him come to some of the talks." Men need information about contraceptive methods for women as well as about those for men. Well-informed men can use a method themselves or support their partners in using a method. Well-informed men also can talk with their wives and cooperate in assessing their needs and choosing a family planning method.

Men especially need information about sexually transmitted diseases since men play a big role in the spread of sexually transmitted diseases including AIDS. Although there is much variation among cultures, except for female prostitutes men are likely to have more sexual partners than women. Men have more control over condom use. Men are more likely to control the frequency of sexual relations and the possibility of abstinence within a relationship. To reduce risk, men can: (1) reduce the number of sexual partners, (2) use condoms, and/or (3) practice sexual fidelity or abstinence.

Encouraging Communication between Spouses: Men can support women's choices better when couples can talk about reproductive health and family planning. But surveys show that even men who approve of family planning do not always discuss it with their wives.

For example, in Burundi 94% of surveyed men approved of contraceptive use, but only 48% had discussed it with their wives in the preceding year. Family planning communication campaigns can change men's role in contraceptive decision-making. The Zimbabwe Male Motivation Project in 1988 and 1989 sought to inform men, promote more favorable attitudes, increase contraceptive use, and promote male involvement and joint decision-making. The project appeared to increase condom use particularly. Its impact on men's attitudes about decision-making was ambiguous, however. Men who heard the campaign radio soap opera, attended a lecture, or saw a pamphlet were more likely to say that the man alone should make the decision to practice family planning. At the same time, these men also were more likely to say that the couple should decide jointly how many children to have. Researchers concluded that future campaigns should put more emphasis on joint decision-making and discussion between spouses.

Some family planning programs welcome husbands and wives who seek family planning counseling and services together. While counseling a couple, a provider can encourage the woman to ask her own questions and express her own opinions. The provider also can encourage the man to understand and respect the woman's opinions and choices. Program managers seeking to improve women's situation need to make clear, however, that the program also welcomes women and men who come alone, does not require a husband's permission before serving a woman, and keeps the names of clients and all information about clients confidential, even from spouses.

Designing Convenient, Appealing Services: Men cannot share responsibility for reproductive health and family planning if services and information do not reach them. Few men go to facilities that offer services primarily for women. Men must be reached in other ways. There are five main approaches:

- *Separate Clinics*: Male-only clinics can inform men about all family planning methods and provide condoms and vasectomy. Separate male clinics have been successful in Asia and particularly in Latin America, including Brazil, Colombia, Guatemala, Honduras, Mexico, and Peru. Some offer a range of reproductive health services including care for sexually transmitted diseases and infertility.
- *Better Service for Men at Existing Clinics*: Some conventional family planning clinics have hired male staff, offered hours convenient for men, and offered additional reproductive health services for men. In Colombia Profamilia serves men at its women-oriented family planning clinics as well as in clinics for men only.
- *Workplace Services*: In India, Kenya, the Philippines, Turkey, and elsewhere, employers or trade unions provide family planning services to workers, often as part of broader health services. Other possibilities include working with male-oriented educational or fraternal organizations, cooperatives, or the military.
- *Community-based Services*: Male community-based distributors can provide men with condoms and information about family planning. For example, in 1987

the Katibougou Family Health Project in Mali recruited men from the community who distributed condoms from stocks kept in their homes, just as female community health workers distributed supplies to women.

- *Commercial and Social Marketing*: Commercial sales have long been men's chief source of condoms. To make supplies more affordable and to increase promotion, social marketing programs, which sell contraceptives at subsidized prices through established commercial outlets, operate in more than 20 countries. Men can buy social-marketing condoms along with other goods. In many Muslim countries particularly, men do the household shopping.

Providing Contraceptive Choices: Currently, there are only two contraceptive methods for men-vasectomy and condoms-and there are two methods in which male cooperation is crucial-periodic abstinence and withdrawal. Research on new methods for men is underway, but it is unlikely that a radically new male method will be available for at least 10 years. In the meantime, family planning programs and the private practitioner should make sure that current methods are readily available.

In most developing countries neither condoms nor vasectomies are widely used. Just under 5% of married couples in developing countries use each of these methods. Condoms probably are more widely used outside marriage than in marriage, however, and use may be growing because of concern about AIDS. Neglect by policy-makers and providers may help explain the low prevalence of vasectomy. Where the procedure is accessible and promoted, men use it. For example, in Colombia the annual number of vasectomies performed by Profamilia rose by 77%, to more than 1,000, after the organization opened its first two men-only clinics in 1985. In 1991 Profamilia's eight men-only clinics performed about 5,000 vasectomies.

Promoting Male Methods and Men's Services: Promoting men's family planning methods and services boosts their use. For example, in Turkey a social marketing campaign to promote condoms involved a television comedy, video tapes, sponsorship of a soccer team and tournament, billboards, and gift packs to medical schools. The program sold 4.5 million condoms in 1991, its first year of sales. Men's response suggests that some men are willing to take responsibility for contraception if programs make the effort to reach out to them.

Social marketing programs have been directed more to men than to women. They have emphasized the economic value of small families. They also depict men as the protectors of their families. While most promotion has touted condoms, some social marketing programs now address advertisements for oral contraceptives to men as members of the "contraceptive decision-making team." In Morocco radio and print advertising, display boxes, and posters depict condoms as offering men the opportunity to share responsibility for reproductive decision-making.

Promotion also has Brought Men to Clinics: In Colombia Profamilia has promoted its men's services in the mass media and through field workers. In Brazil Pro-Pater increased the number of vasectomies performed monthly in 1989 at its Sao Paulo clinic by nearly 80% with television spots, billboards proclaiming that "vasectomy is an act of love," and resulting press coverage.

Promoting Positive Images: Family planning communication can depict new images of men as well as of women. Also mass-media depictions of couples discussing family planning and making joint decisions suggest to the public that such discussions are appropriate. They also suggest to both men and women how to discuss family planning and sex and can even provide an occasion to start discussion.

Men's Organizations are Involved, Too: In Jamaica, Fathers Incorporated assists men who want to help children. The group points out that in the past men have been seen solely as providers of goods for their children. To change that image, group members are holding workshops to promote men as care-givers as well.

4

Family Planning Programs and Women Initiative

By employing women, family planning programs provide many thousands of women with new roles and opportunities. Family planning programs make a point of hiring women, especially as front-line providers. In most societies a woman-to-woman approach is the best way to communicate about family planning and to offer services. Female family planning providers can talk to other women and understand their needs better than men can.

The United States Agency for International Development estimates that currently about 500,000 women work in family planning programs in developing countries-about half of the nearly one million family planning workers estimated by the World Bank to be employed in both developed and developing countries. Jobs held by women range from community-based distributors to program administrators to doctors, nurses, and midwives.

Benefits from Family Planning Employment

What do women gain by working in family planning? Almost all research has concerned community-based distributors. Studies in seven countries conclude that women working as community-based distributors benefit because they earn money, receive useful training, and gain status in their communities. Of course, other kinds of work, outside family planning, might benefit women similarly or more, while still other kinds of jobs can make life worse.

Income: The salaries, honoraria, or fees for service paid to family planning workers can make a difference to their quality of life. In a survey by the Center for Development and Population Activities (CEDPA) of 305 field workers employed in 11 family planning projects in Bangladesh, India, Kenya, Mali, Nepal, Pakistan, and Turkey, 76% reported that the income they received from their jobs improved their economic status.

Most of these women use their income to help their families. In the CEDPA study 51% used their earnings largely for general household expenditures; 29%, for their children's education; 10%, for themselves; and 6%, for other miscellaneous, unessential expenses. The remaining 4% gave the money to their husbands.

By earning money, some women improve their position in the household. Most women in the CEDPA study gained more control over their children's education, medical care, and household expenditures. Many also found that relations with husbands and in-laws improved. Just earning money does not guarantee better status at home, however. Some case studies of women earning money in the informal sector (not in family planning) experienced no increase in household influence.

Of course, many programs ask women to work as volunteers. Even if women cannot be paid for their work, programs can make special efforts to recognize their contributions and publicly honor their contribution to their communities.

Competence in new skills: Family planning providers can learn new information and skills. In the CEDPA study community-based distributors' reports suggest that their leadership and communications skills improved, as did their knowledge of family planning methods and service delivery. For many, this is their first paying job. Unlike physical labor such as sewing, farming, or typing, family planning field work teaches women skills that meet the social needs of the community and that enable women to teach others. Community-based family planning providers often help people obtain medical care at clinics. Some are trained to provide directly and/or to teach oral rehydration therapy, immunization, nutrition services, safe delivery practices, and broader maternity care. Professional status and respect. Female family planning workers often win respect for their knowledge. These women become community authorities in family planning and other health matters.

In Matlab, Bangladesh, both field workers and community members report that field workers are important community resources not only for family planning services but also for general medical advice and referral. Community members even seek field workers' advice on financial matters and neighborhood disputes. Respect is not always easily earned, however. New roles for women sometimes threaten community norms, and those who break the rules may be scorned. For example, in Muslim countries where purdah is practiced, custom prohibits women from moving about alone in public, and yet family planning field workers must visit homes and clinics.

In the face of initial hostility from the community, female workers often find ways to maintain their self-respect. For example, Bangladeshi family planning workers redefined for themselves the traditional norms of purdah and female modesty. They spoke of "inner purdah," shifting emphasis from physical seclusion to an internalized moral code of conduct.

In various cultures and countries, female family planning workers have experienced initial rebuke, then gradual acceptance, and eventual respect. For example, in Bangladesh the field workers initially scorned for violating purdah eventually regained their prestige and at the same time legitimized family planning services. In a few cases female field workers have been unable to win community respect. A study of auxiliary nurse-midwives who provided family planning services in Maharashtra, India, found that many of the women had been abandoned by their husbands or had difficulty finding a husband.

In general, women working as community-based distributors feel strengthened by their work. They reported in the CEDPA study that their achievements and value to the community enhanced their self-esteem and sense of autonomy. Particularly in cultures that generally isolate women, work in family planning is a gateway to new ideas, new information, and new opportunities.

MODELS OF CHANGE

Women working in family planning offer other women more than family planning information and supplies. They often are agents of change and new role-models for their communities.

By persevering and winning respect, women working in family planning set an example for other women. They legitimize women's employment, and family planning workers can serve as examples that young women can aspire to emulate.

Family planning workers can stimulate change in their communities in many ways. Their work can loosen taboos detrimental to women and even help other women assert themselves. For example, after three years of a women-staffed community-based project in Mali, villagers were more willing to discuss such previously taboo topics as family planning and contraceptives. In Nairobi, Kenya, female volunteers in a family planning project spoke with confidence in public gatherings. In both India and Bangladesh community acceptance has enabled female field workers to intervene in family disputes, rebuking and advising men and providing moral support to women.

CHALLENGES FOR FAMILY PLANNING PROGRAMS

Through careful selection, training, and support, family planning programs can make special efforts to see that their female employees benefit from their work. Women's employment in family planning needs more study. Other female providers, not just community-based distributors, need to be surveyed. Also, pay scales, working conditions, and potential for training and career advancement should be analyzed with an eye to increasing opportunities for women.

Workers selected with their communities' input may have a better chance of being accepted than workers chosen by outsiders, as a review of community-based programs in Africa suggests. In some cases newly employed family planning workers may displace traditional practitioners, such as traditional birth attendants and midwives, who play a vital social role. Collaboration may be important to win support from traditional practitioners and avoid resistance that could make the task of family planning workers more difficult. Promoting family planning providers helps women win community respect as qualified, trustworthy professionals. Strengthening both the image and the skills of providers can attract and keep clients. Johns Hopkins Population Communication Services has dubbed this the PRO approach-Promoting Professional Providers. A survey in Kenya showed that people who had heard the radio drama in the Haki Yako ("It's Your Right") PRO approach campaign were less likely to have a negative image of family planning providers than people who had not heard it.

Visible symbols of family planning employment help, too. In Kenya and Zimbabwe, for example, female community-based distributors wear uniforms and have signs outside their homes signifying official endorsement of their work. Recognized as community leaders and authorities, family planning workers are often the only women who sit on the podium at official village events.

SHAPING POLICIES TO MEET CLIENT'S NEEDS

While family planning programs can do much to help women meet their needs, debate continues about how meeting women's needs can be made more central to population policy. Some have criticized population policies as aiming at national goals such as slower population growth, environmental protection, or economic development while neglecting the needs of women as individuals and as a group. Some critics argue that such policies focus on only one aspect of women-their ability to bear children. Ruth Dixon-Mueller has argued that population and development policies must change to reflect "a thoughtful engagement of the difficulties that women face around the world in the struggle to take control over their own fertility and their own lives."

How can population policies better reflect women's interests? Improving the quality of care and protecting women's health have long been concerns of family planning advocates. The United Nations has declared that the goal of family planning should be "the enrichment of human life, not its restriction," pointing out that women in developing countries need a broad range of economic, health, and social rights and services. Many family planning programs are still struggling to meet more modest goals, however. As demand for contraception has risen rapidly in developing countries over the past two decades, programs often have not been able to serve all the people who want family planning.

Recognition is growing that population policies--and development policies in general-must pay attention to their clients' needs and preferences if they are to succeed. J. Brian Atwood, Administrator of the United States Agency for International Development, describes the need in this way:

Attention to gender roles is fundamental to the success of programs we assist. We must support full participation of women at all levels of family planning and-indeed-all health and development programs. We must help women overcome the obstacles they face in obtaining services or using contraceptive methods. We must see that programs are designed to benefit women. And, we must help programs strengthen men's support and participation.

To accomplish this at the program level, family planning program managers are increasing their efforts to learn from clients. At the same time, women's advocates are seeking more opportunities for women to participate in planning services. Thus program managers and women's groups have begun to work together. At the policy level, policy-makers, family planning organizations, women's groups, and other nongovernmental organizations have been building links between population policy-makers and women's advocates. This discussion and debate has grown as world attention has focused on the United Nations International Conference on Population and Development (ICPD) in Cairo in September 1994.

In this discussion diverse policy-makers are recognizing that their various goals can be achieved by the same means-offering services that people want. Policies that serve clients:

- Recognize that reproductive choice is a human right,
- Focus on meeting clients' unmet needs for reproductive health services, and
- Involve clients, especially women, in program design.

REPRODUCTIVE CHOICE IS A BASIC HUMAN RIGHT

Today there is widespread agreement that reproductive choice is a human right. This means that women have the right to control their own fertility and the right to refuse unwanted sexual intercourse, including the right to protect themselves against the violence of men, including husbands, who force intercourse.

Women's advocates have had to struggle to gain recognition of women's reproductive rights. Early in the 20th century women's advocates established the first programs to provide contraceptive information and services so that women could exercise their rights to protect their own health and control their own fertility. Often religious, medical, and government leaders stood in their way. It was not until the 1940s that contraception began to be accepted in developed countries as a medical service and become more widely available.

In recent years international organizations have recognized the right of all individuals and couples to make reproductive choices. In 1968 the International Conference on Human Rights in Teheran affirmed the right of reproductive choice. This right was reaffirmed at the first UN World Population Conference, held in Bucharest in 1974, and again at the second such conference, in Mexico City in 1984. In the words of the report of the Bucharest conference, "All couples and individuals have the basic right to decide freely and responsibly the number and spacing of their children, and to have the information, education, and means to do so."

International institutions consider securing reproductive choice to be an important part of improving women's well-being. For example, the Committee on the Elimination of Discrimination Against Women (CEDAW), established by the United Nations to gauge progress toward ending discrimination against women, monitors access to family planning as an important indication of women's situation.

The declarations of international institutions and global conferences put governments on notice that women should have the right to control their fertility and their own lives-and that family planning programs can help women to achieve these rights.

Governments and reproductive health programs face the challenge of turning these broad principles into policies and programs.

Meeting Unmet need for Reproductive Health Care

Over the past decade the percentage of surveyed women who say they do not want to have more children has grown substantially in every region except sub-Saharan Africa. Even in Africa, although most women want large families, there is great interest in spacing births. In nearly all sub-Saharan countries surveyed by the Demographic and Health Surveys (DHS), between one-third and one-half of married women said that they wanted to space their next births by at least two years.

Such statistics imply large potential demand for family planning services. Even though contraceptive use has risen substantially in recent years, in most surveyed countries between 20% and 30% of married women of reproductive age report that they are not using contraception but do not want any more children or else want to delay their next birth at least two years. Rates of abortion, even where abortion is illegal and unsafe, also testify to women's strong desire to control their own fertility.

Demographers describe women who are not using contraception but want to space or limit births as having an unmet need for family planning. Using this definition, Population Reports has estimated, based on DHS data, that 120 million married women of reproductive age in developing countries have an unmet need for contraception. Ruth Dixon-Mueller and Adrienne Germain suggest widening the definition of unmet need to include unmarried women, women who need better or more suitable contraceptive methods, women who need abortion services, and women who need more comprehensive reproductive health services than are currently available. These numbers cannot be easily estimated, but they would surely add substantially to the 120 million figure.

Men also have unmet needs for family planning. In DHS in Burundi, Egypt, Ghana, Kenya, and Pakistan, over half of men approve of family planning, but very few are using a contraceptive method. In smaller, qualitative studies as well, men have asked for more information about reproductive health services including both contraception and treatment for sexually transmitted diseases. Effectively serving all who want to avoid pregnancy but are not using contraception could help reconcile the dual goals of (1) serving individual clients and (2) slowing global population growth. Steven Sinding has suggested that family planning programs replace demographic objectives with the objective of meeting unmet need. In 9 of 12 countries studied, levels of contraceptive use would be higher if all unmet need were met than if current demographic objectives were reached.

To translate this unmet need to control fertility into utilization of reproductive health services, policy makers must let clients know that these services are a safe and effective way to achieve their personal goals.

Reproductive health programs can identify the obstacles that prevent women from using services and can design services and communication that will help overcome some of those obstacles. Obstacles may range from lack of supplies and services to dissatisfaction with current services to fears of contraceptive side effects, to social limits on women's mobility or decision-making. Beyond the need to control their own fertility, women also need other reproductive health services, and family planning programs may be able to meet these needs, as well.

INVOLVING CLIENTS IN PROGRAM DESIGN

Serving clients' needs requires learning and heeding what clients want. Since most family planning clients are women, women should be involved at all levels in population and reproductive health programs and policy-making. Women can offer valuable insights as policy-makers, program managers, and health professionals. Most importantly, programs should consult with clients about their reproductive health care priorities.

Policy-makers can use various means to learn what clients and the public want. A recent review has identified a range of approaches. Many of these approaches are routinely used in the audience research that is part of designing and monitoring family planning communication programs:

- Observation of client-provider interactions,

- Feedback from "mystery" or "simulated" clients-people who use services and then report on their experience,
- Patient flow studies to determine how long patients spend in such activities as waiting and talking to providers,
- Focus-group discussions with clients and potential clients about their experience and their preferences,
- Exit interviews or other post-service interviews with clients,
- Interviews with service personnel about what they think would constitute a good client visit and what they see as difficulties,
- Involving women directly in program design as program administrators or on advisory groups,
- Working with women's health advocacy groups to benefit from their analyses of women's health needs,
- Open discussion meetings in the community, sometimes specifically for women or for men, and
- Learning from other programs with services that clients like.

In Chile, for example, researchers interviewed women who had come in for clinic services. The clients wanted cleanliness, a reasonable waiting time, accessible services such as pharmacies, enough time with providers to ask questions about such topics as physiology and childrearing, and staff with a positive, respectful attitude toward clients.

Some women's grass-roots organizations have identified their own reproductive needs and responded to them. For example, the Working Women's Forum in India and the Mothers' Clubs in South Korea offer family planning services that complement the economic help and other services that they provide to members. The seven clinics run by the Bangladesh Women's Heal'h Coalition each have a local advisory committee to ensure that the clinics meets local needs. Some women's organizations have focused on informing other women. In 1991 a collective of Egyptian women wrot? a nontechnical book on women's reproductive health. In Peru women in focus groups helped Peru Mujer, a nongovernmental organization, design educational materials for nonliterate women like themselves. Women in Fiji made videos for women's groups on topics that they wanted discussed, such as sexually transmitted diseases and women's attitudes toward menstruation and family planning. Other family planning organizations can learn from such groups and perhaps collaborate with them.

Involving women more deeply in program design should not mean excluding men. Men and women share responsibility for reproductive health. Policies and programs will work best if they are planned by, and for, both women and men. Ideally, the insight and experiences of both women and men will create better programs that improve the lives of all clients.

Improving the lives of women and men should be a primary goal of population policy. Reproductive health care programs contribute by enabling men and women to live healthier lives and to plan when they will have children. Women, and men who enjoy better health and more control over their reproductive lives can have more opportunity to fulfill their hopes for their children, themselves, their families, and their communities.

OPPORTUNITIES FOR WOMEN THROUGH REPRODUCTIVE CHOICE

Women around the world hope for the future-for better lives for themselves, education and prosperity for their children, and security for their families. A broad array of social and economic changes is necessary to overcome the poverty, lack of education, and limited control over their own lives that often keep women's hopes from coming true. But women can take an important step forward when they make their own reproductive choices-about marriage, sex, childbearing, and contraception. The great majority of women want to control their own fertility. Growing contraceptive use in nearly every developing country attests to women's desire to plan their pregnancies. Many other women want to space or limit births but are not using contraception. The continuing high number of abortions, often undertaken illegally at great risk, also testifies to women's desire to control their own fertility.

How can reproductive choice improve a woman's life? Making choices about the course of one's own life asserts a person's fundamental dignity. Thus family planning is a basic human right, although many women are unable to exercise that right. Also, the woman who chooses when she has children, and how many, exerts an important measure of control over her own physical, emotional, and economic well-being. She contributes to her children's well-being too.

Health: More than half a million women die each year from causes related to pregnancy. Many of these deaths follow unwanted pregnancies: 20% to 40% result from unsafe abortions. For women who want to avoid pregnancy, using contraception means avoiding the risks of pregnancy and childbirth or of unsafe abortion.

Planning: By determining when she will have children and how many, a woman takes a step toward deciding how she will spend much of her life-whether to finish school, to give more attention to each child she has, to better manage household duties, possibly to earn income so that she and her family can live more prosperous lives, or even to contribute more to her community and society as a whole. Internationally comparable surveys find that, in countries where levels of contraceptive use are above average, women start childbearing later, end childbearing sooner, have fewer children, and spend fewer years caring for young children. Of course, a woman's decision to control her fertility does not guarantee her new opportunities. It does, however, help enable her to take advantage of opportunities that present themselves and to provide new resources to the family.

How can Family Planning Programs Help?

Family planning programs contribute most by helping women prevent unwanted pregnancies. Well-designed, high-quality programs can do even more by delivering services in ways that help women meet other needs as well. They can:

- Show by example that women should be treated with dignity: their opinions, valued; and their decisions, respected;
- Provide additional contraceptive and other reproductive health services that can meet common and serious needs-possibly care for sexually transmitted diseases and information and services for young people, for example;

- Influence public perceptions of women's roles by depicting in the mass media women who act with courage, take responsibility, and succeed in new roles;
- Encourage men to understand their own and women's reproductive health needs, share reproductive decision making, and take more responsibility for reproductive health, contraceptive use, and their families' welfare; and
- Employ women as family planning professionals, treat them equitably, and offer them opportunities to lead.

With the advice and involvement of the women they serve, well-designed reproductive health programs can help women in a variety of ways to improve their quality of life for themselves, their families, and their communities.

THE ASPIRATIONAL CULTURE AND IMAGES OF WOMEN

Whether or not the world actually has a growing appetite for 'non-political entertainment and sports is largely irrelevant. In a global information and communication system whose corporate managers characterise their output as 'product' (rather than content) and view people as 'demographics' (rather than audiences), appetites and aspirations can if necessary be created. Women are often a central target in this process of opening up markets. 'Polish women have been crying out for a magazine like this' insisted advertising manager Jack Kobylenski at the 1994 Polish launch of the glossy fashion and beauty magazine Elle, owned by French publisher Hachette. Of course no woman in Poland ever took to the streets to 'cry out' for Elle, but the Polish version of the magazine is now the third biggest edition, second only to France and the USA (Meller 1994).

In Russia, the American Hearst Corporation's Cosmopolitan entered the market cautiously in April 1994 with a monthly press run of 60,000; by 1995 this had risen to well over 500,000 and the Russian Cosmo was commonly described as a 'publishing miracle'. Says its Moscow-based publisher: 'I knew Cosmopolitan could work here. You looked at Russian women, and you saw... how they wanted to improve themselves. I knew if there was one magazine that shows you how your life can be, a shop window you can look in... it was Cosmo' (Hockstader 1995).

If women's magazines are fantasy-like shop windows that 'show you how your life can be', the products they display are of course also meant to be purchased-in real shops. But since actual buying power is often extremely limited, this step in the global marketing process requires a more long-term strategy. 'I take a decade's view', said company president Leonard Lauder at the opening of the first Este'e Lauder store in Prague in September 1994. 'I am a lipstick imperialist. You can't underestimate the long-term value companies like Este'e Lauder bring to Eastern Europe... One person, one family, can change the whole aspirational culture' (Menkes 1994). Helping along the process of change is Lauder's Central European Development Corporation which has a 75% stake in Nova TV, the Czech Republic's first-and hugely successful-commercial television station. The most popular items in its foreign-dominated programme schedule include Dynasty, M*A*S*H and Disney animations (Gray 1995), all of whose representations of women have been the subject of much criticism.

Interestingly enough, in his lengthy study of Dynasty Jostein Gripstrud makes a direct comparison between its female 'anti-heroine' Alexis Carrington Colby (played by Joan Collins) and the Disney creation Cruella de Ville in One Hundred and One Dalmations, who wanted to skin little puppies to make herself a fur coat (Gripstrud, 1995, p. 193). These are the 'bad' women of male fantasy, the villainesses whose function is to confirm the proper characteristics of 'good' women-passivity and powerlessness, which are the essential attributes of any woman who is to achieve happiness in popular media fiction. The female audience is encouraged to emulate submissive, long-suffering heroines not simply by a media narrative which suggests that this is how they will 'get their man'. Women are also encouraged to literally 'buy in' to the (fantasy) world of such heroines by purchasing products marketed by the shows' producers.

Disney was one of the first to recognise the power of 'merchandising'. From Alice's Wonderland in 1924 to Pocahontas in 1995, Disney products-films, television, publications, character dolls, theme parks-have become mutually reinforcing links in a powerful narrative of consumption. During the 1980s the multimillion Dynasty merchandising operation included not just clothes (fans of the programme used to 'dress up' to watch the show), but also luggage, linens, jewellery, home furnishings and even optical wear. One of the most successful items was the perfume 'Forever Krystle', named after the 'good', sympathetic female character Krystle Carrington (played by Linda Evans).

In the first series of Dynasty Krystle, then a subservient secretary, married her brutal boss Blake Carrington and the marriage went through numerous tribulations. In the ads for 'Forever Krystle' several years later, Blake is portrayed as an adoring husband who presents his wife with a fragrance specially created for her. Krystle will be happy 'forever' after-and by implication so will the women who buy the perfume.

GENDER AND THE POLITICAL ECONOMY OF COMMUNICATION

Any consideration of gender portrayal in the media must take account of these wider issues of political economy if existing patterns of representation are to be properly understood and challenged. For as Kamla Bhasin has rightly pointed out: 'We are not just concerned with how women are portrayed in the media or how many women work in the media. We are also concerned about what kinds of lives they lead, what status they have, and what kind of society we have. The answers to these questions will determine our future strategies for communication and networking. Communication alternatives therefore need to emerge from our critique of the present world order and our vision of the future' (Bhasin 1994, p. 4).

Certain trends in the information and communication system of the present world order are set to have a considerable impact on the future of people throughout the world. The media mergers of the past decade have not only consolidated huge power in a decreasing number of corporations with global reach. They have also begun to erode old distinctions between information and entertainment, software and hardware, production and distribution. It is this fusion of communication forms, which constitutes a radical break with the past, that presents such a challenge for the future. For although the influence of a single medium such as television is clearly limited in many ways, it is the 'panoply of cultural means together' (Schiller 1989, p. 151) that is central to the ability of large media conglomerates to present a world-view that bolsters and reinforces their position in the modern economic system and that system itself.

In this context the significance of 'lipstick imperialism' becomes clear. The term puts an intriguing new spin on a concept that dominated much of the debate on international communication during the 1960s and 1970s. 'Cultural imperialism'-the rallying cry of communication scholars and activists who sought to defend indigenous cultural identity and economic independence-now has a rather anachronistic ring. Yet the free-market economic policies adopted by many countries around the world in recent years have opened the doors to new forms of consumerism, driven by increasingly commercial, increasingly transnational communication media. Reflecting on the current situation in Latin America, Gabriel Escobar and Anne Swardson take the example of MTV Latino, whose 'message is powerful and still growing, an influential cultural tool in a market already saturated with images and products from the north.

But what is most striking about this loud invasion is the silence that has greeted it. Three decades after the Latin American left led a call against cultural imperialism... the continent has unabashedly embraced-cultura lite'-a universal, homogenised popular culture in which touches of Latin American rhythm or-Spanglish' accent a dominant North American diet of songs, words and images' (Escobar and Swardson, 1995). To explain the lack of opposition to this contemporary cultural invasion, Uruguayan writer and journalist Eduardo Galeano echoes Schiller's 'panoply' thesis. By stimulating consumption, he argues, the neo-liberal policies which the countries of the North passionately promote simultaneously stifle resistance and creativity. They have helped to develop in Latin Americans a trend towards imitation and what he describes as a 'mentality of resignation' (see Hamelink 1994, p. 132).

Such an analysis is equally applicable outside Latin America. MTV Asia-with 28 million viewers in the region-is said to have triggered a change not just in musical tastes, but 'in social style.

In fashions, behaviour, language and morals, more and more youngsters are falling to the thrall of MTV and are drawn into aping the West' (Menon 1993a, p. 29). Again, this cultural invasion is dictated by economics-as MTV's director of international programme sales explains: 'The youth audience is the most sought-after and most lucrative demographic internationally' (Jenkinson 1994, p. 104). Again, the representation of women plays a particular role in the channel's iconography. Sut Jhally, in his educational documentary Dreamworlds, argues that MTV works systematically to deny women subjectivity. Jhally demonstrates how the channel constructs an image of women through a patriarchal discourse of 'nymphomia'-as ever-available objects in an endlessly repetitive male adolescent fantasy world. Other studies agree that, despite the presence of strong female images in some music videos, it is hard to fault the essential truth of this argument.

MEDIA COMMERCIALISATION AND THE WOMEN'S MARKET

If music television targets the 'youth demographic' by using highly sexualised male fantasy images of women, the 'female demographic' is itself an increasingly important market in today's commercial media environment. According to Tor Hansson, managing director for Universal Media in Norway, 'the most sought-after demographic group in Norway is women between the ages of 25 and 45-and especially professional and middle management women' (Edmunds 1994, p. 4). With advertisers in Norway and Sweden complaining that this lucrative market was not being delivered to them, the powerful Kinnevik media group launched TV6-Scandinavia's first channel targeted solely to women-in April 1994. Three weeks before its launch, all advertising spots for TV6 had been sold out.

Most of the new channels aimed at women adopt the style and mode of address of women's magazines-the vehicle through which advertisers have traditionally reached the female consumer. Not surprisingly, publishing giants such as Hearst (USA), Hachette (France), D.C. Thompson (United Kingdom) and Bertelsmann (Germany) were among the first to grasp the additional routes into the female market opened by a proliferation of new cable channels. In 1993 three channels aimed at women were launched in the UK alone. The most successful has been UK Living, providing 'practical and entertainment' programmes for women. The output is 'comforting, non-threatening and promises not to over-tax your senses, sensitivities or brain-cells. It smacks of tabloid television-the agony aunts, the special offers,... the game shows, the cult of the minor celebrity as social pundit. There are no documentaries or news' (O'Brien 1993, p. 20). Apolitical and uncontroversial, these channels fit perfectly within the framework of consumerism. To paraphrase the (male) director of Germany's first women's television channel TM3, launched in August 1995, they pursue an ideal viewer who is 'feminine rather than feminist'.

Gems, the first transnational television channel aimed at women, was launched in April 1993 for distribution in the USA and Latin America. The (male) president of International Television which produces the channel's shows, all made in Spanish, describes it as 'programming that's relevant to women, showing musicals, movies and mini-series featuring women's unique roles' (Burnett 1993, p. 25). Particularly revealing of the Gems ideology is an advertisement for the channel, run in the trade magazine 'TV World' in April 1994: 'She's a romantic and a realist. A caretaker and an emerging power. She's the gatekeeper of more than $260 billion in the U.S. alone. And she has just one international Spanish-language cable television service talking directly to her. GEMS Television.... GEMS is her TV. Because we empower her in a way cable programming never has before. And because we know she is a treasure. GEMS is her TV. That's its brilliance'. Telenovelas feature prominently in the schedule, ensuring-according to marketing director Grace Santana-success against any competition: 'We've programming that's proven-novelas have been around for 40 years' (see Lindsay and Millichip 1994, p. 4).

That such a channel will 'empower' women seems improbable. What does seem likely, however, is that Gems will indeed open up a new gateway to capital-potentially '$260 billion in the U.S. alone'. With an audience of 600,000 subscribers shortly after its launch, by early 1995 the Miami-based channel was reaching a potential audience of almost five million viewers throughout the Americas (Weinstock 1995, p. 39).

While male-owned commercial women's channels like these are flourishing, the Canadian Women's Television Network (WTN)-launched in January 1995 as 'a dynamic alternative to mainstream viewing: a channel run by women, for women'-is attempting to succeed in the same market, but on quite different terms. In May 1995 Barbara Barde, WTN's first Vice President of Programming outlined some of the channel's distinctive features: 'WTN has no victims, no violence.... We have women as chief protagonists, women who drive the stories, are in control of their lives.... For us, it is very important that women form part of the creative team of producers, directors and writers... We also have a foundation to which we pledge three-quarters of 1% of our revenues. Its job is two-fold.

The first part is research rojects, looking at issues relating to women in broadcasting. The second is concerned with mentoring, apprenticeships, etc.... not only mentoring women within our own organisation, but also encouraging conventional broadcasters to do the same.... I think we can be a role model' (Barde 1995, pp. 18-19).

The philosophy has little in common with that of the male-controlled channels described earlier and-almost inevitably-WTN has met with hostility from male media establishment. When industry ratings, released in July 1995, showed that WTN was the least-watched of Canada's new cable channels, male critics rushed to the attack. An article by John Haslett Cuff in the Toronto 'Globe and Mail' declared that 'WTN was born with a large chip on its padded shoulders'; in his view, no-one would be surprised by the ratings.

On the other hand, Cuff was surprised and disappointed that Bravo, an arts channel, had tied for second-last place in the ratings since it was 'easily the most stimulating and original of all the new specialty services'. It is instructive to contrast this review with another in 'TV World', by Claire Atkinson. She noted that both WTN and Bravo were 'still finding their audience, although both have won recognition for their programming philosophies.... For WTN.. the problem is that TV viewing is a family affair during primetime, and it isn't until after 22.00 that women will watch channels on their own'. .

The gendered nature of these two reviews is illuminating. Cuff's comments display a deep and subjective antagonism to the channel; Atkinson reveals a knowledge of the context in which female viewing takes place, and uses this knowledge to interpret the ratings. For WTN itself the ratings would have come as little surprise.

As Barbara Barde remarked two months before they appeared, 'We always expected that our audience would grow slowly, and that we would have to change habits in a large number of households, because guess who controls the remote controls? Not women' (ibid.). Whether the finances of WTN will allow the channel sufficient time to build up its audience remains to be seen.

Rosalind Coward has argued that during the 1980s, series after series of women's television programmes in the United Kingdom were simply 'allowed to fail', while other genres were protected and preserved until they had established themselves (Coward 1987, p. 100). In the 1990s it is clear that any venture of this kind faces an even more formidable array of obstacles, most of which will never be experienced by channels which treasure women as the gatekeepers of dollar bills.

RESISTING THE MENTALITY OF RESIGNATION

The immensity, facelessness and apparent impregnability of today's media conglomerates undoubtedly help to foster a 'mentality of resignation', as Galeano puts it. The mentality of resignation is a sign that people are being, or have been, disempowered. But if certain forms of communication and culture can disempower, others can empower. Over the past twenty years women have not been content merely to denounce biases and inequities in the established media.

Women have created and used countless alternative and participatory communication channels to support their struggles, defend their rights, promote reflection, diffuse their own forms of representation. Pilar Rian argues that this process has made women the primary subjects of struggle and change in communication systems, by developing oppositional and proactive alternatives that influence language, representations and communication technologies. Standing outside the mainstream, 'women's movement media' have certainly played a crucial role in women's struggle around the world. Part of a global networking, consciousness-raising and knowledge creation project, they have enabled women to communicate through their own words and images. If print and publishing have been the most widely used formats, in the past two decades other media such as music, radio, video, film and-increasingly the new communication technologies-have also been important. Over the same period, in most regions there has been a steady growth of women's media associations and networks, and an increase in the number of women working in mainstream media. Yet as Donna Allen points out 'there is still a wide gap between the women who have formed networks outside of the 'mainstream' media and those women who are employed in mass media who hold the key to reaching the larger public'. The closing of this gap, she argues, 'is a crucial step toward the advancement of all women.'

The building of such alliances, and the merging of women's diverse experiences of working with and in the media, is surely one of the most urgent tasks for women struggling for a more diverse and democratic world information and communication system.

GENDER PORTRAYAL IN THE MEDIA

Clearly the debates around gender representation in the media have moved on since the content analyses of 'sex-roles and stereotypes' which typified studies of the 1970s in North America and in countries such as Japan, Korea, the Philippines where quantitative social science methods were favoured. These studies certainly documented women's exclusion from or silencing in many media forms, and helped to show how media images reinforce notions of 'difference'-in behaviour, aspirations, psychological traits and so on-between women and men. Studies of this kind are of course still carried out, and they remain important in recording some of the basic elements in a very complex situation. In an ambitious global monitoring exercise, women from 71 countries studied their news media for one day in January 1995. More than 15,500 stories were analysed, and the results were dramatic. Only 17% of people interviewed in the news were women. Just 11% of news stories dealt with issues of special concern to women, or foregrounded any gender perspective on the events reported (MediaWatch, 1995).

National monitoring studies, over longer time periods, show similar patterns. The particular power of these studies lies in their potential to document change. In fact, regular media monitoring in Canada and the USA shows surprisingly slow progress towards equal representation of women and men in the media. Studies since 1974 indicate that 'peaks' may be followed by 'troughs', with no sustained pattern of improvement (see CRTC, 1990; Stephens 1994; Women, Men and Media 1995). Indeed, according to one of the longest running studies of trends in gender portrayal on US television (carried out since 1969 by the Cultural Indicators research team at the Annenberg School of Communication, University of Pennsylvania), 'the demography of the world of television is impressive in its repetitiveness and stability:... women comprise one-third or less of the characters in all samples except day-time serials where they are 45.5%, and in game shows where they are 55.3%.

The smallest percentage of women is in news (27.8%) and in children's programmes (23.4%). As major characters, women's role's shrink in children's programmes to 18%... A child growing up with children's major network television will see about 123 characters each Saturday morning but rarely, if ever, a role model of a mature female as leader' (Gerbner 1994, pp. 39, 44). The world depicted by the media 'seems to be frozen in a time-warp of obsolete and damaging representations' (op. cit., p. 43).

INTERPRETING PATTERNS OF PORTRAYAL

Obvious numerical imbalances in media portrayals of women and men tell only a small part of the story-and not necessarily the most important part. Of course most studies go further, investigating gender differentiation in social and occupational roles, psychological and personality traits, physical attributes and so on. The results have been extensively documented for most world regions and will not be detailed here. Perhaps the more interesting questions concern the implicit messages which are woven into these media portrayals of women and men. Why is the pattern as it is, and why does it so stubbornly persist despite two decades of research and action aimed at changing it? There are many ways of approaching such questions. For example, I have already argued that discrimination or imbalance in gender portrayal is not an isolated phenomenon which can be studied-or changed-in a compartmentalised way. Media representations of women and men take shape within particular, and changing, socio-economic formations which must themselves be analysed and understood. But there are other issues to consider too.

One is the question of political ideology. In most parts of the world, at different times in history, representations and images of women been used as symbols of political aspirations and social change. An obvious example was the widespread use of particular asexual, 'emancipated' female images in Soviet culture: the confident, sturdy woman on her tractor, on the farm, or in the factory. As various recent commentators have pointed out, images of this kind never reflected existing reality. In the words of Olga Lipovskaya, 'the social realist tradition was intended to create an ideal reality and utilised this model to portray the exemplary woman of the radiant Communist future' (Lipovskaya 1994, p. 124; see also Voronina 1994; Azhgikina 1995). In such a situation female imagery becomes a metaphor for a particular political ideology, rather than a representation of women's lives. In her analysis of the powerful media definitions of womanhood in revolutionary China, Elizabeth Croll maintains that 'imaging' actually became a substitute for living or experience: 'With the gradual exclusion of semantic or visual variations of image and text, the rhetoric of equality and celebration soon became the only language officially tolerated... There were no images of, or words for representing, the inequality of experience' (Croll 1995, p. 80).

In one of the few extensive analyses of female imagery in the Arab States, Sarah Graham-Brown points out that images of women may be used in conflicting ways-as symbols of progress on the one hand, and as symbols of continuity with the cultural past on the other-frequently in reaction to representations of women imposed from outside the society, for instance by the Western media. Major ideological changes obviously affect the use of female imagery to promote national goals. A clear example, cited by Graham-Brown, is the contrast between the way women were portrayed in the media in Iran during the Pahlavi rule and since the revolution. 'In both instances, these images form an important element in the way the regimes promote and legitimize themselves. At the same time, neither kind of image necessarily reflects with accuracy the changes or continuities in the everyday life of women in different classes'. The disjuncture between image and reality becomes profound in situations where governments are attempting to mobilize people for certain kinds of social change.

Graham-Brown gives examples from post-independence Algeria and Nasser's Egypt, where 'modernist' and westernised images of women were used as emblems of progress and enlightenment. Yet 'on the whole, these images of emancipation, while they might promote the idea of the progressive nation, did not challenge basic gender relations in society, particularly male domination of the family structure' (Graham-Brown 1988, p. 245). In contemporary Egypt, according to Lila Abu-Lughod (1993), there is a similar gap between the ideological message of certain 'national interest' television serials and experience of life in particular communities. The interpretation of such images is thus fraught with complications. This does not mean that no indication of changing status, or changing attitudes to women can be gleaned from them. But they cannot be 'read' according to any simple formula whereby changes in imagery are assumed to equate with changes of the same magnitude in women's lives.

DIVERSITY AND CHANGE IN GENDER PORTRAYAL

These examples illustrate the limitations of a framework which sets out to critique 'negative' images and to demand 'positive' media representations of women. Such a juxtasposition assumes that there is a norm against which images can be judged. In reality, things are much more complicated. The same kind of image can embody a variety of different meanings, depending on the context. A more promising route seems to be offered by the search for greater 'diversity' in gender portrayal. But here again, the situation is not completely straightforward. Media representations of women and men in the 1990s may indeed be more diverse than they were twenty years ago. Lawyers, doctors and police officers are no longer inevitably male; and we may even see the occasional male character in the kitchen, weeping into the washing-up bowl. But how important is this change, and what is its significance?

It is true that drama-including popular fiction, soap operas and telenovelas-has to some extent begun to respond to new currents and complexities in gender relations, with occasional portrayals of the 'new man' (gentle, supportive, emotional) and the 'modern woman' (independent, assertive, resourceful). But detailed analyses suggest that such innovations are often simply a modish facade, behind which lurk old-fashioned formulaic assumptions. Longitudinal studies of Italian television drama show that, despite a scattering of 'anti-heroes', output remains overwhelmingly male-centered and success-oriented.

In Germany and the United Kingdom, studies have called into question claims that 'progressive' soap operas have actually introduced radically different points of view (for example, Externbrink 1992; Geraghty 1995). In Latin America most of the independent new heroines of recent telenovelas, on closer examination seem to have been introduced as a means of changing the 'outer wrappings' of the genre rather than its core messages. In the USA several studies of the successful prime-time series thirty something have concluded that despite claims that it articulates a 'new view of manhood', the show's construction of reality is substantially conservative (see Hanke 1992; Heide 1995). Even the trail-blazing 1980s female detective series Cagney and Lacey does not escape criticism. Julie D'Acci's detailed study reveals that although the writers struggled to maintain the show's original feminist orientation, in the face of pressures imposed by commercial network television, the series gradually became more conventional, 'feminine' and exploitative-in the sense of promoting stories that literally 'cashed in' on issues of great complexity for women, such as rape, abortion, marital violence and so on (D'Acci 1994).

Sightings of the 'new man' in media portrayals have been recorded in countries as different as India, Italy and the USA (Shelat 1994; Buonanno 1994; Douglas 1995). Again, this phenomenon can not automatically be taken at face value. Milly

Buonanno sounds a note of caution, pointing out that the 'new man' in Italian drama is winning the central position in the family and domestic domain at the expense of women, whose overall share of central roles has fallen over the past four years: 'Even the domestic sphere, the traditional stronghold of the female character in drama, now seems to be increasingly inhabited by males who show themselves more in command of emotional life than the women do' (p. 82). A similar concern is expressed by Susan Douglas. Both she and Manisha Shelat question the extent to which these images actually reflect reality in their societies, though for Shelat they are a 'welcome change' from the role stereotyping that predominates in the majority of Indian media. But Douglas is less sanguine, seeing the development as a 'bizarre twist on the real world, where many women have changed, but too many men have not' (p.81).

This review raises important questions about the extent to which the mainstream media are capable of reflecting diversity and complexity in a way which would properly respond to the current criticisms of women media activists. For this reason, some women remain sceptical of any engagement with the mainstream. But others-like film-maker Michelle Citron-regard it as an essential step forward, providing a possibility of 'subverting' and changing mainstream media content, despite the compromises involved: 'These are risks we need now to take. We will lose a certain amount of control, despite our best intentions and preparedness... But we need new-data' in order to refine our understanding of (the media) and our relationship to it' (Citron 1988, p. 62).

THE MEDIA AND VIOLENCE AGAINST WOMEN

In a detailed analysis of how the press covered four prominent sex crimes in the USA over the period 1978 to 1990, Helen Benedict concludes: 'During the 1980s and 1990s, the quality of sex-crime coverage has been steadily declining... Rape as a societal problem has lost interest for the public and the press, and the press is reverting to its pre-1970s focus on sex crimes as individual, bizarre, or sensationalist case histories' (Benedict 1992, p. 251). Benedict offers a useful set of suggestions to improve the reporting of sex crimes-covering language, balance, context, focus on attacker rather than victim, and so on. On the specific question of language Ann Jones, author of Next Time, She'll Be Dead: Battering and How to Stop It, gives numerous examples of crime reporting in which women are victims but their attackers' violence is masked in the language of love. Says Jones, 'this slipshod reporting has real consequences in the real lives of real men and women. It affirms a batterer's most common excuse for assault: "I did it because I love you so much" (quoted in Media Report to Women 1994). It does seem justifiable to suppose that what we see and hear in the media has real consequences in our lives. However the issue of 'media effects' raises many complicated questions which I will not attempt to take up in this short paper. Instead I will approach the question of violence primarily from the perspective of the female consumer. How do women react to the portrayal of violence? It seems fair to conclude that if women are made uncomfortable, anxious or frightened by depictions of violence, then their views deserve to be heard.

In fact, the presentation of violence in the media is an issue which provokes quite divergent reactions between women and men. Women are less likely than men to watch violent programmes and films. And even if they do watch, women may not actually enjoy what they see. In the words of one woman interviewed in a recent British study, 'women don't enjoy watching violence in the way that men do, judging by the popularity of violent films. I don't know any women who get a kick out of watching the after-effects of violence' (Hargrave 1994, p. 20). Research in the USA shows that women (47%) are much more likely than men (24%) to object to the level of violence on television (see 'Marketing to Women' 1993, p. 6). A survey of women viewers in Canada found that violence was what concerned women most about television: 34% selected this from a list of seven items of concern, and 36% said they avoid violent programmes on television (MediaWatch 1994).

In India women were found to have a 'strong dislike for (television) films which show violence, and admit to just waiting for the violent scenes to be over so that they could enjoy the next violent-free scene' (Media Advocacy Group, 1994). Women are also more concerned than men about the possible impact of violent messages. Research in the United Kingdom has shown that 59% of women-compared with 45% of men-would be prepared to give up their freedom to watch violent programmes if it was widely believed that these caused some people to be violent (Docherty, 1990). Of the Canadian women questioned in MediaWatch's 1994 survey, 82% said they believed that violence in the media contributes to violence in society. More informal reports have found that women in many countries around the world express high levels of anxiety about media violence, and groups such as the Tanzania Media Women's Association (TAMWA) and Women's Media Watch in Jamaica have launched campaigns and activities to address the problem (see Davies 1994).

For women who have actually experienced violence, subsequent exposure to scenes of media violence against women-particularly when portrayed as 'entertainment' may be especially painful: 'There are things that bring it back... I can't watch extremely violent things, I just want to turn off because the thoughts start and I just don't want to know' (see Kelly 1988, p. 193). But even if they have not been victims themselves, seeing violence on television is an extremely disturbing experience for many women. Recent audience research in Germany found that more than half of all female viewers are frightened and feel threatened by the kind of violence presented on television (Roser and Kroll, 1995).

Similar findings emerged clearly from an in-depth study in the United Kingdom (Schlesinger et al., 1992) in which women were shown various kinds of violent material, including an episode from Crimewatch UK (a series which reconstructs crimes: the reconstruction used was of a young woman's rape and murder), and the Hollywood film The Accused (which includes a graphic portrayal of gang rape). One of the most striking findings was 'the fear of male violence, particularly of rape. This was generally found across all of the viewers, despite class or ethnicity, as was the concern about the possible impact upon children of viewing violence against women on television. In relation to the rape/murder in Crimewatch and the gang rape in The Accused, group discussions revealed a profound anxiety about personal safety' (op. cit., 166). In the case of The Accused, 'there was considerable concern about the appropriateness of a Hollywood film-essentially premised on entertainment values-as the most suitable vehicle for dealing with this troubling subject... and worries (which) centred upon what-men' were likely to make of this film' (op. cit., 163).

The Center for Media and Public Affairs in the United States analysed the incidence of violence on television over a twenty-four hour day in April 1994.

The number of violent scenes ranged from a low of 71 in the hour between 2 p.m. and 3 p.m., to a high of 295 scenes of violence in the hour from 6 a.m. to 7 a.m. (Kolbert 1994). An eight-country study of television violence in Asia conducted by the Asian Mass Communication Research and Information Centre classified 59% of all the programmes studied as 'violent', with particularly high levels of violence in India, Thailand and the Philippines (Menon 1993b).

George Gerbner, who has studied television violence for the past twenty years, maintains that 'Constant displays of violent power and victimization cultivate an exaggerated sense of danger and insecurity among heavy viewers of television.' Clearly, many of the women in the studies mentioned earlier experience this sense of danger and insecurity. Strong sentiments were also expressed by these women about the extent to which it is acceptable to show representations of violence against women to the general public without adding special safeguards.

Such ideas deserve to be taken seriously, and to enter the public domain so that they become part of the debate on regulation and self-regulation. Satellite communication, by weakening the control of national governments over a growing proportion of media messages and images beamed into their territories from elsewhere, has given this debate a new urgency. But proposals for a global code of practice have been met with general scepticism by the media community (see Shaw 1993). At the national level only a few countries-for example, Australia, Canada and New Zealand-have so far taken a new, tougher stand on television portrayal of violence against women (see Racine 1995; Mills 1995).

The United Nations Declaration on the Elimination of Violence Against Women-which defines the term 'violence against women' as 'any act of gender-based violence that results in, or is likely to result in, physical, sexual, or psychological harm or suffering to women'-certainly provides scope for actions aimed at reducing or eliminating media violence in general, and scenes of violence against women in particular. Here it is important to bear in mind that media depictions of dramatic aggression against women are at one end of a continuum of media images of women which build up from an apparently benign starting point. For instance the educational video Dreamworlds, mentioned earlier, demonstrates how an accumulation of images in which women are presented as submissive objects of male fantasy in music television may contribute to a perception of the ultimate act of sexual violence-rape-as justifiable and 'natural'. At the very least, the development of further materials of this sort should be undertaken with a view to documenting how patterns of media violence against women are constructed, and what their implications may be for the lives of women everywhere.

PORNOGRAPHY AND FREEDOM OF EXPRESSION

Pornography has for many years been a multi-billion dollar international industry. In the United Kingdom alone, œ52 million was earned from the sale of pornographic magazines in 1993 (Davies 1994). Recent developments in the information and communication system have made pornography more widely available than ever before.

For instance television deregulation, combined with transborder satellite channels, has resulted in a tenfold increase in televised pornography over the past decade in Europe, and the demand is escalating (Papathanassopoulos 1994). New information technologies have introduced various forms of 'on-line' pornography. Interactive computer porn is a particularly menacing development. This is quite different from earlier forms, in that the user becomes a participant-a 'doer' of pornography rather than merely an observer. Male fantasy myths about women's sexual availability feature strongly in these products.

In cyberspace and elsewhere, pornographers routinely use 'freedom of speech' arguments to defend their right to distribute material which is nothing other than a violation of women's human right to safety and dignity. In 1986 British Member of Parliament

Clare Short tried to introduce a Bill to make illegal the display of naked or partially naked women in sexually provocative poses in newspapers (known in the UK as 'Page 3 girls'). 'Killjoy Clare', as she was dubbed by the Sun newspaper, was accused of 'authoritarianism', of wishing to deprive people of one of their few 'pleasures', of wanting British newspapers to resemble Pravda. Compared with the displays used in hard-core pornography, Page 3 may seem relatively innocuous. But Clare Short received 5000 letters of support for her proposal, the overwhelming majority from women. Twelve women who had been raped wrote that their attackers said they reminded them of a woman on Page 3, or said they ought to be on Page 3 (see Short 1991, p.xxi). Since 1986 one major British tabloid newspaper has abandoned its 'Page 3 girls', but others maintain the practice.

Pornography is a central issue for the women's movement, especially in relation to violence against women. It is regarded by many as the key site of women's oppression. Yet disputes over the regulation of pornography have split women's groups, raising the spectre of censorship-a weapon which could be used against minority groups and against women themselves. In this respect, recent developments in Canada are of note. In February 1992, in a milestone decision, the Canadian Supreme Court upheld a conviction against a pornography dealer and, in so doing, recognised a new definition of obscenity. The Court 'recognised the harms to women, children and society arising from pornography as justifying constraint on the free speech rights of pornographers. The expression found in obscene material, the Court concluded, lies far from the core of the guarantee of free expression' (Easton 1994, p. 178). The Butler decision, as it became known, has had important and not entirely predictable consequences. Women saw it as a huge step forward, opening up the possibility of convictions in other areas of media content which could also be proven to degrade or dehumanise women. But the unforeseen consequence was a crackdown on works by prominent homosexual and lesbian authors and, for a time, Andrea Dworkin-one of America's fiercest opponents of pornography, whose book Pornography: Men Possessing Women was temporarily seized by the Canadian customs.

The regulation of pornography is also a contentious issue for women partly because the term 'pornography' has been confused-even in legal instruments-with the concept of 'obscenity'. The definition of obscenity-filthy, disgusting, indecent-implies a moral judgement with which women may feel uncomfortable. The definition of pornography in most feminist literature follows that of Catharine MacKinnon and Andrea Dworkin: 'the graphic sexually explicit subordination of women through pictures or words' (MacKinnon 1987, p. 176). This perspective shifts the arguments against pornography away from the terrain of morality, towards an interpretation of pornography as a violation of women's rights. Yet even here there are problems. One criticism of the civil rights Ordinances of Minneapolis and Indianapolis, drafted by MacKinnon and Dworkin in the 1980s as a means of regulating pornography, was that terms such as 'sexual objectification', 'degradation', 'subordination'-on which appeal to the Ordinances depended-left too much scope for judicial interpretation and could be used against women. As Carol Smart (1989) argues, traditional judicial attitudes reflect a legal framework which is essentially incompatible with the definitions of feminism, and which cannot accommodate the complexity of feminist arguments. However, Susan Easton (1994) takes the view that-rather like the mainstream media-this is an area of challenge for feminists, who must work to infuse new ideas into established legal frameworks. As one of a number of strategies to deal with pornography, she advocates the enactment of a law to prohibit 'incitement to sexual hatred'.

Of course the polarisation of the pornography debate in terms of 'free speech' versus 'censorship' fails to take account of the fact that freedom of expression is limited in all sorts of ways for most people, most of the time. As A.J. Liebling remarked many years ago, 'Freedom of the press belongs to those who own one'. In today's media context, the aphorism rings particularly true. Eastman points out that the feminist argument against pornography 'is not an isolated assault on free speech rights, but could be seen as a recognition of the difficulty and undesirability of an absolutist position on free speech in a pluralist society' (1994, p. 174). Since they have relatively restricted access to the channels of communication, it is hardly surprising that women's attitudes towards 'free speech' differ from those of men. For example, a study of attitudes among journalism students in the USA found that the women see the free speech issue from a dual perspective. While they value the operation of a 'free press', they also believe that absolute freedom of expression can be harmful to them and to others. The authors conclude optimistically that if the female students carry their attitudes towards free expression with them into the journalistic work force, 'society may see a somewhat different set of professional values in the future.'

WOMEN AS USERS OF MEDIA AND NEW TECHNOLOGIES

Gender differences in media access are linked with patterns of discrimination in society at large, and with patterns of power relations within the home. In many parts of the world, high female illiteracy rates mean that women have little access to the print media. As for television and radio, women may not always be able to watch or listen to their preferred programmes. Research in countries as different as Mozambique, Zambia, India, the USA and the United Kingdom shows that, in family viewing and listening situations, the decisions of the adult male in the household tend to prevail. Nevertheless, these and other studies show that women are enthusiastic media users. In Egypt certain groups of women are particularly avid television viewers: one study found that 21% of women-compared with 11% of men-spent on average more than four hours a day in front of the small screen (El-Fawal 1991). In a study of relatively low-income, poorly educated women in Nigeria, 96% had access to radio within the household or compound and television was available to 89%. More than two-thirds of the women listened to the radio every day, and just under one-third watched television daily (Imam 1992). In Ecuador, Rodriguez (1990) found that 94% of the working-class women she surveyed had radio in their homes, and over half listened at least three hours a day. In Brazil almost every woman in three low-income areas studied by Tufte (1992) had television in her house, and the women watched an average of three to four telenovelas a day, six days a week.

These Brazilian women's heavy viewing of telenovelas reflects a universal, gendered pattern of media preferences. All over the world men prefer sports, action-oriented programmes and information (especially news); women prefer popular drama, music/dance and other entertainment programmes (see Cooper-Chen 1994; Lull 1988; Sepstrup and Goonasekera 1994). These programme choices are most easily explained in terms of the extent to which women and men are able to identify with various types of media content. One of the most obvious reasons for women's preference for serialised drama, soap opera and telenovelas is the exceptionally high proportion of female characters in such programmes. Nor is it surprising that men favour genres such as action drama which feature powerful, dynamic male characters, or sports and news which revolve almost exclusively around male figures. It is reasonable to wonder what impact these repetitive patterns of gender representation have on the female- and the male-audience. During the 1980s there was a vogue for research into 'women's genres'-soap opera, melodrama, magazines-leading to the conclusion that these could 'empower' women. Recent studies have criticised such claims as being wildly exaggerated, and have focused on the fundamentally conservative and patriarchal frameworks within which these genres operate.

The problem is that in most other types of media content women simply do not see or hear any reflection of themselves, or of their experience of life. Television sports coverage in Europe provides a good example of the ways in which women's media choices are limited. Audience data for six countries in 1992 showed that, in all six, the sporting events most watched by men were football matches (Akyuz 1993). But women watched other sports. In France, the event which got the top female audience-over 8 million viewers, which was higher than the male audience for any sporting event-was women's figure skating at the Winter Olympics. According to the same data, the event which attracted the largest female audience in the United Kingdom was the women's 10,000 meters final in the Summer Olympics, though this reached only 8th place among male audiences. So it is not that women don't like watching sport, but that they like watching different sport. In particular, they like 'women's sport'. Unfortunately for women, the television sports schedules are built around male and not female preferences.

Similarly, news and current affairs programmes reflect a hierarchy of values in which the issues that concern women are given low priority, if covered at all. Recent research with British viewers shows that although women feel ambivalent about the concept of 'women's issues'-believing that once an issue becomes labelled as being of exclusive concern to women, it is in danger of being marginalised-there is also a shared understanding among women about issues that do concern them, and a feeling that these are not given priority in the news media. As one woman put it: 'Women's issues don't always get enough airtime on the so-called serious programmes. They don't have the same weight as world politics-which they should do, because they are about changing society in fundamental ways' (Sreberny-Mohammadi 1994, p. 69).

When asked directly, many women are clear that their preferences are not catered for by the media. In common with women recently surveyed in Canada and Germany (MediaWatch 1994; Roser and Krull 1995), most of those interviewed in Annabelle Sreberny-Mohammadi's research said that women should have more visibility on television, that there should be stronger female characters in drama and entertainment, and that there should be more women of authority in news and current affairs output. The participants felt that more women journalists and more female experts voicing opinions across a variety of issues would act as significant role models for other women, stimulate female interest in public issues, and-perhaps-sometimes speak in the interests of and for women (op. cit., p. 75).

The potential of the new information and communication technologies for the advancement of women is considerable. Networking, research, training, sharing of ideas and information-all these could be made infinitely easier through relatively affordable computer-mediated communications such as E-mail, Internet, hypertext and hypermedia (Steffen 1995). However, the obstacles are formidable. Unequal access to computers at school and in the home; highly male-dominated computer languages and operating systems; a hostile environment in which sexual harassment, sexual abuse and pornography flourish; these are just some of the factors which deter women from entering cyberspace. Gender-differentiated data on access to the new technologies are scarce, but those available do indicate that women are more reluctant users than men. In the United Kingdom in 1992 27% of women (compared to 37% of men) owned a home computer. Almost identical figures were reported in 1994 for the USA, where just 9% of women (and 15% of men) also had a computer modem-essential for use of E-mail and Internet. However 46% of women in this survey were dissatisfied with their level of technical know-how, suggesting that women may be frustrated users rather than completely uninterested in the new technologies.

Women comprise only about 10% of the Internet population in the USA. On the other hand Women's Wire-a commercial on-line service-has 90% to 95% female subscribers. Aliza Sherman recommends this kind of service-'providing women-specific information on topics such as women's health, politics, news, technology, business, finance, and family'-as a good starting point for women wary of cyberspace (Sherman 1995, p 26). Dale Spender claims that there are literally thousands of women's groups now on-line, though it seems that most of them are located in-and relatively limited to-North America. An exception is Virtual Sisterhood, described as a 'network for women around the world to share information, advice and experiences' which claims to have links with women's networks in a wide range of countries in Asia and Latin America (op. cit., p. 238). At the international level, the Association for Progressive Communications (APC) is among the most actively involved in supporting women through electronic communication. Women in Latin America as well as Canada and the USA have been using the APC networks for information exchange, and the APC Women's Networking Support Program has provided training workshops for women in Africa and Asia. The presence of a 40-strong all-women APC team at the United Nations Fourth World Conference on Women in 1995 introduced countless women to the possibilities of electronic communication, creating connections-technological and human-which will doubtless flourish in the years ahead.

But despite the hyperbole, it is important to remember that these new technologies are inherently no 'better' than the old ones-print, radio, television etc. For example, to claim-as British scholar Sadie Plant does-that the Internet is an inherently equalizing, non-hierarchical, even liberating communication system (see Spender, op. cit., p. 229) seems somewhat overstretched. Already, as Herman Steffen points out, 'large corporations are trying to turn cyberspace into a televised shopping mall where communications is one-way (entertainment) unless the consumer wishes to buy something; if so, he is welcome to communicate by punching in his credit-card number' (op. cit., p. 16). In that sense, cyberspace merely provides women with a new terrain on which to wage old struggles.

CHANGING THE PICTURE

As we reach the close of the twentieth century, there is little evidence that the world's communication media have a great deal of commitment to advancing the cause of women in their communities. Although the presence of women working within the media has increased in all world regions over the past two decades, real power is still very much a male monopoly (see Gallagher 1995). And while it is relatively easy to make proposals for the implementation of equality in the area of employment-and to measure progress-the issue of media content is much more problematic. Who is to decide what is acceptable in this domain? What criteria should be used to evaluate progress?

Research (and experience) has shown that purely quantitative measures are completely inadequate to describe gender portrayal in the media, much less to interpret its meaning or significance. There may be fairly widespread agreement that certain types of media content-for example, violent pornography or child pornography-are completely unacceptable and degrading to women, and should be strictly regulated. But what about the routine trivialisation and objectification of women in advertisements, the popular press, and the entertainment media? What about the prime-time television shows, watched by millions, in which women are regularly paraded as the mute and partly-clothed background scenery against which speaking and fully-clothed men take centre-stage? And how many women feel uneasy, or downright fearful, if they are alone at night in a taxi which stops at traffic lights beside an advertising poster adorned with a semi-naked, pouting female image? There are important rights and responsibilities involved here, and the conflicts are obvious. We have hardly begun to address them, much less find ways of reconciling them. In terms of strategies for change, there are perhaps five broad areas in which simultaneous and coordinated activity could bring results. Within each of these, I will merely indicate the types of action which seem particularly important, rather than explore the many approaches and initiatives which have already been tried.

First, there needs to be pressure from within the media themselves. More women must be employed-at all levels and in all types of work-in the media, so that we do finally achieve the critical mass of female creative and decision-making executives who could change media output. Numbers are important, if long-established media practices and routines are to be challenged. To quote the veteran American journalist, Kay Mills: 'A story conference changes when half the participants are female... There is indeed security in numbers. Women become more willing to speak up in page-one meetings about a story they know concerns many readers' (Mills 1990, p. 349). There is evidence that, when they do constitute a reasonable numerical force, women can and do make a difference.

For instance, in the United States a 1992 survey of managing editors of the largest 100 daily newspapers found that 84% of responding editors agreed that women have made a difference, both in defining the news, and in expanding the range of topics considered newsworthy-women's health, family and child care, sexual harassment and discrimination, rape and battering, homeless mothers, quality of life and other social issues were all cited as having moved up the hierarchy of news values because of pressure from women journalists (Marzolf 1993). In their study of press coverage in India during the 1980s, Ammu Joseph and Kalpana Sharma (1994) conclude that female journalists played an important role in focusing attention on issues of crucial importance to women: dowry-related deaths, rape, the right to maintenance after divorce, the misuse of sex determination tests, and the re-emergence of sati.

But it is not just a question of introducing 'new' topics (though they are age-old concerns for women) on to the news agenda. As we know from the example of war reporting in the former Yugoslavia, women have also succeeded in changing the way in which 'established' issues are covered. Similarly, in the Asian context, Joseph and Sharma note a qualitative difference in reporting of the conflict in Sri Lanka by Indian women journalists who 'focussed on the human tragedy unfolding in that country while also dealing with the obvious geopolitical aspects of the ethnic strife. By contrast, the latter was the sole preoccupation of most of the male journalists covering the conflict' (op. cit., p. 296).

The second need is for pressure from outside the media, in the form of consumer action and lobbying. One of the many paradoxes of the move towards the market-led media systems that are developing all around the world is that in some respects it places more power in the hands of the consumer. Not surprisingly, this was recognised long ago in North America, where strong media lobby groups already exist. In Canada for instance, MediaWatch-established in the early 1980s-has secured the removal of numerous sexist advertisements, has worked with national broadcasters and advertising associations to develop guidelines on gender portrayal, and has effectively lobbied to secure a strongly worded equality clause in Canada's 1991 Broadcasting Act.

Elsewhere the Tanzania Media Women's Association (TAMWA), Women's Media Watch in Jamaica, and the Media Advocacy Group in India have all made an impact with both the media and the public. In Europe initiatives of this sort have barely started. In Spain the Observatorio de la Publicidad (created in early 1994 by the Instituto de la Mujer), and in Italy the Sportello Immagine Donna (established in 1991 by the Commissione Nazionale per la Parita`) have begun to provide mechanisms through which complaints can be organised and channelled.

However, these are rare examples. Strong women's media associations do exist in a many countries, but often their primary purpose is to defend women's professional interests as media workers. There is a real need to develop monitoring and lobby groups which could organise effective campaigns and protests on a national and-when necessary-a regional and even a global level.

The third area is media education. It is astonishing how little the public in general, and even media professionals themselves, understand the subtle mechanisms which lead to patterns of gender stereotyping in media content. This emerged clearly from recent research by the Broadcasting Standards Council in the United Kingdom.

For instance, they found that women viewers had even 'no concept of the scriptwriter developing characters in a particular way and accepted with little question the presentation of women that they were offered.' There is a great deal of talk-particularly in academic and political circles-about the portrayal of women in the media. But abstract discussions about 'sexist stereotyping' and 'negative images of women' are unlikely to promote true understanding of what is involved, much less lead to real change. What is needed are effective, practical workshops built around specific media examples. In this sense, the NOS Portrayal Department in the Netherlands is exemplary. It was launched as a five-year project in 1991, and has built up a unique collection of audio-visual examples-as well as specially produced material-which are used in training sessions and workshops with programme-makers. Media education is a key strategy. The development of national and regional banks of examples and materials, which illustrate the many ways in which gender stereotyping occurs, would be a tremendous contribution to its success.

The fourth need is for pressure from above so that, for example, media organisations are encouraged to adopt guidelines and codes of conduct on the fair portrayal of women. The media in most countries already have guidelines that govern particular aspects of their output such as the portrayal of violence, or the regulation of advertising. In some countries-for instance Canada, the United Kingdom-certain media organisations also have guidelines covering the ways in which women are portrayed (see Mariani 1994, for a review of relevant European regulations). These guidelines have been made to work, and they could work in other organisations too. Given the development of transborder and global communication systems, there is also an urgent need for regional and international codes of practice.

This is a delicate matter, which would undoubtedly provoke immediate and vociferous objections from the media communities. For example, in 1995 the European Union adopted a Resolution on the image of women and men portrayed in advertising and media. As a result of fierce lobbying by the media industry, the final text is very much weaker than the initial draft. However, it is still a useful document. Despite the inevitable opposition, it is important to work towards the development of regulatory texts and codes of conduct in all countries and regions.

The final need is for international debate aimed at a reinterpretation of 'freedom of expression' within the framework of a women's human rights perspective, and the subsequent development of a global code of ethics based on this new interpretation. Such an undertaking would certainly provoke controversy. Cees Hamelink points out that the pursuit of democracy in world communication has been all but abandoned because 'the gospel of privatisation... declares that the world's resources are basically private property, that public affairs should be regulated by private parties on free markets' (Hamelink 1995, p. 33). Moreover the belief that a free market guarantees the optimal delivery of ideas and information means that-in a bizarre way-the terms 'free market' and 'free speech' have become almost interchangeable.

With more and more communication channels in the control of fewer and fewer hands, it is surely time for a fundamental reinterpretation of the doctrine of freedom of speech, and the search for a new definition of this 'freedom' which takes full account of the contemporary global economic, information and communication system and of women's place within it. The 1995 report of the World Commission on Culture and Development provides a lead here. The Commission points out that the airwaves and space are part of a 'global commons'-a collective asset that belongs to all humankind, but which is at present used free of charge by those who possess resources and technology. It goes on to suggest that 'the time may have come for commercial regional or international satellite radio and television interests which now use the global commons free of charge to contribute to the financing of a more plural media system' (World Commission on Culture and Development 1995, p. 278).

CONCLUSION

The World Commission on Culture and Development makes a number of very concrete proposals aimed at 'enhancing access, diversity and competition' in the international media system (op. cit., pp. 278-281, emphasis added). But its view of 'competition' is a radical one, whose starting point is human and cultural diversity, rather than financial markets. Radical as it is, this approach offers women more hope than the information superhighways of the Global Information Infrastructure extolled by Vice President Al Gore. The Vice President, it will be remembered, envisions 'a new Athenian Age of democracy forged in the fora the GII will create'. But the Vice President seems to have forgotten that Athenian democracy did not extend its membership to women.

5

Exploitation Against Women

Globalization has changed the world. Commodities are bought and sold across national borders and continents with unprecedented frequency. Unfortunately, one of the hottest commodities in this new world order is young women.

The profits gained from trafficking women exceed $8 billion annually. This is comparable to the lucrative trade in guns and drugs. In addition to the considerable financial gains, there are also fewer risks in trafficking women than in trafficking other illegal goods such as arms, drugs, and endangered species of animals and plants. These factors combined draw many people into the business, including well-established crime syndicates such as the Japanese Yakuza and the Hong Kong Triad.

Law enforcement has generally proved inadequate in combating this problem, both nationally and internationally. This is because of a general perception that trafficked women migrate willingly and allow themselves to be sold. According to Lois Chiang, Assistant Dean at U of T's Faculty of Law, "The impediments [to combating trafficking] are first a lack of understanding of what trafficking is--and this in not purely a legal issue. We need a better understanding of this phenomenon, and this gets intimately tied up with issues around women's agency and women's sexuality."

The causes of trafficking are complex and multifaceted. The intensification of international trade and foreign direct investment was intended to improve the economies of developing countries. Unfortunately, it appears that the opposite has occurred and poverty is rising in many developing countries. Large numbers of women are now leaving their home countries in the hope of finding better wages in developed countries.

In addition, the sexual division of labour has also intensified the vulnerability of young women (aged 15-25) to trafficking rings. Girls are often educated to lower levels than boys and have fewer work opportunities in skilled professions. The jobs available to them are often limited to domestic service and factory work.

The merchandizing of women takes a variety of forms including forced labour, mail-order brides, arranged marriages and slavery-like practices in prostitution. As such, trafficking may be defined as the exploitation of women for their labour, with or without pay and with or without their consent.

Surprisingly, many of the manifestations of trafficking can be found in our own backyard. According to Chiang, "There are many instances of trafficking in women in Canada-both as a domestic issue and a cross-border issue. As a domestic issue, we have seen in the press stories of young girls being deceived or coerced and kept forcibly confined and then raped by either the abductors or others and forced into prostitution. We see similar stories about women being brought over to Canada by traffickers and also forced into prostitution."

EQUALITY OF MEN WOMEN: A NEW REALITY

Over a century ago, and for the first time in the history of revealed religion, Bahaullah, Prophet-Founder of the Bahai Faith, proclaimed the equality of man and woman. He did not leave this pronouncement as an ideal or pious hope but wove it, as a basic factor, into the fabric of His social order. He supported it by laws requiring the same standard of education for women as for men, and equality of rights in society.

Equality of the sexes is, for Bahais, a spiritual and moral standard essential for the unification of the planet and the unfoldment of world order. Without the qualities, talents, and skills of both women and men, full economic and social development of the planet becomes impossible. The world of humanity is possessed of two wings the male and the female. So long as these two wings are not equivalent in strength the bird will not fly. Until womankind reaches the same degree as man, until she enjoys the same arena of activity, extraordinary attainment for humanity will not be realized; humanity cannot wing its way to heights of real attainment.

In the present transition of humanity from adolescence to maturity, signs of this evolving equality can be observed everywhere. In the Bahai view this is hardly surprising, for "As long as women are prevented from attaining their highest possibilities, so long will men be unable to achieve the greatness which might be theirs."

The character of this unique age we are entering is further brought into focus in the following statement from the Bahai BIC Document #93-0405 Writings:

The world in the past has been ruled by force and man has dominated over woman by reason of his more forceful and aggressive qualities both of body and mind. But the scales are already shifting, force is losing its weight, and mental alertness, intuition, and the spiritual qualities of love and service, in which woman is strong, are gaining ascendancy. Hence the new age will be an age less masculine and more permeated with the feminine ideals, or, to speak more exactly, will be an age in which the masculine and feminine elements of civilization will be more properly balanced.

UNITY AND EQUALITY IN THE FAMILY

The Bahai world community has, for more than one hundred years, accepted as truth the principle of equality of the sexes and has understood the importance of implementing this standard in individual, family, and community life. The institution of marriage, the basis of the family in the Bahai community, is part of this process. Before a Bahai marriage can take place the couple, who have freely chosen each other, must obtain the consents of all parents and transmit them to the communitys governing body.

The couple then weds in an atmosphere of loving parental approval and acceptance by the community. With the exchange of vows, in which each partner repeats, "We will all, verily, abide by the Will of God," the newly wedded begin their lives together on a basis of true spiritual unity and equality.

This unity and equality, rooted in the rights and responsibilities of every person before God, unfolds in the family. Here, values and attitudes essential for the development of the individual, the community, the nation, and humanity must be taught from early life. In the Bahai view the family being a human unit must be educated according to the rules of sanctity. All the virtues must be taught the family. The integrity of the family bond must be constantly considered and the rights of the individual members must not be transgressed.... All these rights and prerogatives must be conserved, yet the unity of the family must be sustained. The injury of one shall be considered the injury of all; the comfort of each the comfort of all; the honor of one the honor of all.

Equality in Education and Training

Although both parents share in the overall responsibility of educating the children, the mother is given recognition as the first educator of humanity, and she must be carefully prepared for this task. Her education, in fact, from the Bahai point of view, is more necessary and important than that of man, for woman is the trainer of the child from its infancy. If she be defective and imperfect herself the child will necessarily be deficient; therefore imperfection of woman implies a condition of imperfection in all mankind, for it is the mother who rears, nurtures and guides the growth of the child.

Since Bahais do not separate life into religious and secular compartments, and since faith must be expressed in social action, education for men and women, in all its facts, "holds an important place in the new order of things." For this reason, the education of each child is compulsory. If there is not money enough in a family to educate both the girl and the boy the money must be dedicated to the girls education, for she is the potential mother. If there are no parents the community must educate the child. In addition to this widespread education each child must be taught a profession, art, or trade, so that every member of the community will be enabled to earn his own livelihood. It is also significant that, in the spirit of this new era of human evolution, Bahaullah has "promulgated the adoption of the same course of education for man and woman," making clear that "daughters and sons must follow the same curriculum of study, thereby promoting unity of the sexes."

Contribution of Women to Peace

The Bahai Writings promise that "the entrance of women into all human departments is an irrefutable and incontrovertible question. No soul can retard or prevent it"; that in "no movement" will women "be left behind; that they "will attain in all such a degree as will be considered the very highest station of the world of humanity and will take part in all affairs"; that "when women participate fully and equally in the affairs of the world...war will cease." This contribution of women to the establishment of world unity and peace will inevitably be recognized and developed.

In past ages humanity has been defective and inefficient because incomplete. War and its ravages have blighted the world. The education of woman will be a mighty step toward its abolition and ending for she will use her whole influence against war.... In truth she will be the greatest factor in establishing Universal Peace and international arbitration. Assuredly woman will abolish warfare among mankind.

An Equal Voice

A great responsibility is, however, placed on woman to develop her potentialities fully.

She must make every effort to attain greater perfection, to be mans equal in every respect, to make progress in all in which she has been backward, so that man will be compelled to acknowledge her equality of capacity and attainment.

Certainly the well-being of mankind depends on the development of the potential virtues and abilities of every individual, regardless of race, nationality, class, religion, or sex. For this reason prejudices, which cause division and oppression, are systematically abolished in Bahai community life. A unique administrative system, rooted in the concept of unity in diversity, both insists on education for all members of the community and allows for the immediate assimilation of all those who in the past have been deprived of their rights. The Bahai electoral system, operating by secret ballot, with no nominations or electioneering, encourages universal participation: every adult Bahai is eligible for election to local and national administrative bodies responsible for decision in the conduct of Bahai affairs. The ease with which women, long deprived of equal opportunities, can now be integrated into the life of society, is vividly evidenced by the participation of women in all areas of Bahai community life.

Today, in the Bahai world community, in over 200 nations and territories, women are joining with men in building a global society. Their full contribution toward the establishment of a world civilization is possible, Bahais believe, because of the all-pervasive spiritual power released in this age by Bahaullah, Who has erased all limitations preventing the fulfillment of human potentialities. For in the Bahai view, since this is the century of light, it is evident that the Sun of Reality, the Word has revealed itself to all humankind. One of the potentialities hidden in the realm of humanity was the capability or capacity of womanhood. Through the effulgent rays of divine illumination, the capacity of woman has become so awakened and manifest in this age that equality of man and woman is an established fact.

RAPE AND SEXUAL ABUSE OF WOMEN IN INTERNATIONAL LAW

This paper will consider the international legal response to rape and other forms of sexual abuse committed against women during the course of an armed conflict: its incidence, impact and consequences. Although both men and women can be and are raped, causing severe injury for both, in terms of numbers rape is essentially a crime committed against women. Further, women suffer from particular after-effects in rape that are not shared by men.

Women are raped in all forms of armed conflict, international and internal, whether the conflict is fought primarily on religious, ethnic, political or nationalist grounds, or a combination of all these. They are raped by men from all sides-both enemy and `friendly' forces. There have been reports of rapes and other forms of sexual abuse committed by members of United Nations peacekeeping forces; women are not free from interference even from those who are in the territory with an international mandate to restore international peace and security. International media attention has been directed towards the widespread rapes, torture and forced pregnancies in the former Yugoslavia. The `mobilization of shame' which has been identified as the primary means of enforcing international humanitarian law has to some extent been activated in this instance. Nevertheless, the international response in itself carries the risk that violent offences against women will be perceived as something exceptional, peculiar to this particular conflict. The reality is that rape and violent sexual abuse of women in armed conflict has a long history.

Numerous incidents of women raped in other international and internal armed conflicts can be cited to illustrate this point. During the August 1990 invasion of Kuwait it is estimated that at least 5,000 Kuwaiti women were raped by Iraqi soldiers. After the liberation large numbers of foreign domestic working women in Kuwait were attacked and subjected to sexual violence from subsequently returning Kuwaitis; women in Rwanda who are caught up in the vicious civil war in that country; women in Kashmir who have suffered rape and death under the administration of the Indian army. The following has been reported concerning a civil conflict in South America.

> Throughout Peru's 12 year internal war women have been targets of sustained, frequently brutal violence committed by both parties to the armed conflict... Women have been threatened, raped and murdered by government security forces; and women have been threatened, raped and murdered by the Communist Party of Peru-Shining Path. Often, the same woman is the victim of violence by both sides.

Liberian women have been repeatedly raped in the ethnic violence of that country's civil war and women from East Timor have been raped as well as killed since the occupation by Indonesia commenced in 1975. Another example which occurred longer ago, but which has only recently received serious attention, was the continued sustained rapes of the so-called `comfort women' by the Japanese military during the Second World War.

Numerous other examples could have been cited but this selection illustrates that women are attacked in conflicts across the globe by men of all colours, religions, nationalities and ideologies.

Rape in war is not merely a matter of chance, of women victims being in the wrong place at the wrong time. Nor is it a question of sex. It is rather a question of power and control which is `structured by male soldiers' notions of their masculine privilege, by the strength of the military's lines of command and by class and ethnic inequalities among women'. Radhika Coomaraswamy has identified a number of reasons for sexual violence against women, two of which are especially applicable to rape in armed conflict: violence against women may be directed towards the social group of which she is a member because `to rape a woman is to humiliate her community'.

Complex, combined emotions of hatred, superiority, vengeance for real or imagined past wrongs and national pride are engendered and deliberately manipulated in armed conflict. They are given expression through rape of the other side's women. For the men of the community rape encapsulates the totality of their defeat; they have failed to protect `their' women. Second, studies have indicated the connection between militarization of the nation State and violence against women.

Other connections have been drawn between `normal' peacetime attitudes towards women and rape in armed conflict; one that has been controversial in the context of the former Yugoslavia is the direct causal link that has been made by Catharine MacKinnon between pornography in that country and the mass rapes of Muslim women. The connection between pornographic projections of women and the use as war propaganda of these and other media images can be readily accepted; but to identify these as the sole, or even major cause of the abuse of women throughout that area is simplistic and misleading.

Licence to rape has been included as a term of employment for mercenary soldiers. In determining why such a condition is repugnant, Walzer discounts the utilitarian argument that it acts as a spur to military courage. Instead he goes to the heart of the matter:

Rape is a crime, in war as in peace, because it violates the rights of the woman who is attacked. To offer her as bait to a mercenary soldier is to treat her as if she were not a person at all but a mere object, a prize, a trophy of war. It is the recognition of her personality that shapes our judgment.

Rape has also been directed as an instrument of war. In the former Yugoslavia rape has been `massive, organized and systematic'. It was perceived by the Special Rapporteur appointed by the United Nations Commission on Human Rights not only as an instrument of war but as a method of ethnic cleansing `intended to humiliate, shame, degrade and terrify the entire ethnic group.'

THE CONSEQUENCES OF RAPE

The consequences of rape continue beyond the actual attack or attacks, often lasting for the rest of the women's lives. As well as the degradation, pain and terror caused at the time, the fear engendered remains long after. This fear is also experienced by other women who were not themselves attacked but are aware that they might have been, or might be in the future. Rape centred within a community undermines the well-being and secure existence of the community. For survivors, rape carries the risk of sexually-transmitted diseases, including of course AIDS. It also can result in pregnancy. Women have to face the prospect of bearing the child of the invader (of their State, their community and their bodies), or of seeking an abortion at a time of intense social dislocation and when scarce medical supplies are directed as a priority to military personnel.

This same factor reduces availability of treatment of sexually-transmitted diseases. Abortion is restricted under the teachings of a number of religions, or women have been forcibly detained to prevent abortion. Other women have been so badly internally injured that they will never be able to bear the children they would have chosen to have; infertility and loss of virginity make women unmarriageable in some societies. Still others have been unable to bear their shame and have committed suicide. Where the effects of conflict have caused shortages of food and shelter, and priority health care is directed towards the military, child bearing can impose an impossibly high additional material, as well as psychological, burden upon their mothers. This can be further exacerbated by the child-being seen by family or compatriots as `proof' of the woman's collaboration with the enemy, or of her immoral behaviour. Women fear they have become unacceptable to their families and communities, a fear which may be enhanced where the rape was committed publicly in the presence of members of these communities. Public rape terrorizes and traumatizes the civilian population. There is also only just beginning to be some understanding of the psychological damage caused by the trauma of violent sexual abuse.

INTERNATIONAL LEGAL RESPONSES

Substantive Law

One response has been to call municipal and international legal systems into play, which in turn raises the questions of the adequacy of legal norms and the effectiveness of their implementation.

A number of substantive international legal regimes are currently applicable. States are liable for harm done to individuals which constitutes violation of the laws and customs of war by troops under their authority and command, for violations of internationally guaranteed human rights, including genocide and torture, and for wrongdoing to aliens under the normal principles of State responsibility. These different legal regimes allow for analysis of rape through different lenses: violations of the laws of war, violence against women as a violation of women's human rights, and protection of ethnic groups against genocide. In addition to State responsibility there is individual criminal responsibility for the commission of war crimes and crimes against humanity. The plea of superior orders is not available as a defence to such actions.

Meron has demonstrated that rape has long been prohibited by the laws of war and has been incorporated into various modern Codes of Military Conduct. The currently applicable laws of war are contained within the 1949 Geneva Conventions, the 1977 supplementary Protocols, and in the body of law arising from the judgment of the Nuremberg Tribunal and the Military Tribunal for the Far East. Unfortunately, in these documents the position with respect to rape is ambiguous.

Rape was not included in the listed war crimes in Article 6 of the Nuremberg Charter, although the list was specifically stated not to be exhaustive. The Fourth Geneva Convention provides protection for civilians in international armed conflict and specifically provides that women should be protected against rape. This provision is almost exactly reiterated in Protocol I. It is noticeable that these provisions do not impose a blanket prohibition against sexual abuse, but rather oblige States to offer women protection against attacks on their honour and to accord them special respect. Article 4 of the Fourth Geneva Convention applies to those `who at a given moment and in any manner whatsoever find themselves, in case of a conflict or occupation, in the hands of a Party to the conflict or Occupying Power of which they are not nationals'. Article 76 of Protocol I enhances this protection by extending its scope to all women in the power of a Party to the conflict including a Party's own nationals.

In non-international armed conflict, Article 3 to the Geneva Conventions provides a minimum standard of behaviour that applies both to government and non-government forces. Prohibited actions include violence to life and the person, cruel treatment and torture, and humiliating and degrading treatment. It is easy to interpret these Articles so as to include rape, but it is nevertheless unfortunate that it is not spelled out as an explicit prohibition. For this reason the affirmation by the World Conference on Human Rights in Vienna in 1993 that `violations of the human rights of women in situations of armed conflict [with no distinction drawn between international and non-international armed conflict] are violations of the humanitarian principles of international human rights and humanitarian law' is to be welcomed. The Declaration and Programme of Action continues that violations, including systematic rape and sexual slavery `require a particularly effective response'.

The same is true of the enforcement provisions. States are under an obligation to make grave breaches of the Geneva Conventions and Protocols subject to the jurisdiction of their own courts and punishable by severe penalties. Rape is not however explicitly listed as a grave breach of the Convention, although acts wilfully committed and causing great suffering or causing injury to body or health do constitute grave breaches. Protocol I includes among its list of grave breaches `degrading practices involving outrages upon personal dignity based upon racial discrimination' but makes no reference to gender discrimination.

War crimes, that is violations of the laws or customs of war, are not the only possible legal regime for the prosecution of rape committed during international armed conflict. There is also the concept of a crime against humanity and, it has been argued in the context of the former Yugoslavia, genocide. A crime against humanity was defined in the Nuremberg Charter as:

> murder, extermination, enslavement, deportation, and other inhumane acts committed against any civilian population before or during the war, or persecutions on political, racial, or religious grounds in execution of or in connection with any crime within the jurisdiction of the Tribunal whether or not in violation of the domestic law of the country where perpetrated.

A number of points require special mention. First, although crimes against humanity were established as a separate category from war crimes, the crimes in question were inevitably associated with the occurrence of the Second World War. This association between armed conflict and crimes against humanity has been continued in the case of the former Yugoslavia. Second, despite the enormous incidence of rape of civilian populations during the Second World War, prosecutions of crimes against humanity were limited to persecutions on racial, political or religious grounds, in accordance with the wording of Article 6. These words import a requirement of discriminatory behaviour into the concept of crimes against humanity, which is equally well provided by the gender discrimination inherent in violent crimes against women. Thirdly, for actions to come within the category of crimes against humanity they had to be committed against a civilian population, not against individual civilians. Fourthly, in contrast to war crimes, it has been necessary to establish systematic government planning for crimes against humanity. Crimes against humanity are not easily established in light of these restrictive requirements. Nevertheless, when the four occupying powers in Germany adopted Control Council Law No. 10 they departed from the Nuremberg precedent and incorporated rape as a crime against humanity.

Genocide is defined in Article II of the Genocide Convention. There must be an intention to destroy, in whole or in part, a national, ethnic, racial or religious group through the commission of such acts as killing or causing serious bodily or mental harm to members of the group; deliberately inflicting on the group conditions of life calculated to bring about its physical destruction in whole or in part; imposing measures to prevent births within the group; or forcibly transferring children of the group to another group. At first sight rape does not appear to fall within this definition, but it has been forcefully argued that where it has been carried out on a massive and systematic basis for the purposes of producing babies of the ethnic class of the rapists, of destroying the family life of the victims and of cleansing the surrounding area of all other ethnic groups rape becomes genocidal. This categorization has been further supported by allegations that impregnated women were forcibly detained until it was too late to abort.

Despite this impressive body of formal prohibition, the incidence of rape in armed conflict has been widely ignored, underplayed or tolerated. Rape is too frequently regarded as an unfortunate but inevitable side-effect of conflict, or as an anticipated bonus for soldiers on all sides. Rape did not figure prominently at Nuremberg, `not because the Germans were not guilty of rape, but because the allied forces, especially the Russians and the Moroccan forces under French control, were also guilty of many rapes'. Rape was also largely invisible in the trials of the Japanese war criminals.

This silence by international law enforcement agencies denotes a double irony for women. Feminist writers have argued that the distinction drawn in international law between public acts of the State and private actions has been an important factor in its failure to address denial of human rights to women. Violence against women for example has not been readily viewed as torture, or as being imputable to the State, because of its widespread commission by private actors within the private arena of the home. Yet rape in international armed conflict, which is largely committed by military agents of the State under public authority, has also been ignored.

Law Enforcement

However, in the context of the former Yugoslavia there has been widespread pressure to ensure that this long silence is broken. The substantive law on rape in armed conflict has now become entangled with the question of arenas for its application. Condemnation of violations and calls for compliance have been made within international political fora, notably the Security Council, the Human Rights Commission, the Commission on the Status of Women, and the Committee on the Elimination of Discrimination Against Women. Proceedings have been commenced against Yugoslavia (Serbia-Montenegro) in the International Court of Justice by Bosnia-Herzegovina. Yugoslavia (Serbia-Montenegro) has counter-claimed in similar terms. Since under Article 34 of the Statute of the Court only States can be parties before it, this litigation will deal with the question of the responsibility of the State under the relevant treaties and customary international law. The options for the prosecution of individuals alleged to have committed such crimes are the domestic courts of any State, or an international war crimes tribunal on the precedent of Nuremberg.

Criminal proceedings have been commenced in domestic courts, for example in Germany, France and by a Bosnian military tribunal in Sarajevo. In the United States civil proceedings have been commenced under the Alien Torts Claims Act and the Torture Victim Protection Act against Radovan Karadzic, who has command authority over the Bosnian-Serb military forces. These claims rely upon the jurisprudence following the case of Filartiga v. Pena-Irala.

There Judge Kaufman accepted civil jurisdiction within the United States for offences violating the law of nations, in that instance torture, irrespective of where the offence had been committed and the nationalities of the accused and victim. While there may be concerns about the extension of United States' extra-territorial jurisdiction, there are advantages for the plaintiffs in such civil actions. Jurisdiction can be established for the violation of international law provided personal service can be achieved.

Amicus briefs from interested third parties, including non-governmental organizations, which set out many aspects of the issue can be admitted. A default judgment may be entered against an absent defendant on the basis of the burden of proof appropriate in civil cases. While it is highly unlikely that any award of damages would ever be forthcoming, the proceedings prevent free access to the United States for the defendant and allow a domestic court to assert its understanding of customary international law.

In Resolutions 808 and 827 the Security Council, acting under Chapter VII of the United Nations Charter, established an International Criminal Tribunal for the prosecution of persons responsible for serious violations of international humanitarian law committed in the territory of the former Yugoslavia since 1991. The Tribunal has been accorded jurisdiction over war crimes, genocide and crimes against humanity. Since a prevailing principle is that of nullum crimen sine lege, the definition of each offence relies upon pre-existing customary and conventional humanitarian law. In addition, all the parties to the conflict have largely accepted the application of the Geneva Conventions and Protocols to it. Thus the Tribunal can determine whether grave breaches of the Geneva Conventions have been committed. As already stated these do not explicitly include rape, although as a matter of interpretation it can be readily included.

The Tribunal also has jurisdiction over violations of the laws or customs of war. These include `employment of... weapons calculated to cause unnecessary suffering'. If rape is correctly regarded as a weapon of war in the way described above, it can readily be brought within this prohibition. The definition of crimes against humanity follows that of the Control Council Law No. 10 and therefore includes rape. The Secretary-General's report makes it clear that to constitute a crime against humanity the acts must be of a very serious nature and be committed as part of a widespread or systematic attack against any civilian population.

The purpose of the International Tribunal is to put an end to the commission of war crimes in the former Yugoslavia and to provide effective measures for bringing to justice those responsible for them. In accordance with the requirements for Chapter VII action, the Security Council has stated that the establishment of the International Tribunal will help to restore and maintain international peace in the area. There are enormous legal and practical questions relating, inter alia, to the identification, arrest and detention of accused persons, the collection and presentation of evidence, and the rules of evidence and procedure to be followed, which will have to be resolved for the Tribunal to become effective.

While the practical and deterrent effect of such a Tribunal may be questioned, the importance of an authoritative public articulation of the relevant norms of international law cannot be understated. In a decentralized legal system where principles of customary international law are generated through State practice and opinio juris, the conclusions of the Tribunal resting upon the authority of the Security Council will inevitably have normative and educative effect. It is for this reason that it is essential that rape is considered separately from the other charges and is explicitly condemned. It is not sufficient for it to be regarded as an add-on to other offences.

INTERNATIONAL LEGAL REMEDIES

Despite the importance of an affirmation of the illegality of rape in armed conflict, some reservations about the role of the Tribunal from the perspective of the survivors of rape must be expressed. Some of these can be addressed by sensitivity towards the process and procedures of the Tribunal, while others go directly to the inadequacies of international legal remedies in the case of rape.

The focus of the Tribunal is on punishing the wrongdoers, not on providing compensation and support to those who have suffered the harms described above. Admittedly this is a defect shared by municipal criminal legal systems, but these may be backed up by other domestic support services. A war crimes tribunal must be supplemented by long-term practical assistance from governments, such as medical care, shelter, support and counselling. Survivors of rape must be provided the space to specify their own needs within their own communities.

Appropriate support must be made available to all concerned within the community to enable survivors to regain control of their own lives.

The health and emotional needs of those who were not themselves raped must also be given consideration. Indeed it has been argued that to concentrate only upon the survivors of rape can be `counter-productive by possibly stigmatizing and further traumatizing' those women. It cannot be assumed that all women will share the same needs. For example, some who feel that crimes committed against them have been disregarded may feel a sense of empowerment in the establishment of the Tribunal, while others may consider this a further intrusion into their lives, or fear the consequences of proceedings. Responses must take into account both individual preferences and the needs of the harmed society. The traditional exclusion of women from decision-making with respect to the use of force must not be here continued.

Those performing these tasks must receive adequate and relevant training, including psychological counselling. The international community must ensure that survivors do not become victims of, or become manipulated by, a well-meaning international reaction to the offences committed against them which fails to take account of their own concerns. It is important that fact-finding missions report their findings accurately and objectively and that research into the conflict reflects the complexities of its historical and ethnic origins. The fears of the Zagreb-based Centre for Women War Victims need to be taken seriously and responded to:

> ... we fear that the process of helping raped women is turning in a strange direction, being taken over by governmental institutions... and male gynaecologists in particular. We fear that the raped women could be used in political propaganda with the aim of spreading hatred and revenge, thus leading to further violence against women and to further victimization of survivors.

The pain of women raped and abused in armed conflict has often been appropriated by males for propaganda purposes. Suzanne Gibson discusses the examples of how rape of women in France during World War One became `transformed into a representation of France as an innocent female natior assaulted by a barbaric and brutishly male Germany' and British military conscriptors used the image of `the Hun' violating their sisters. She concludes with a warning that must be borne in mind throughout any criminal proceedings:

> ... rape has not throughout most of recorded history, been a crime against women. It has significantly however been a heinous crime against men: a humiliation inflicted upon a nation, an affront to a man's pride as guardian of his women,...

It is essential that prosecutions are brought against accused people from all sides. While the International Tribunal is unique in that it was established during the continuation of the conflict and is therefore untainted by notions of `victor's justice', it must not be used to prosecute offenders from only one side. Prosecutions must be brought against the alleged perpetrators and those higher up in the chain of command. It is essential that the message is made clear that rape of women is illegal and will be punished whoever is responsible for the commission of the offence.

There are various aspects of the Tribunal's composition and procedure that must be considered. Only two women judges have been nominated to it. While this is an advance on the composition of the International Court of Justice which has never had an elected woman judge, it is still far from the goal of 50% female judges sought by women's groups. Attention must be paid to gender distribution of all other personnel of the Tribunal, including prosecutors and investigators. Women may be fearful of retribution and publicity and thus be reluctant to testify before the Tribunal. The Special Rapporteur has pointed out that there are many reasons why survivors may be reluctant to testify as to their experiences. These include `severe traumatization, feelings of shame, lack of trust, fear of awakening bad memories as well as fear of reprisals against themselves and their families'.

A balance will have to be drawn between the rights of the accused to due process and the needs of the survivors. There has long been criticism in domestic criminal proceedings of the ways in which women in rape and other sexual abuse cases have been subject to intense and distressing personal questioning by investigators and defence lawyers. Procedural reforms have been introduced in some countries. The international tribunal should draw upon these experiences in determining its procedures. As a minimum, all people involved in the work of the tribunal, and especially those involved in judicial, investigatory or prosecutorial work should receive gender sensitivity training.

There are other still more fundamental questions that need to be addressed. The jurisdiction of the Tribunal is limited to offences in the former Yugoslavia; it will not assist women who have been raped or will in the future be raped in other conflicts all around the world, although its effectiveness is likely to impact upon its future precedential value. Further, rape and sexual violence against women occurs along a continuum of seriousness. The widespread and systematic nature of the offences committed in the former Yugoslavia place these offences at the far end of the spectrum, as is recognized by their inclusion as crimes against humanity in the Statute of the Tribunal. The focus on these rapes and the failure to make explicit that any rape committed in armed conflict is a war crime entails the risk of creating the assumption that `lesser' rapes may still be committed with impunity.

CONCLUSION

The measures here proposed are reactive, where what is primarily needed are positive steps to implement international humanitarian law in international and non-international armed conflict. The obligations incurred and learned in peacetime need to be sufficiently strongly imbued so that they hold fast in the social disruption of armed conflict. Even more urgently, commitment to preventing armed conflict and thus to eradicating the environment conducive to the occurrence of such offences is needed.

The maintenance of international peace and security relates to social and economic justice and the observance of human rights in peacetime, as well as to enforcement action in response to a breach of the peace or an act of aggression. This has been recognized by organs of the United Nations. The General Assembly has accepted it in the context of decolonization; nor has the Security Council limited its understanding of acts detrimental to international peace and security to external acts but has recognized the interlocking relationships between systemic oppression, deprivation, terrorism and breach of the peace. The Secretary-General has acknowledged the connection between armed conflict and sustained structural injustice in his analysis, `Agenda for Peace'.

Despite the willingness of United Nations' organs to move beyond a narrow concept of the causes of international conflict, and in particular the recognition of the threat to international peace caused by apartheid and racial discrimination policies, the global denial of basic rights to women has not been similarly recognized. This denial of rights has been largely ignored by mainstream human rights bodies which have failed to interpret their conventions in ways which are relevant to women's lives. Any rape of women in armed conflict is not the end of the spectrum, but it continues through to the constant attacks and sexual abuse of women in `normal' peacetime conditions. Physical, psychological and economic violence against women is manifested in many forms but is a constant fact of life for millions of women. It must be recognized that the climate of fear created through oppression and domination and the reality of violence is part of the patriarchal State structure and is a threat to international peace. Thus recent steps within the international community to ensure that women's rights are recognized as human rights and to enhance the accountability of governments for violence against women are as much an integral part of the overall counter-attack on the war against women as are the more publicized and dramatic responses to events in the former Yugoslavia.

CHILDREN WITHOUT SEX

Let us take a journey through time to the year 2050. Our time machine has landed in the spacious drawing room of Barbara, the 45-year-old owner of a smart advertising agency, and Michael, her equally high-flying husband, in their London townhouse.

Barbara's career ambitions have been realised, and she is at the top of her game, wealthy and happily married. The time is right to start a family. If she'd had a baby in her 20s or 30s, setting up her own agency-what with all those 15-hour days-would have been virtually impossible. But now it's not a problem. Barbara simply puts in a call to the baby bank, where her eggs are kept in "cryopreservation". Barbara deposited them there when she was 20, when they were in their prime.

Sex without children; children without sex-who knows what the future may hold.

The eggs are transported to the lab, along with Michael's sperm-which he has taken the precaution of having frozen, too-and an embryo is produced and returned to her womb. Nine months later, their "ice baby" is born.

Barbara is not alone. In the year 2050, thousands of middle-aged women like her-and some even older-are putting motherhood on ice until the time is absolutely right.

One might think this Huxleyesque vision of a Brave New World just a few years from now sounds a little fantastical. Yet it is the prediction of one of the world's most eminent scientists, Carl Djerassi. Professor Djerassi is the man who invented the Pill, the first oral contraceptive, which triggered the sexual revolution of the 1960s, and which many would argue changed the face of society and sexual morality for ever-and not necessarily for the better.

The Pill gave us sex without children. Now Djerassi has turned that concept on its head. He believes the developed world is heading towards its next cultural revolution-children without sex.

"It is my own prediction that within the next 30 to 50 years in the Western world, many women, when young, will bank their eggs or ovarian tissue, have them frozen, and use them when they feel the time is right for them to have a child," he says. "It will become commonplace.

"The world has changed. The days are past in which women in countries like Britain have economic dependence on their husbands and take care of the children.

"The days are past when women looked after children and nothing else. Women have careers now. They are better educated, more affluent and healthier on the whole, and many are now living into their 80s.

"They postpone having children until later and then they forget-or remember too late. Soon there will be nothing to stop a woman freezing her eggs when they are at their healthiest and then using them later on in life."

Less than a decade ago, such a scenario would have seemed impossible. But even now, there are indications that Professor Djerassi's prediction will come true. A handful of babies have already been born using frozen eggs.

A couple of years ago, freezing and thawing human eggs was a highly-complicated procedure used only as a last resort-for example, when a woman has been made infertile through cancer treatment.

There was no guarantee of success because while sperm freezes well, when an egg is frozen, its high water content means the ice crystals that form inside can severely damage or destroy it.

Egg-freezing techniques are being increasingly refined. A new process called vitrification, in which water is drawn out and anti-freeze chemicals added, is improving success rates to the same level as normal IVF treatment.

Widespread freezing or eggs, if Djerassi's prediction is correct, is bound to prove controversial. Is it ethical for women to have children in their 60s? How will the child born using such a procedure be affected both emotionally and physically? Even today we do not know what the long-term consequences of IVF will be on those children it has helped to create.

And then, of course, there is the question of women choosing to defrost and fertilise eggs without bothering to find a partner to help raise the child. Do we really want science to create a generation of ageing mothers who've chosen to corrupt nature for the sake of their careers by having children late in life-with or without a man?

Djerassi is dogmatic in his rejection of these moral and social concerns. Controversially, he believes advances in egg freezing techniques would be greatly beneficial to the human race. "There are so many unwanted children in the world," he says. "This would be a way of helping to reduce the number of unwanted children. Every child born to a woman who has taken a conscious decision to have a child at that time would be wanted and loved and properly cared for.

"Is there not something to be said for wisdom, affection and maturity? Why shouldn't a woman have a child when she is older if the science is there to help her? Nowadays it is not thought peculiar if a man in his 50s or 60s has a child. So should it be different for a woman?"

Today, Djerassi is a sprightly 83. Until just last year he was still skiing but has had to put any sporting adventures on hold after falling and breaking his hip.

LOOKING INTO THE FUTURE

He lives with his wife, the author and poet Diane Middlebrook-whom he met in 1977-in a spacious apartment which covers two floors of a grand townhouse in North London. Djerassi, whose family fled Vienna for America after Hitler's troops marched into Austria, remains consumed by his work and locks himself away for ten hours every day in his study.

These days he is a playwright and novelist, specialising in what he terms "science in fiction". To date he has written five novels, seven plays, two memoirs and a book of essays. He has just returned from New York following the Broadway premiere of his play Phallacy.

Djerassi believes putting eggs on ice will have benefits to the health of "babies born to older mothers".

Biologically, the ideal age to have a child would be 18-20, after which the woman could go to university and have a career.

"In those circumstances, society would have to make arrangements for childcare, which it is does not do, so women are waiting till their careers are established and they can afford good childcare," he says.

"The problem with this is that the moment a woman hits 35 the risk of her having a child with Down's syndrome increases four to six times. "At that age she has lost 90-95 percent of her eggs, and those that are left are ageing rapidly. Storing her eggs is her insurance policy against the future. I think you will get the odd woman of 60 or 70 who will decide to have a baby, but most will be in their 30s and 40s."

But isn't the idea of mass child production without sex somehow, well, cold?

"Women, especially, romanticise the moment they conceived," he says, "but the truth is many don't actually know. And besides, is it such a high price to pay for a healthy child born at a time that is right for the mother?"

It is certainly a radical idea, but then Djerassi has always been a radical. History was made in a small laboratory in Mexico City on October 15, 1951, when he synthesised norethindrone, the first oral contraceptive, recognised worldwide as one of the most significant advances in steroid chemistry.

He was stunned by the impact it had on society: "I could not anticipate the impact the Pill would have. No one really knew that women would accept the Pill so readily."

The Pill gave women freedom from the fear of pregnancy and the horror of backstreet abortion, but many see it as a cursed invention that is almost single-handedly to blame for the sexual revolution which brought about-as its critics see it-a wholesale collapse of moral values across the Western world.

Djerassi does not concur with this damning verdict on the legacy of his invention. He argues that society was changing anyway; the Pill just smoothed the way.

"The sexual revolution of the Sixties coincided with the introduction of the Pill-the Pill did not bring it about," he says bluntly. "The Pill came along at the right time, in the same period as hippy culture, the drug culture and rock 'n' roll culture.

"That the Pill facilitated that direction is absolutely true, but I believe it would have happened anyway. Not as explosively, but more gradually. It would have happened in exactly the same way." And he says it is a myth that everyone started having a lot more sex with multiple partners-that his invention effectively allowed the risk-free one-night stand to flourish as it never could before.

"Women were having sex before the Pill, but they were getting pregnant and having abortions. The Pill helped to stop that," he says.

What about the side effects of the Pill? "There is nothing without side effects," says Djerassi. "Does it increase the risk of breast cancer? Well, there have been thousands of studies and the question is still debated. But we must not forget that it has been proven that the Pill reduces the risk of ovarian cancer by 50 per cent-that is crystal clear."

He has been unable to escape his "father of the Pill" tag, though he prefers to think of himself as the "mother of the Pill". "In order to give birth to anything, you need three people," he says. "A father, a mother and a midwife."

Djerassi was the chemist who provided the raw chemical ingredients-the "egg". The biologist Gregory Pincus, who co-ordinated its experimentation as a contraceptive, might be seen as the "father". And the physician John Rock, who oversaw the first clinical trials, was the "midwife".

Djerassi's invention made him a very wealthy man. Unlike many, he had enough belief in what he was doing to buy shares in Syntex, the small Mexican company where he did his research.

"They were shares I bought on the open market," he says. "Other people could have bought them but no one believed in the future of the company, which developed very much because of work that I and other colleagues conducted. We deserved it."

With his fortune he bought a 1,200-acre ranch near San Francisco and indulged his passion for art, becoming a leading collector of the works of the painter Paul Klee. He also became a professor of chemistry at Stanford University-which he is to this day.

With his second wife, Norma Lundholm, Djerassi has a son, Dale, a documentary filmmaker. He and Norma also had a daughter, Pamela. It was her suicide at the age of 28 that has been the great tragedy of his life. It came a year after he met his third wife, Diane.

After Pamela's death, her father set up an artists' colony on the ranch. He sold his Picassos, Giacomettis and Henry Moores in order to fund the colony, which continues today. Djerassi's London flat is filled with artwork produced by artists who've lived there. He also bequeathed his entire Klee collection to the San Francisco Museum of Modern Art. "Well, you can't take it with you," he says.

But it is not his art collection for which Djerassi will be remembered: the Pill will be his true legacy. Given that he has already fundamentally altered the relationship between sex and procreation, perhaps we should take seriously his alarming predictions for the future.

WHY MEN ARE LOSING INTEREST IN WOMEN

THE RAVAGES OF FEMINISM

ABC's flagship public affairs program "20/20" was devoted to the "biggest secret of American marriage" Friday.

"As many as 20% of American marriages are sexless," host Barbara Walters intoned. "It's not women who don't want sex as you might expect, it's the men!"

The program focused on two couples. In both cases, feminist mind control is responsible for their problem but the TV show wouldn't admit this.

One man was married to an attractive 30-something woman who is a stripper! Reporter John Stossel thought this made her husband's indifference even more astonishing. The show's marital therapist, Michele Weiner-Davis, ignored this as an explanation for his impotence.

Feminist groupthink says a woman's sexuality is just like a man's, hers to enjoy (or sell). In this essentially lesbian mindset, the male's ability to respond is irrelevant.

I beg to differ. The stripper's husband is impotent because he is a cuckold. Sex is an act of possession. The husband cannot possess his wife because she gives herself to hundreds of other men every day. She makes part of their living this way. When a woman's sexuality is her own, essentially it belongs to any man. She is a public utility, which is what the framers of the Communist Manifesto envisaged. (Children also would belong to the state.) She is unfit for a long-term monogamous relationship.

A woman can thrive only in the context of a loving marriage. Despite what feminism says, most women want to belong to one man, their husband.

The Second Couple

Here the wife criticizes and nags.

"I can't be myself," the husband says. "I'm walking on eggshells all the time."

By controlling her husband, the wife is emasculating him. He compensates by riding a Harley and volunteering at the local fire department.

The therapist suggests that the wife stop nagging and the husband listen. She doesn't notice that the husband responds only after the wife starts to cry.

Men respond to vulnerability in a woman not power. As I have said before, heterosexual love involves the exchange of power for love. Men want power. Women want love. The female surrenders and allows the male to protect and possess her.

In return for her acquiescence, the male loves her in the full sense of the word. He is in charge but he also wants her to be happy. This is natural when someone makes you happy.

My wife's mother gave her good advice: "Look for a man to take care of you but be able to take care of yourself."

Penis Equals Power

In the film The Crying Game, director Neil Jordan captures the experience of the modern male when the protagonist tries to make love to his girlfriend and discovers she has a penis. He runs from the room and vomits.

This film notwithstanding, today's female impersonators are mostly women. By encouraging them to be "strong and independent", feminism has given them a psychological phallus. They have become men and thus made men redundant. They try to coerce men to love them anyway as if we were their hand puppets.

In reality, a woman's power consists in being without penis, being everything a man is not. Not aggressive, forceful, dynamic, muscular and driven.

Feminine power consists in persuasion rather than force. A real woman relies on moral authority and her attraction, i.e. beauty, grace, charm, love and devotion. These women are extremely rare and in great demand.

Men and women are different. Jonathan Swift remarked that women love flattery but men are embarrassed by it. This is because men are active and women are passive. The universe is held in balance by these positive (active) and negative (passive) principles. Marriage is the way heterosexuals achieve cosmic balance.

Men Need to Take Charge

Men have been emasculated by feminism. An Australian man recently wrote to me: "For too long I have made girlfriends insecure by not telling them what I wanted because of a fear of appearing overbearing."

Another man told me that after he has spent the day doing home renovations, he is afraid his wife will "go ballistic" if he asks her to do the dishes. Men need to assert their just leadership and dump women who don't like it. There are plenty of fish in the sea and they are biting. With patience and firmness, some feminists can be saved. The rest can be thrown back.

Generally speaking, men need to figure out what they want to accomplish with their life. We need to ask what God wants us to do. Then define the role we want our wife to play and find a woman who is eager to play the part.

This is want women want too. Women are attracted to dynamic men whom they cannot control. He must have a wholesome vision of life in which she plays an important role and is cherished for it.

FEMINIST ROAD KILL

Feminist propaganda teaches that sex roles are merely "stereotypes". As a result, millions of people are clueless about their sexual identities and suffer from arrested development. I was one of them.

At age 53 normally I would have had at least three children by now. Instead, I have been divorced three times. I have one child from my first marriage. It took me until age 50 to figure out what was happening and make a successful marriage.

Feminism corrected some abuses and gave women more opportunity. But these reforms mask its real agenda. It is a psychological warfare program to depopulate and destabilize society, invented by the same Illuminists who gave us Communism. They exploit any grievance to advance their "New World Order" a system that doesn't include democracy.

Contrary to what media and educators would have us believe, the world is run by occult perverts and super rich criminals. This sounds outrageous I know. If it were fiction, I would have made up something more credible. For a concise background, read William T Still, New World Order: The Ancient Plan of Secret Societies, 1990.

The Illuminists control us using the education system and mass media. We are conditioned to listen to others instead of trust our own instincts and common sense. Generally speaking, we are very gullible.

THE MATRIX OF DOMINATION

The Middle Passage-the transatlantic transition of Africans from their native land into slavery-was one of the most decisive and formative phases in the history of the New World. The onset of a reidentification process predicated on the European construction of race segued into the collectivization of Africans from a previously defined, ethnically-based identity.

The sexual exploitation of African women aboard the slave ships, and later, on the plantation, functioned similarly, as it cohesively oppressed all passengers of the Middle Passage.

Having embarked upon one of the most difficult experiences in recent human history, the Africans who endured the Middle Passage transition formed a unique bond based on the shared experience of suffering. The memory of anguish and violence inflicted on survivors was seared permanently into the conscious of the African and her American-born offspring.

The high incidence of rape and sexual coercion of African women by European men became one of the major contributing factors in the process of reidentification and collectivization that began aboard the slaver or slave ship itself. In fact, Angela Davis points out in her pioneering work on female slavery, it was common practice among many vessels to permit their crews access to such sexual exploits as a matter of policy.

The assertion that rape was simply expression of white men's sexual desire is an oversimplification. Nonetheless, Robert Hayden's 1962 poem entitled "The Middle Passage," appropriates lust as a means to reflect rape as a tool of oppression and dominance. The following excerpt is taken from the poem:

That Crew and Captain lusted with the comeliest/of the savage girls kept naked in the cabins;/that there was one they called The Guinea Rose/and they cast lots and fought to lie with her.

Thus the institutionalized pattern of rape of African women by European men was a well-established before the Africans who survived the Middle Passage transition ever arrived in the New World.

Regardless of the extent of violation or the total number of women abused, all aboard the vessel faced the same predicament: first, that African women (or young girls in some cases) became completely vulnerable and incapable of protecting themselves; second, the African men who attempted intervention endured tremendous hardship. Davis' reflections on sexual coercion during slavery and the way it fostered political aims are equally as applicable to the slave ship itself, where a system of repression and violence was also crucial to the successful suppression of revolts and other forms of resistance. At the core of this argument lies the contention that the sexual coercion of women also functioned by targeting African men, who unavoidably suffered from their inability to protect the women and children, who were their own wives, daughters, sisters, and friends. As Michael Gomez puts it in Exchanging My Country Marks, "Those who reacted to the rape of women moved into the continuum" (167).

Thus, the institutionalized pattern of rape, as it entered the framework of the slaver, provided the means to destroy the women's will to resist and, by corollary, to demoralize their men. A curious irony of this tactic, Davis points out, is that despite slaveowners' attempt to render women unequal to their male counterparts by increasing the intensity of their brutality-for they were not only raped but whipped and mutilated as well-the oppression was still equally distributed over both males and females. This indeed rendered black women's positions equal within the slave community and formed the groundwork upon which their resistance to slavery occurred with a passion equal to their men's.

It is the bond caused by the shared experience of affliction that prompted these Africans to conceive the foundation of a community, separate and distinct from that of slaveholders and other whites. Following the correlation between the grounds on which African men and women suffered aboard the slaver and what they and their offspring would suffer on the plantation, the transition demanded the inception of a reorientation of identity, a reassessment of who and what formed the community. Gomez reminds us that "For in order to suffer at all, an identification with those so violated had to take place. In order for there to be any anguish, there would have necessarily been some reflection on the loss of power, on the inability to defend" (167). In turn, the feeling of subjection and the indignation over the incapacity to protect was grounded in the need for power and the obligation to safeguard. The formation of a new black community, took place on the grounds of joint humiliation and reflecting a movement away from a previously defined, ethnically based identity, therefore becomes apparent even prior to arrival in the New World.

MISGUIDED WOMEN

The ninjas. The burqa brigade. The women in black. For some years now I've been hearing such terms thrown around with disdain by "burqa-unfriendly" sections of Pakistani society to describe the women who swathe themselves entirely in black. The terms are disparaging, but until recently they were a joke, not invested with the property of fear invoked by the ninjas' male counterparts: the beards, the fundos, the jihadis. In the past few weeks, all that has changed.

The first sign of trouble occurred in January when the female students of Islamabad's Jamia Hafsa madrasa occupied a children's library to protest against the demolition of 80 mosques encroaching on public land. Rather than resorting to its usual brute-force tactics, the government sent in the minister for religious affairs to promise that those mosques already demolished would be rebuilt. Many voices started grumbling about the government's inability to stand up to "a group of girls". But it didn't take much to imagine the PR fallout for Musharraf's government if he sent in baton-wielding police officers after a group of teenaged girls objecting to the razing of mosques in a country where illegal buildings are hardly out of the ordinary.

Then, in March, dozens of girls from Jamia Hafsa kidnapped three women and a baby from a house they claimed was a brothel. Next they kidnapped two policemen. Newspaper front pages were splashed with pictures of the ninjas chasing away plain-clothes policemen while wielding long sticks. They have also taken to patrolling the bazaars, threatening the owners of DVD and CD stores, which they claim spread pornography and vice. Every few days the papers now carry pictures of DVD bonfires.

The girls of Jamia Hafsa have their male counterparts at the adjoining Jamia Fareedia madrasa for men. But "Jamia Fareedia" has not entered Pakistan's vocabulary in the way "Jamia Hafsa" has, and the part that the male students play in their campaign of "virtue" has gone comparatively unremarked on, though they, too, were present at the kidnappings and are part of the intimidation of video store owners. In fact, the femaleness of the female students seems to be causing almost as much consternation as the decision by the brothers who run the two madrasas to impose a parallel sharia system of justice within their premises and their warnings of suicide attacks if the government doesn't also impose sharia law

The gendered nature of the commentary about the Jamia Hafsa students cuts across many sections of society-from the radio DJ who, tongue firmly in cheek, declared the theme of his show "girl power-in honour of the ladies of Jamia Hafsa", to the highly respected journalist deploying the phrase "chicks with sticks", to the head of Jamaat-ud-Dawa (the offshoot of the banned militant party Lashkar-e-Toiba) opposing the students' actions on the grounds that it is un-Islamic for women to take a leadership position, to General Musharraf dismissing the vigilantes as "misguided women"-which seems to suggest that they wouldn't or couldn't behave as they were doing if not for someone else (presumably male) guiding their actions. Musharraf has also used gender as an excuse for not taking action against their flagrant violations of the law. "We respect women," he intoned with great sincerity, putting aside the fact that women are being harassed and kidnapped by the JH students.

Repent and be Forgiven

If Pakistan's outspoken feminists are not rising up in objection to the sexist subtext of all these comments it is because they're far more concerned with the threat that the JH students pose to other women. They have already announced that they know of 30 other "brothels" in Islamabad that they're going to raid, though the male head of the madrasa has generously added that any prostitute who turns herself in and repents will be forgiven (he will set the example of forgiveness by marrying one of them). Not content with threatening alleged prostitutes, the JH students have also declared a fatwa against Pakistan's tourism minister after she was shown on television paragliding and then hugging her French coach. Both actions are deemed to be un-Islamic.

It's easy to think of the paragliding minister and the burqa-clad militant as opposite poles of Pakistan's complex pictures of womanhood. Newspapers have taken to juxtaposing "oppositional" photographs in support of this thesis: a tracksuit-wearing female athlete with a javelin beside stick-wielding women in black; a bare-headed, short-sleeved female protester holding up a sign saying "No to Extremism, Yes to Music" taking the front-page space given the previous day to more stick-wielding women in black (the photographs of the JH students are taken from different angles, in different places, but are ultimately always the same photograph). The more complicated truth is that the real opposites are the women who appear on the front pages and those who don't appear anywhere at all, except in a small column tucked away inside, detailing a story of a woman raped, a woman killed for "honour", a woman stoned alive.

"Obscured" women in Pakistan are a metaphor to a greater extent than they are a literal presence. (Sometimes, as in the case of the JH students, when they are literally obscured, they are also front and centre of the nation's view.) Though Pakistan's women are, in temperament, probably more powerful than its men, they are also almost entirely absent from the structures of power-and on the rare occasions when they do enter those structures, it is often as some man's wife or daughter. Small wonder, then, that when they enter the public sphere with any gesture of defiance-be it progressive or regressive-their femaleness attracts particular attention. Women should stay tucked away in the local news section of newspapers, is the implicit message of all this gendered scrutinising; to behave otherwise is simply not appropriate.

PREPARATION FOR LIFE IN PEACE: THE CONTRIBUTION OF WOMEN

A consideration of components that must be included in the process of preparing for life in peace deals more frequently with the structure of society that needs to be reordered or re-created, rather than with the disturbing flaws in individual behavior that make impossible-or at least improbable-acts of cooperation that must underlie a stable world society enjoying international security and peace.

The Bahá'í International Community would like, therefore, to touch on some of the elements in the human personality that need to be addressed if a harmonious interaction between the individual and society can come into being.

Education from childhood in a basic understanding of the connection between peoples and cultures, insisting on a search for the common denominator in all persons, is, in our view, the basic prerequisite. To strip human beings of their accidental identities of race, nationality, religion, class, or sex, and to find within each person the basic intellectual, emotional, and physical needs and potentials is, we believe, a necessary process leading to the eradication of the whole range of prejudices preventing human beings from working together to build a peaceful world.

For it is the conviction of the Bahá'í International Community, as expressed in the Bahá'í Writings, that man's glory lieth in his knowledge, his upright conduct, his praiseworthy character, his wisdom, and not in his nationality or rank. And further, that they that are endued with sincerity and faithfulness should associate with all the peoples and kindreds of the earth with joy and radiance, inasmuch as consorting with people hath promoted and will continue to promote unity and concord, which in turn are conducive to the maintenance of order in the world and to the regeneration of nations.

In the educational process earlier referred to it is important to consider the contribution that women can make in strengthening international peace and security, and in bringing about a world society that embodies the noblest characteristics and aspirations of the human race, a society that in turn nourishes the unfoldment of the full-range of individual talents.

It will be, in our view, only with the full participation of women in the affairs of the planet that we can bring about world peace. And the key to this essential involvement of women in the establishment of world order will be the provision of education for every human being, regardless of sex, race, nationality, class or religion. The need for such action is clearly expressed in the following passage from the Bahá'í Writings:

When all mankind shall receive the same opportunity of education and the equality of men and women be realized, the foundations of war will be utterly destroyed. Equality between men and women is conducive to the abolition of warfare for the reason that women will never be willing to sanction it.

The principle of the equality of rights, privileges and opportunities for both sexes is one of the central principles of the Bahá'í Faith. Essential to the unity of mankind and the establishment of universal peace, this principle has been actively promoted by Bahá'ís for over one hundred years. As women have become more involved in helping solve the many world problems that confront us today, it is encouraging to note, as the Bahá'í International Community mentioned in a statement submitted to the 30th session of the Commission on the Status of Women (E/CN.6/1984/NGO.1) on the relationship of women to peace, that the non-aggressive tendencies in women, who by nature seek cooperative means in solving such problems, are beginning to be appreciated by societies attempting to solve conflicts by peaceful means.

In our stage of human civilization, cooperation is seen as a vital element bringing about a complex but challenging unity through diversity, a garnering of the riches of human backgrounds and cultures to be integrated into a planetary pattern of international law and world order, and the emergence, eventually, of a world civilization. In the first quarter of this century, the pattern had already been witnessed with full clarity by `Abdu'l-Bahá, the son of Bahá'u'lláh, Founder of the Bahá'í Faith, when he observed:

The world in the past has been ruled by force and man has dominated over woman by reason of his more forceful and aggressive qualities both of body and mind. But the scales are already shifting, force is losing its weight, and mental alertness, intuition and the spiritual qualities of love and service, in which woman is strong, are gaining ascendancy. Hence the new age will be an age less masculine and more permeated with the feminine ideals, or, to speak more exactly, will be an age in which the masculine and feminine elements of civilization will be more properly balanced.

It would seem quite clear, however, that it will not be possible for civilization present and future to benefit from this balance between masculine and feminine if an extraordinary effort is not made to provide education to women throughout the planet-even to favor the education of women from earliest childhood-so that the potentialities of this half of the human race can be developed fully and brought to bear in the resolution of world problems and the establishment of world peace. This could be, indeed, in our view, one of the thrusts of the International Year of Peace-to fully explore ways, and recommend action, that will bring about this fair balance of education for boys and girls in the family, in the community, and in the nation. For not only is the participation of women as mothers and parents crucial to develop the proper qualities in children to become agents for peace, but the influence of women in the affairs of the world, through their participation in all areas of activity on a full and equal footing with men is also an essential element to make war once and forever obsolete.

Further, women could help reverse a prevalent philosophy of life that assumes that human beings are captive of the natural world, and that human behavior must therefore resemble that of animals; since the resultant struggle for material wealth is one with which women are very familiar, having long been victims of a system that values material productivity as the mark of success, but does not lead to security, happiness, or well-being for anyone.

It is the view of the Bahá'í International Community that the struggle of one group, class or race for control or advantage over others for economic benefit serves only to increase divisiveness, deepen prejudices and enhance the competitive side of human nature. Instead, a philosophy based on the nobility of human beings and on the development of their higher spiritual nature can give a new vision and education essential to peoples and governments in our time.

If women-and men-could by every means available to them promote such a view of life, a rapid transformation of society might soon be possible. This action would, as we expressed in our statement to the Commission on the Status of Women mentioned earlier, ensure the development of moral and spiritual values, which are so essential if education is to promote peace; it would help to bring about the equality of the sexes, cementing the partnership which must exist between men and women; it would lessen the competitiveness and struggle for power between warring groups seeking to exercise dominance over others; and finally it would make possible the building of an effective system of collective security to maintain peace among states: for in a united world no aggressor nation could destroy any other, since all other countries would act in unison, through an international agency, to prevent that aggression.

There is a great need in our world today to include in education cooperative approaches involving respect for the potential realization of the highest qualities in every human being. We have found that cooperative attitudes and respect for others in the family will encourage the acceptance of rights for everyone: the respect for children and for women is enhanced in families where moral and spiritual values underlie the concern for material well-being. In addition, when these attitudes are extended from the family to the nation and the world, they hold great promise for lessening and eventually abolishing those divisive prejudices that have seriously inhibited growth and development.

Although the Bahá'í International Community supports special programmes for the development of women, the experience of Bahá'í communities has shown that if these programs do not also educate men in the equality of the sexes, leading to their acceptance of this just principle, they will fail, since the healthy condition of the family, as the basic unit of society, requires the shared contribution of both men and women. Wherever the family structure and influence are weak, problems will multiply-especially for children, those adults of the world of tomorrow.

If International Year of Peace can encourage programmes that stress an increasing awareness of the interdependence and organic unity of humanity, it will be fostering conditions in which peace is possible. For, it seems to us, we need urgently a spreading wave of people who learn respect for the rights of others, assume responsibility to build good character, and are willing to dedicate themselves, in the spirit of service, to the interests of the whole of humanity.

6

Status of Women in Developed World

It is clear that women in America enjoy much more personal freedom and independence than women in many other parts of the world. This freedom is something we hold dear and one of the things that define contemporary American culture. However, it is also clear that many immigrants, coming from very different-thinking cultures, view such women with at least suspicion and at most contempt. Acquiring a functional view of the women in America might take some re-thinking on the part of some immigrants who may have had little exposure to women in the workplace, women in charge, or even women operating on their own. It might give a more accurate view of the real character and status of American women if you think of them as "honorary men."

Different cultures espouse widely variant ideas of the proper role and place of women within a society. One coworker, from Egypt, informed me that women did not typically live outside of their parents' homes there unless they were married. There, a woman setting up "house" by herself is assumed to be setting up a place of prostitution. Why else would she leave the guidance and protection of her family? This way of thinking was completely new to me and would be to most Americans. Here, females, just like males, are expected to move away from parents' homes and set up on their own in order to prove themselves successful, fully functioning adults. True, a woman can more easily remain at home with her parents than a man can here, but past about age

25 others would begin to look at her askance. So expect the women here to live on their own, in apartments or homes that they own, and consider such a situation to mean simply that such a woman is an adult and that she can afford such accommodations.

Further, in many other places in the world, women are expected to hold marriage and children as their primary goals and interest. Here, women are generally more interested in these things than the men are, but they do not necessarily place them first on their "to do" lists. In America, a woman is just as likely to decide that her education, for instance, needs to be completed before she can consider marriage or family. She may decide that her career needs to develop to a certain point first. In short, an American woman may have the same kind of broad concerns about conducting her life that men have around the world. In the case of men, most folks would consider holding such priorities as prudent in preparing for life's challenges, but women can still come under scrutiny for the same priorities. Here, it should not be surprising to find women delaying marriage and family into their thirties, forties or even fifties.

Finally, many cultures associate a female's independence with evidence that she is morally and/or sexually slack. The title of this article is "honorary men" for a reason. It suggests that independent women in America should be viewed through the same lens through which most folks would view men. A young man, living independent of his parents, working on his education or his career, may be morally upright or morally depraved; he may be sexually chaste or sexually promiscuous. His status as an independent man cannot tell you these other aspects of his character. Rather, one would need to meet him and get to know him before one could make such judgments. This scenario is exactly the same for American women. A woman living on her own and conducting her own personal and professional business can run the whole gamut from dutiful, traditional and chaste to self-involved, nontraditional and sexually free. One would need to engage the individual woman in order to find out the truth.

Similarly, American women tend to wear jewelry and make-up, and to many immigrants, too revealing clothing. Yet American women are typically dressing within the norms of social correctness (and beauty) that all women follow in their own cultures. American women of all types even dress more conservatively as they meet the requirements of various workplaces. The few women who violate such codes receive the same shocked and negative reactions from other Americans that they do from immigrants. So, despite the make-up and high-heels, the skirts and the hairdos, remember that these women are meeting the norms of the society. American's women's style of dress, then, has little to do with her morals or her character. In short, it might make more sense just to think of us all as honorary men,. and proceed accordingly.

THREE VALUE SCALES IN MODERN WORLD

In modern world, values are measured on three coexisting scales: non-materialistic, materialistic, and postmaterialistic. The latter term was introduced by American sociologist R. Engelhart (Silent Revolution, 1997, and Cultural Shift in Developed Industrial Society, 1990). His studies are based on worldwide surveys of public opinion. The core ides is that material well-being of postwar period resulted in major shift in large populaces' perception of values. Engelhart calls former values "materialistic" and the new one-"post-materialistic". Respondents in the surveys were offered a wide range of values and should check those of them they perceived as their own.

"Materialistic" values included: "national-level order", "price regulations", "economic growth", "national defence", "stable national economy", "crime containment". "Post-materialistic" values included: "more public participation in government", "freedom to communicate one's opinion", more public participation in decision-making at community level", "improve public and environmental health", "make society more friendly and diversified", "make ideas overpower money".

"Post-materialistic" values, in Engelhart's sense, differ from their "materialistic" counterparts rather in quantitative than quality characteristics. To qualify the new system of values widely adopted today by modern western youths, it would take a combination of two words: "post-materialistic" (which is already in place) and "post-patriarchal" (which is not). In these terms, non-materialistic values are described as "patriarchal" (which is essentially the same). The term "patriarchy" was initially introduced by feminists to designate men's supremacy over women carried out through variety of public institutions. Today this term is widely used by all type of ideologists as reference to societies based on rigid hierarchy. "Post-patriarchal" society produced new values that can be described, according to a German sociologist H. Z. Betz, as "mixture of left-libertary and non-materialistic." It means that post-materialistic values should include all rights and freedoms of today's democracy-and that is the main feature distinguishing post-materialistic set of values from the non-materialistic set.

Non-materialistic values were placed in almost every culture throughout human history. These values included struggle, victory, unity, mutual support, unselfishness, honor and other concepts of the same row. Past cultures having shifted to materialistic values (Carthego, for instance) were usually renounced and sometimes demolished by their neighbors. Only with industrial revolution, Western Europe and USA made their final choice of materialistic values and eventually overruled non-materialistic values both at home and abroad. Materialism established new values: individual, his rights and liberties, personal benefit. It was materialism that gave start to concepts of equal rights for men and women, women's "entitlement" to artificial abortion, liberty to choose one's sexual orientation, etc.

"Post-materialists" plan to keep all these gains of democracy. For this reason, post-materialistic system of values is strikingly different from non-materialistic paradigm of the past. It can be argued that the idea of returning to pre-materialistic values is both attractive and repulsive for "post-materialists". Therefore, they check each value for its compatibility with emancipation trends. There seem to be no other explanation why one would protest against drugs being tested on animals and stand for artificial abortions at the very same time.

The same reasoning helps explain why patriarchal ethics is deemed "egotistic" by post-materialists. Whereas an individual feels that he belongs to his kind-be it a nation, a class, a tribe, or a family-he becomes a part of self-sufficient "collective ego", while true unselfishness, to their opinion, means belonging to entire humanity without any discrimination between human groups.

New values-either post-materialistic or post-patriarchal-are publicly promoted by so-called alternative movements (ecologists, ecofeminists, communitarians and some others). Their goal is to help evolve new political culture. Political culture is known to be always "stratified" to some extent. Today politicians operate in terms of traditional culture (based on concepts of authority, hierarchy, law and so on). However, other strata of political culture exist today within the global framework of the prevailing authoritative one. They are, for example, rural and community self-government culture, "guerilla warfare" political culture of left radicals, and others. Western "civic" and Eastern "patriarchal" political cultures cause abundant discussions. For post-materialists, however, these distinctions and deviations seem to not exist at all. They assert that what we have today is solidified "oppressive" political culture.

Therefore, they visualize future political culture to be "soft" and feminine as opposed to "hard" and masculine culture of today. Alternative movements associate crisis of the western civilization with dominance of masculine ethics and thinking. Masculine way of thinking is essentially dualistic in its perception of the world; hence, reality is fragmented into pairs of opposing concept: Nature/culture, body/spirit, manhood/womanhood, I/other, etc. Moreover, horizontally fragmented world is subjected to vertical classification by hierarchy, assigning elements the more importance and power, the higher their standing is. Values prevalent in masculine ethics are freedom, personal autonomy, equality, equity, etc. In addition, for all his life a man has to prove his sexual identity, and for this end he fervently competes with others of his like to confirm his standing.

Feminine culture and thinking may be generally characterized by the following features. First, it is integrated perception of the world inherent in women. "Femininity is determined through unity," writes Caroline Gillighan. Second, feminine ethical values are primarily those of mutual dependence, compassion and care. A female does not have to constantly prove her status (it is soundly based on her reproductive function); consequently she is not inclined to construct hierarchical chains and promote herself to higher standing in them. Third, women acquire essentially different socialization experience. Right from the beginning, they are taught how to care for others, make decisions that would incorporate others' interests, keep her family clear of conflicts, etc.

Many think that with building-up women's role and representation at all levels of power a "bloodless revolution" may occur through gradual replacement of masculine "terror-based political culture" with feminine culture of universal care, pacifism, ecological thinking, etc.

If males remain prevalent at power any longer, the global catastrophe will follow inevitably, as Elizabeth Gray believes, because for male politicians "steadfastness is a cult." Male politicians are almost incapable of compromise, as their primary concern is to play self-assured winners.

Alternative movements' adherents largely agree that most women (not to say about men) are yet unready to accept most of "feminine" values. To spread new values, it will take a worldwide effort-"New Enlightenment" as it is often called. Of course, skeptics may say that all attempts to remold human psychology are utopian. The same label used to be attached to the Enlightenment ideas. Nevertheless, so prominent a sociologist as Alexis de Toqueville in his The Old Order and the Revolution acknowledges that it was enlighteners who had prepared the Great French Revolution, as the latter was grounded in abstract concepts, rather than in realities of that time. Apostles of new values openly declare themselves to be new enlighteners, and since the old ones succeeded in their mission, it's not improbable that their conceived inheritors will be successful too.

Education is the main tool to reengineer human mind and morale. From standpoint of new social values, school education systems that we presently have are "estrangement-producing machinery". Moreover, not only education system requires complete restructuring, basic principles of what and how is taught in school must be revised. That is why new schools are among major concerns of projects implemented by alternative movements. One of them (movement for humanistic education) entirely focuses on this problem. The movement sees its mission in opening schools of new type which would be deeply rooted in local communities.

Children are brought up on entirely new principles, often contradictory to those practiced elsewhere. For example, children are taught to play new games that do not imply competition and winners, while unisex-style clothes prevent boys and girls from evolving "sexist templates" of how they should behave. As mentioned above, "non-materialistic" values do not imply "feminine" or "mild" political culture.

With the exclusion of "the golden billion", majority of earth's population keep on living with non-materialistic values (or rather pre-materialistic from European standpoint). Whereas collectivism, care for neighbors, and-to some extent-"femininity" (harmoniously combined with women's' secondary role) are natural attributes of the third world, it is absolutely free of any motives of liberation and emancipation. Moreover, there is no evidence that, on having achieved understanding of solidarity and collectivism as values to be unconditionally preserved in the future, these nations would want to adopt democratic values in their common sense (e. g., equality in face of the Law).

Most humans still live in communities that profoundly disprove materialistic values, including their manifestations in form of human rights and freedom so cherished in the West. Far more doubtful prospect is of political culture feminization, especially if looked upon from the standpoint of ethnic psychology. L. N. Gumilev wrote in his In Trouble of Illusion, that "history evolves not in itself, but in every particular ethnos... For universal human values to take possession of the entire humankind, multiple nations of today should merge into a single hyperethnos. However, as long as levels of passionate tension vary across superethnoses already present, as long as land-scapes and climates vary from country to country and require specific skills to adjust... chances for such merger are narrow..."

Though in somewhat peculiar (not in his days) language, Gumilev makes it clear that prevalence of feminine (care, peace, cooperation, security) or masculine (aggression, struggle, quest, self-assertion) qualities depends on age of an evolving entity-be it an individual or a nation. In this sense, Nietzsche was absolutely correct when he wrote that, in certain periods, "manly, belligerent, victorious instincts take over all others, such as 'happiness' instinct..." while at other times other instincts dominate, those of "contemptible prosperity of which minor shopkeepers... women and other democrats dream." Putting aside Nietzsche's disregard to shopkeepers' values, he was absolutely right about their feminine origin. Getting back to Gumilev's terms, we see that whenever feminine values prevail in political life of "ethnos", it has already entered its "autumn" characterized by declining livelihood and overall sluggishness of the nation. In other words, we witness a nation that has passed its activity peak and is getting prepared for dissolution. At this stage, nations become peaceful; moreover, they seek harmony with the Nature. Iceland and Norway were the two nations Gumilev had chosen as examples of declining ethnoses. Today these two countries are at forefront of "feminine" political culture.

In this context, feminine domination is associated with rather pessimistic expectations for the future. Therefore, post-patriarchal values and political culture may be expected to spread only over those ethnic systems driven by inertia, while other nations will stick to masculine values at practically any cost.

As for Russia, most recent surveys reveal a bizarre picture: romantic elders oriented towards collectivism and pragmatic youths oriented towards individualism.

In 1995 survey undertaken by Russian Independent Institute of Social and National Problems, 93.4% Russian respondents backed the statement of "clean conscience and inner harmony" as a major human value; 90.7% supported "family and friends"; while only 35.4% mentioned "well-paid job", and 8.1%-"public cognizance and fame". However, of younger respondents (22-26 years old) only 89.2% the first statement, while elders (>60) were much more consonant (98.9%). Young vs. elder score in support of the three other values was: 89.8% vs. 91.8%; 38.1% vs. 25.2%; and 6.5%.

Separately stands the assertion that a person should "make his way into power, in order to have influence upon others". Among younger people this statement gained approval of 9.1%, while of older citizens it was supported by 0.0% precisely.

Obvious analogies may be drawed between this survey and "materialistic" and "non-materialistic" values. So far, a certain part of Russian young generation is quite happy with "materialistic" values which have already produced strong repulsion in their western counterparts (e. g., "competition drives development", "the strongest survives", "consumption above all" and other market-oriented values). All others (note, that they are not "elders" in American Medicare sense, for this group included everyone of 35 and above) simply reject these values as if they were non-existent, for experience of all their previous life suggests that these values are not actual values, but rather channels for fraud and corrupt behavior to take place of morality. In addition, middle-aged and elders had lucky opportunity to grow up while enjoying far better social and economic standards (which, in turn, theoretically means more openness to "post-materialistic" thinking).

Nevertheless, compatibility of "post-materialistic" values and Russian thinking is a thing that would take much insanity to believe in. Engelhart's evaluation method was developed for nations with developed market economies only. Having been applied in transition-market Russia, it produced the outstanding score, "Materialists-9 vs. Post-materialists-1" (while in Western Europe the average ratio is 4:3). What we observe, however, is rather non-materialism than post-materialism as opposed to "western materialism". Post-materialistic values depend on age of ethnos. Finally, they include libertary values which are understood as formal rights and negative freedoms (not to...). In Russian tradition, however, freedom is understood as positive "freedom of will", and rights are understood as a "gain for being rightful".

Despite of all, alternative movements exist in Russia. They attract persons of diverse (but always non-materialistic) orientation. As for post-materialistic values, they are inherent in a few-mostly representatives of intelligentsia with interests lying in fields of technical engineering, applied and natural sciences (for education in liberal arts always results in excessive self-esteem and lack of appropriate collectivism). Though unmistakable enemies of alternative values and movements include primarily those who constitute the bunch that has recently been designated as "the middle class in process of formation" (corrupt officials and businessmen who had finally attained/hope to attain western living standards). This powerful group is enthralled by gains of materialistic period and shows no sign of being bored of capitalizing.

It was back in 70's when certain social groups in the former USSR (primarily those who used to go in rounds with communist-future messages) silently adopted western values (while keeping on discrediting them in public) and began to practice excrescent consumption, unlimited (shadow) business development, private and public competition and so on. This phenomenon was then publicly labeled and disrupted as "veschism".

One point of this article is to assert that "post-materialistic values" are products of unprecedented growth of wealth resulting in incredible formal liberties that have evolved in the West. This unique process cannot be reproduced elsewhere on the earth (at least, in this and following generations). Therefore, standards of living that made western youths (and sometimes elders) to believe in "post-materialistic values" are non-attainable on the global scale. For this simple reason, "post-materialistic" values are doomed (at least, as they are today). Sooner or later, traditional non-material values that prevail in the most of human culture will take over (though with certain western-inspired modifications). Anyway, libertary impetus will never regain equal strength that we witness today in alternative movements. "New" Islam fundamentalism is, probably, one example of what future alternative movements will be like. While claiming to promote "true" Islam values, fundamentalists, in fact, have largely modernized tradition Islam to the extent that it might be as well designated as "post-materialistic religion". (After all, fundamentalism evolved as a substitute for Western values once so popular in the East.) For example, modern fundamentalists do not disclaim freedom and democracy; they just emphasize that they understand them differently. In this sense, new values may come into dominion over the world under any conceivable name.

WOMEN AS CONSUMERS AND PRODUCERS IN THE WORLD MARKET

Globalisation has had adverse effects on women in the South. As consumers, women are the targets for a host of dangerous products and a consumer culture which reduces them to commodities. As producers, they are exposed to work exploitation and occupational hazards.

Health is humankind's most basic consumer need and the most precious possession, next perhaps only to life itself. Good health is particularly important to women because lack of it affects them for a variety of reasons.

As potential mothers requiring care and attention, women need specialised services related to the reproductive system. As mothers they become responsible for the health of their children and families. And as workers outside and inside the house, they often have to shoulder double burdens; consequently they are overworked, subject to poor working conditions and suffer undue overstrain and mental stress. They are more dependent on the health system than men, and are major consumers of health care due to their many roles.

In recent years many products related to women's health have been found to be dangerous or giving rise to illnesses which in some cases have led to deaths. Many of them have been banned or restricted in the developed countries although they continue to be marketed in the Third World.

Third World countries have become convenient dumping grounds for products and medicines peddled by the transnational corporations (TNCs). Most of these products do not meet the safety standards in their countries of origin in the North and many Third World women have become unfortunate guinea pigs and victims. Some of these products include dangerous contraceptives like Depo Provera, the Dalkon Shield and Norplant.

Not only have the TNCs affected the health of Third World women with their marketing of dangerous contraceptives, they have also introduced new food and new tastes at the expense of wholesome traditional nutrition. Many of these foods are hawked by the TNCs as fashionable items of consumption.

Across the Third World today can be found a wide array of costly beverages, packed in attractive cans and bottles, canned foods, frozen foods, fast food and processed foods which not only swamp supermarkets, but are also often prominently displayed in the remotest village shop.

The irony is that in most Third World countries, the basic needs of some two-thirds of the population are yet to be satisfied. Yet impoverished families have been persuaded by the sales tactics of TNCs to spend their hard-earned money on junk foods and products which they do not need.

Coca Cola is sold in every village shop and even the families of fishermen buy canned fish which is advertised on radio, television and in glossy magazines. Farmers who can hardly make ends meet are known to spend a third of the family income on cigarettes and alcoholic drinks thus siphoning off a valuable portion of their hard-earned money which could be used for family nutrition instead.

Bottled drinks and junk food have become essential items not only in the urban but also the rural areas and not only during festivals and celebrations but also in everyday living. In recent years, the American fast food culture has spread to many Third World countries, which are now savouring the delights of hot dogs, pizzas, McDonald's beefburgers, Kentucky Fried Chicken and A & W root beer.

In Third World countries when people with limited budgets are influenced by the prevailing culture to switch from traditional and nutritious foods to high-cost low-nutrition foods, there is an adverse effect on their health.

BOTTLE FEEDING OF INFANTS

One outstanding and well-known example of the detrimental influence of introducing new foods to replace traditional practices is the case of infant formula and sweetened condensed milk. Due to aggressive sales promotion by the milk companies, many poor mothers in the Third World have switched from breast-feeding to bottle feeding their babies. Because of this pressure from the milk companies and the prevailing consumer culture, women lose confidence in breast-feeding and themselves as mothers. Breast-feeding is no longer considered modern and a mother is led to believe that she is denying the best for her baby if she does not give the bottle. As a result, breast-feeding rates have been declining in the Third World.

THE TOBACCO EPIDEMIC

With smoking declining in developed countries, the tobacco industry is shifting its operations to the Third World. Many Asian countries, including Thailand and South Korea, have had to open up to imports of foreign cigarettes in the name of free trade under pressure of Western governments and tobacco companies.

As a result, there has been a rise in the number of smokers, women included. Besides the adverse health effects, there is also a negative social impact. An ordinary worker or farmer smoking one packet of cigarettes a day may spend a quarter of his income on cigarettes.

In most Third World societies, when there is not enough food to go around, it is the women who have to give up their share. And when the men in the family are sick or die, it is again the women who have to bear the brunt of the family burdens and responsibilities.

THE IMAGE OF WOMEN IN THE CONSUMER CULTURE

The globalisation of culture promotes not only a Western brand of consumption and lifestyle, but also projects an image of women which is discriminatory, oppressive and male oriented. In this consumer culture, women have been reduced to mere commodities for mass consumption.

Women in most Third World societies have inherited the worst of both worlds. The concept in traditional feudal society of woman as the property of her husband subject to male authority in the family, is today made worse by the commercial exploitation of women in our consumer society.

This view of modern woman as a sex object is unprecedented in human history because it is only in our age and time that through the mass media and technology at its disposal the commodification of women has become so pervasive and insidious. This process is linked to a market economy where women are used as sex objects to sell products. This is seen time and again in advertisements where women are almost always depicted as vain and seductive, as sex commodities, dull-witted, in constant need of approval (almost always by men) and ultimately best left in the home or kitchen. It is here that women are most exploited in terms of their sexuality and physical appearance. One has only to look at the advertisements flashing from cinema screens, billboards, bus stops, magazines and calendars to confirm this. Many of these portray scantily dressed women advertising motorbikes, cars or radios-products which bear no relation to the figure of the women in these ads. The commercialisation of the female body as an object to be feasted upon and consumed by eager male eyes, is seen in the semi-nude and nude pictures of women-in suggestive poses and revealing big breasts-on calendars advertising cigarettes, liquor, tractors, paints and machinery. This portrayal of women in mass media is but a reflection, albeit a distorted reflection, of how women are regarded and made out to be in a consumer society.

More important, consumer culture has created an image of woman in terms of her face and body. This in turn helps to shape women's views about themselves and how others view them. In our hearts and minds we begin to believe that the real woman, the meaning of 'femaleness' is the one we see so often in the beauty magazines or the models advertising beauty aids and women's products. Thus the real woman is all beautiful, all glamour, all seduction.

And in the process of trying to attain 'this real thing' women not only compete with each other to outdo one another in sophistication and seduction (for sexual attention from men), women also lose confidence in themselves and their true worth. In this manner, consumer culture manipulates and distorts the personality of women, destroying their self-confidence and makes all of them victims.

WOMEN AS PRODUCERS

In recent years TNCs have located some of their manufacturing plants and industries in the Third World. The main reason adduced for this is the abundance of cheap, hard-working and docile labour.

By this they mean women workers of course. The exploitation of women in this sector in terms of their low wages, poor working conditions, instability of employment, absence of employment benefits and oppressive laws which deny women workers their rights to representation, unionisation and compensation has been well documented in the literature.

This situation is also true in the plantation economy where women workers suffer double oppression and exploitation-working as coolies and labourers in the tea, rubber and oil palm plantations and working as beasts of burden for their other lord and master, the husband in the home.

Plantation society is an enclosed atrophied society. Workers here have almost no control over decisions affecting their lives. Perhaps it is only a little better than the slave plantations during the first wave of colonial expansion in the New World.

Hazards

One of the most serious forms of exploitation that women workers face is the hazards they are exposed to in the workplace. These hazards not only threaten their health, but that of their unborn children if they are pregnant. Although both men and women face hazards at work, women because of their dual jobs-one at the shop floor and the other in the home-have to shoulder more burdens and are therefore exposed to more hazards. Thus the fatigue and stress suffered by most women workers 'is a result of their 80-hour work week-40 on the job, 40 in the house, and 24 hours on-call duty to their families.'

Women workers face four types of work hazards-psychological, physical, biological and chemical hazards.

The most serious psychological work hazard is stress and a major source of occupational stress is job dissatisfaction. The majority of women work in occupations where wages are low and where they have no control over decisions affecting them. This coupled with shift work and poor working conditions result in stress, one of the manifestations of which is mass hysteria-a common occurrence among factory workers in Malaysia.

Physical hazards include noise, heat, ventilation and lighting, vibration, trauma and radiation, and biological hazards include exposure to bacteria, viruses, fungi and infections. Chemical hazards are the most common. They include a wide range of industrial solvents, anaesthetic gases, heavy metals, dyes, inks, asbestos, shampoos, detergents, pesticides and radioactive materials. Women workers at home, in factories, hospitals and shops and whether they work as typists, agricultural workers, teachers or hairdressers are all exposed to these hazards.

For the female worker on plantations, her long and dangerous work as a breadwinner is further burdened by her household work. As a result, women workers suffer immense stress, hardship and strain and a general deterioration in their health.

WOMEN AS SELLERS

Many Third World countries are dependent on foreign trade. This is compounded by the fact that a large share of the exports of Third World countries consists of only a few commodities-raw materials which are more susceptible to price and demand fluctuations than manufactured goods. In the world market, both Third World men and women producers suffer from the low prices they are able to get for their produce. Their incomes are also reduced. And the industrialised countries dominate world trade.

This unequal relationship vis-a-vis the Third World means that industrialised countries (ICs) control the markets of both raw materials and manufactured goods. Third World countries have to take whatever price is being offered-both for their exports of raw materials and the imports of manufactured and industrial products from the ICs.

Thus, Third World countries have poor terms of trade for their commodities vis-a-vis industrial products of the developed countries. Their terms of trade have been declining in the past few decades and continue to do so.

Apart from the poor terms of trade for Third World commodities, a large portion of the export earnings of Third World countries goes to payment for freight, insurance, packing, marketing and shipping-services controlled by TNCs who, through their shipping firms, impose high and increasing charges for freight services.

Although this problem is not specifically related to women, women do suffer as they are also producers of commodities like rubber, tin, tea, bananas, cotton, coffee and sugar. Indirectly, they are also affected if their menfolk who are the primary bread-winners earn less income. With less money being brought home, the quality of life, health, nutrition and general well-being of the entire family is also affected.

SEX TOURISM

There is more insidious exploitation of women which is linked to world tourism. This global industry has given rise to the flesh trade whereby women and even children are made to sell their bodies for sex. Hundreds of thousands of women in Asian countries, forced by socio-economic circumstances, have been sexually exploited working as prostitutes, social escorts, dance hostesses and waitresses in nightclubs and cocktail lounges.

Sex tourism is the most dehumanised form of sex and economic exploitation of women. It has its roots in a Western decaying urban life, where society is alienated and deculturalised, and where the need to consume has become compulsive and devoid of any real meaning. Hence new stimulations, distractions and excitement have to be sought to give one continued satisfaction and what can be better than the fulfilment of sexual fantasies?

This barren existence is best typified by this young carpenter from Amsterdam who returns yearly to Bangkok on the sex tour: 'It's really unbelievable, all the gorgeous dames here. This is the third time I've come here and I swear that in all these times I haven't seen anything else except this bar. They drive you wild and for a few guilders you can pick the most beautiful of the beauties. This is something else, at least, than lying on your back in Spain to get a little tan. You're the king here and all for a few rotten pennies.'

This is also how much Asian women are worth. Through sex tourism, the industrialised countries export their sexual alienation and perversion to the Third World.

MARGINALISATION THROUGH DEVELOPMENT

The impact of the West which began first with colonial intervention and the development decades that followed have had adverse consequences on the role and status of women in traditional subsistence society.

The introduction of Western concepts of ownership of land has deprived women's usufructuary rights to cultivation and control of land. The introduction of cash crop production and Western male concepts of ownership have led to the exclusion of women in the cash economy. The neglect of the food subsistence sector where women were confined, in place of export crops and the new technologies which were introduced in agriculture not only increased her burden but in many instances, led to her redundance in traditional agricultural activities. This has resulted in the increasing marginalisation of women in the traditional rural economy, reducing women to a position of dependence which was absent in the traditional economy.

This discrimination against rural women has led to a steady displacement of women in the traditional sector. Further displacement due to development projects like dam construction, mining activities, aquaculture projects and tourism development, forces women to drift to the towns and cities in search of wage labour. In the factories they are exposed to hazardous and stressful working conditions, sexual harassment and an urban culture and lifestyle.

Despite the various attempts of the UN and the International Agencies to highlight and alleviate the problems of women, a UNESCO study at the end of 1993 revealed that the status of women in the developing nations of Asia had actually deteriorated in the past three decades.

Hence the problems of women must be examined in the light of present development strategies. As such, the solutions to the problems have to be seen and understood within the context of the whole development process that is taking place both in the rural and urban areas.

THELYPHTHORIA OR EXPLOITATION OF WOMEN

The real meaning of sex, the relations of the sexes in the past and at the present time, and the influences that these relations have on the present condition of mankind, are questions that transcend all others in importance, and that have more to do in determining the present condition of humanity than all other questions combined. No more certainly does the race arise by generation than it falls by abuse of the generative powers and functions. So likewise with regeneration, which means literally a new birth. It means not only that the individual shall be born again, but it means that the generative functions, individually and collectively, must be re-formed. There is no human attribute in which man approaches so near to deity as in the power to generate human beings. Here he is a creator.

There is no power in man capable, when perverted, of dragging him so deep into hell, and through which he can degrade so hopelessly so many other human beings as through the sexual life. Neither England nor the "civilized world" have had time to forget the "Pall Mall Gazette's Secret Commission", through which a single glimpse was obtained of the ruined lives and horrible depravity caused by perversion and degradation of the generative power of man. It was as though the door of the bottomless pit had opened for an instant, so that the world could get a single glance and be stifled with one puff of the vapours of the inferno. All that Dante ever painted was as a pleasant dream to this. The inferno is no myth, nor is it in the bowels of the earth, it exists in the body of society, and is eating out the heart of humanity. The present writer has neither the purpose nor the power to paint this realm, this leprosy of society. It would be appalling to even name its departments.

The seduction, desertion, and prostitution of young girls ending in suicide; the most loathsome and demoralizing diseases, scarcely second to leprosy, if not the real cause of that terrible disease; infanticide, only another name for murder; rape with its lynchings, and murder in every form; the pouring out on humanity and in the pure air of heaven daily and hourly of a fathomless, conscienceless, heartless ocean of lust. It is as though there had been poured into the pure stream of life the very dregs of the bottomless pit, and then, as though to prevent a single effort at purifying the stream, the Prince of Darkness has tabooed the whole subject, and attempts to cover with odium everyone who utters more than a mild regret, or who dares to long for the pure waters of life. Ask any old physician, who has had opportunity to know the under-current of society, if the above category is overdrawn, and he will tell you that it is incomplete. Here at the very fountain of all, life is the root of all evil. We are now writing for theosophists, some of whom have expressed a desire for practical instruction, and here are a few hints only.

If the whole stream of life is corrupt, it can be purified only by commencing at the fountain-head. There is but one way in which any man can help to purify or benefit the world, and that is by purifying himself. The whole of humanity is sexually diseased. Only the grosser crimes have as yet been named in this connection. Legalized prostitution and perversion of the highest attributes under the sacred name and in the habiliments of Love have not yet been mentioned. The theosophic life and the highest human achievement has been often declared to involve absolute chastity-purity in thought, word, and deed; and with this condition, love has been declared to be the absorbing element, the crowning glory. Over against this statement stands the record of celibacy in the clergy, and to it may be added the results as ordinarily witnessed of male and female continence both in private life and in various societies, whether as a matter of choice or necessity.

The results desired have seldom flowed from these conditions, and hence the earnest student is often bewildered and left in doubt as to the real meaning and possible results of chastity. Beyond this there are young people greatly interested in studies called theosophic, beside many married persons seeking to know theosophic truths, and striving to lead theosophic lives. To these last-named individuals the present essay is particularly addressed. The reform of the world from the horrible abuses named is not herein attempted. The attempt is made only to throw a little light on this all-important subject, so that those who are really in earnest, and who desire the truth in order to use it and serve it, may receive assistance. Let those who talk of England and America as "Christian Countries", count up the number of prostitutes in the large cities alone; let them add to this the number of cases of seduction, rape, bastardy, suicide, and murder, including abortions, the latter largely among the upper classes, and when they have gone thus far with their statistics, let them pause and read the "

Sermon on the Mount"; then if they are still ready to abuse and ostracise those who hesitate about attaching the sacred name of Christ to "modern civilization", we shall have nothing further to say in that direction.

If the wailing of the slaughtered innocents, the homeless waifs cast out on society, the despair and degradation of the poor prostitutes, and the shriek of the suicide as she rushes into the unseen world, do not blanch his face with horror and force him to cry, How long, O Lord! how long! argument would be wasted and words worse than useless. There are others again who do revere both the Sermon on the Mount and the author of it, and who hold the Bible and real Christianity in reverence, and who feel deeply the awful sarcasm of calling this or any present nation of the world, Christian. If these care to know the real bible doctrine on the subject under consideration, let them consult an old work bearing the title of this essay and printed in London in 1780. The following "memorandum" appears in the second of the three octavo volumes.

"The grand question to be tried is,-Whether a SYSTEM filled with obligations and responsibility of MEN to WOMEN, and of WOMEN to MEN, even to death itself, and this established by INFINITE WISDOM, is not better calculated to prevent the ruin of the female sex, with all it horrid consequences, both to the public and individuals, than a SYSTEM of human contrivance, where neither obligation nor responsibility are to be found, either of MEN to WOMEN or of WOMEN TO MEN, in instances of the most important concern to BOTH, but more especially to the weaker sex? " I have quoted the above as italicized in the original. The author shows the Bible doctrine to be beyond all controversy, that whether a man be married or single, he is "joined by God" to the woman with whom he is carnally intimate, and that "he shall not put her away all the days of his life", and as this necessarily involves polygamy and precludes divorce, the author faces the problem squarely, and shows, not by argument, but by Bible, that is "the law and the gospel". The present writer does not argue nor advocate this point either pro or con, but refers to it for the benefit of those interested in the subject from the Bible stand-point. The book can be found in many libraries, and can be occasionally picked up at old news-stands. One thing is very certain, and that is that the laws and practices of Christendom are widely at variance with the "law of God" as set forth in the Bible, and compiled and annotated in "Thelyphthoria, or a Treatise on Female Ruin".

Every careful student of religions, of occultism, or of theosophy, is aware that the symbols and the god-words of all-religions have a very close relation to sex. Not only Payne Knight, and Inman, but hosts of other writers, have pointed out and abundantly illustrated this fact. The deity to whom was offered divine honours in the various religions, was sometimes male, sometimes female. The God of Christendom today is undeniably male, notwithstanding the fact that the original name in Hebrew is both male and female, and that to a specific degree. The Catholic Church, wise as a serpent, in this as in all other generations, recognises this androgynous God, and god-name, and has elevated a woman to the God-head. If our present civilization be claimed still as Christian, it cannot be called catholic in its treatment of woman, in its practice of abortion or infanticide, whatever may be said of other crimes in this direction. It would surprise most persons to learn to what extent the fast and feast days, and " all the ordinances of the Lord's house", conform to and are derived from the periods of time which are related to parturition, viability, and the like.

Suffice it to say that the mysteries of religion, like the mystery of life, are all involved in the mystery of sex. This fact no one having the least knowledge of the subject can deny, for the evidence is overwhelming. Furthermore, the degradation of religion and the degradation of life has everywhere, and at all times, gone hand-in-hand with the degradation of the sexual instinct, and has sprung directly from the sexual degradation of woman and the bestialization of man. On the other hand, pure religion, pure life, and pure men and women go together. In the degradation of the world, man has always taken the lead, and woman been the victim. Every student of history knows that no more correct measure of any age, or any people, can be made than that which is based on the position and estimate in which women were found at that time. The new age that is just dawning for the human race is called " the Woman's Age". For many centuries, at least, woman has not occupied the position which is open to her today, and it is doubtful if, since written history began, her opportunities have been anything like that which she may now enjoy.

True, this opportunity falls to the lot only of a favoured few. The great majority are still in darkness and bondage, the victims of man's laws and passions. The responsibility and the god-given opportunities of the favoured few are seldom appreciated. These favoured few, who, from larger intelligence or fortunate circumstances, are free to live pure and noble lives, seldom rise to the full stature of conscious liberty. We hear a good deal of the Brotherhood of man, but there is more pressing need of the Sisterhood of women. True the leaven of humanity is beginning to work. Yet, how many of these free and really noble women will pass a poor prostitute in the street without, almost unconsciously, gathering in her skirts for fear of contamination? How many will meet a girl in society over whose fair name has passed a cloud of suspicion, whether true or false, and not shrink into herself? And yet where are they who are so much in need of love and sympathy as these poor victims? To house these outcasts in asylums, feed them, clothe them, pray over them, thus marking them more indelibly as outcasts than even man has done, has seldom permanently reformed one. Ask your woman's soul, my noble sister, how it would regard these things were you to change places, and do not call yourself Christian till you have learned how Christ spake to these, and how he LOVED THEM. You can reform them but by love, and not by cold charity and self-righteousness.

Many of the students of the Higher Life are in every way unprepared for real chelaship, but they can place themselves in training if they so desire, but to begin by abandoning wife and children will be to train in the opposite direction. The very fact that they find themselves so situated is evidence of a needed development through these things, not away from them. Karma has placed them just here to learn, to consider, to overcome. If either man or woman imagines, when so situated, that he or she can draw away from companions and children, from friends and associates, leaving them to take their chances, and so develop the higher life, the first principle of theosophy has yet to be learned.

The nearness of your relation to these gives you the opportunity for helpfulness that no one else in all the world enjoys. There lies your work, you can make home a very paradise by learning the difference between lust and love. Love seeketh not its own but another's good. Love endures all, and bears all, and at last triumphs over all.

As even animal lust may create a human body, so divine love can regenerate a human soul. What we need in the world today is not celibacy, but happy homes in which love reigns, and love pure and simple will make these homes a tabernacle for angels. Husband and wife may so live together as to be a source of joy, of perpetual delight, nay, even of health and physical strength and continual inspiration to each other.

They may learn thus the very secret of love itself, and enter together the higher life, clad in raiments of purity and light, and they may help to uplift their children, and such children as the world sorely needs.

The fountain of life and the fountain of love flow from the same divine source. Both life and love are sexual, but in a sense that the world never even dreams of, and never will, till it learns to put aside the animal attribute egoism, and really exercise and base their whole lives on the principle of divine altruism.

How many men imagine they love the pure girl they "marry"? And how many of these have really down deep in their souls one thought beyond self? Ask the divorce courts of America and the unhappy homes of England. Reform the family, regenerate the homes, and from these will go out an influence that in time will reform the street, the brothel, and prevent at least the participation in these crimes and all the loathsome diseases and penalties of your own children.

If there is a young man or woman who is free from obligations, free to work for humanity, one who appreciates the opportunity, and values it above home or any personal advantage, or possible gain, the time for such an one has come. Their souls will be filled direct from the pure fountains of love, and they may be the blessed medium through whom the Divine Love is to reach the poor, the outcast, the unloved. Would any of these feel honoured and grateful to take orders direct from a Mahatma? to be the chosen medium between such an one and a society of theosophists?

The door is wide open. "Enter ye who will". Act as the messenger of love, of charity, of self-forgetfulness, of helpfulness to every ready soul, to the sinful, the degraded, no matter how low a criminal he or she may be, for by so much the more is help needed. Do this modestly, patiently, persistently, and a new joy will come into your soul, and all mahatmas in all worlds will delight to do you honour, and whenever you need their help or their presence be sure it will not be wanting. The writer, an humble layman, has tried this even in a slight degree, being trammelled on every hand; he has needed help, needed instruction many times, and it has never failed to come. It has come in its own way, often as though it came not. Yet there it was !

The first sentence in a book taken at random when thinking of something else, would perhaps answer a question that I deeply felt the need of knowing. Be not anxious, be not disappointed, only be, faithful, silent, sincere, and patient. Do the duty that lies nearest at hand in the best way you can. Do it as though for love of the dearest one in all the earth; or, better, do it for the sake of Love. So the love-nature will expand and grow. The more you give out the more you will receive.

Love delights to flood the soul of the one who delights to pass it on. Love fills us full at all times; but what little dwarfed and deformed vessels do we present to the Goddess: she fills them full, and is poorer for this gift, for she is entitled to larger vessels and better measure, and less dross than we mix with the pure waters of love. Love bargains not for return, receives nothing back, begs only the privilege of giving. Full-freighted soul! hurry on thy gifts, love waits without to renew thy store. Disappoint her not. Thy store of love will be like Egypt's bondsmen's quails and manna, not alone are the morrow, but in a moment, if thou restrain thy love. Dost thou desire the mysteries of love, to know how she creates, preserves, renews? Fill thy soul full of her, and thou wilt be love, the mystery thine. Shall not he who has the power of love have also the mystery? are these not one? Where use reigns, mystery disappears. Love is the great revealer. Her neophytes walk in her presence as in a blaze of glory; ask what thou wilt in the name of love and it is done. Knowest thou the hierarchic name of love? the unwritten name, low-breathed from ear to ear? I'll give thee then a substitute till in some other fair degree the true Master's Word shall echo in thy soul.

'Tis self-forgetfulness, consideration for others, preferring to be burdened with nought else, that thou mayest be full of love, and only love. Do this, and every zephyr of every wind that blows shall whisper in thy ear the name by which the fair goddess is known in realms elysian. Give all thou hast away but love, and then be quick to give love away: squeeze thy soul dry of love, and then with quick rebound thy love shall span all space, and sitting on thy throne shall be the fair goddess thyself, thy other self, now two in one, and One with all.

FREEING WOMEN FROM EXPLOITATION AND DESPAIR

Imagine a terrible plague--a devastating disease--descending on and ripping apart the fabric of your community, killing, crippling, or otherwise disabling half of your friends, family, and neighbors. Beyond the human pain and suffering this would cause, consider the incredible impact it would have on your community's ability to thrive. How could the economy grow? How would societal institutions function? How stable could things possibly be? The world would be compelled to action.

Yet in far too many places around the world today, there is indeed a plague holding back many communities and keeping untold millions from reaching their potential. It is a plague the world must face, not only because it is the moral thing to do, but because the cost for ignoring it is simply too great. What is this plague? It is the systematic and violent exploitation of women. This exploitation takes many forms, depriving women of their most basic freedom, robbing them of their health, keeping them from the education they need and deserve, and condemning them to lives without economic opportunity.

No country can prosper when women's voices are silenced, their bodies exploited and their rights violated. Around the globe, the oppression of women goes hand in hand with failed societies. Nations, like women and their children, have the best chance to thrive where fundamental freedoms, human rights, and property rights are ensured for all. The United States has been the world's leader in helping to free women from exploitation and despair. Guaranteeing the human rights of women and children is essential to the creation of stable, democratic, and prosperous societies. This is not only in keeping with the deeply held values of the American people; it is strongly in the United States' national interest as well. As Americans, we take our rights for granted. We cannot conceive of being sold into sexual slavery, forced into an arranged marriage at age 5, subjected to female genital cutting as a rite of passage, systematically raped as a weapon of war, or killed with impunity in the name of honor--by a father or brother.

As the U.S. Ambassador to the United Nations Commission on the Status of Women, I have seen how women in many parts of the developing world, especially in regions of conflict, face these very threats today. It is inconceivable that in the 21st century so many women still lack legal protections for basic human rights.

Plight of Refugees

No group is in greater danger than the large number of women refugees and internally displaced persons. They are often single-handedly responsible for the survival of their children, even when their own survival is at stake. Every day provides challenges that increase the risk of physical danger: finding cooking fuel, carrying water (often for miles), obtaining sufficient food at distribution sites, and accessing primary health care for themselves and their families. They are also exposed to violence at every stage in their flight. Secretary Rice has expressed deep concern with the rape of displaced women in Darfur when they venture out to gather food or firewood, a story brought to light in a July U.N. report.

Sexual violence and exploitation, associated psychological trauma, and the risk of sexually transmitted diseases, are among the terrible dangers confronting refugee women today. Violence takes many forms--trafficking in persons, domestic violence, rape, and harmful traditional practices such as female genital mutilation and honor crimes. It shatters the most fundamental human right to which every woman is entitled: the right to be safe.

7

Modern-Day Slavery: Women Treated as Slaves

The most egregious violation of human rights is the modern-day slavery of human trafficking, which affects hundreds of thousands of persons each year, mostly women and children, depriving them of basic freedom and inflicting unspeakable physical and emotional harm.

Ambassador John Miller, director of the State Department's Office to Monitor and Combat Trafficking in Persons notes that 80 percent of trafficked persons are female and nearly half are children. He states "Sex slavery... is the dominant form... then domestic servitude, both of which are largely women or girls. What was once a race issue has become primarily a gender issue."

Women are particularly vulnerable in post-conflict societies with economies in shambles. Faced with lack of opportunity at home, they are easily lured by false promises of well-paying jobs abroad. Many are then coerced into lives of prostitution, domestic servitude, or other types of forced labor.

As President Bush told the U.N. General Assembly in 2003, "Nearly two centuries after the abolition of the transatlantic slave trade, and more than a century after slavery was officially ended in its last strongholds, the trade in human beings for any purpose must not be allowed to thrive in our time."

The Bush Administration has provided more than $295 million to support anti-trafficking programs in more than 120 countries, including a special $50 million initiative that the President announced at the U.N. This funding helps countries to develop laws, investigate cases, rescue and voluntarily repatriate victims, build emergency shelters, run awareness campaigns, and mount rehabilitation and vocational training programs.

Combating trafficking successfully requires educating people on prevention. One such program is run by the U.S. Agency for International Development. USAID/Ukraine's Trafficking Prevention Program has seven regional centers offering job skills training, hot lines, crisis prevention, and referral services to vulnerable women. More than 30,000 women have used the services provided by these centers.

We must remember that without buyers women could not be sold. That is why at the 2005 meeting of the Commission on the Status of Women, the United States introduced a resolution on eliminating the demand for trafficked women and girls. This was the first U.N. resolution addressing how demand--particularly for commercial sexual exploitation, or prostitution--fuels human trafficking. Certain countries do not want to acknowledge the important link between commercial sexual exploitation and trafficking in women and girls. However, the resolution was adopted by consensus with over 50 co-sponsors.

Sadly, women are not just abused by strangers. On a trip to three Central American countries, I found that domestic violence afflicts an astonishing percentage of women and families. In a sample survey of over 300 women in Santiago and in Managua, reports of domestic violence reached 40 percent and 52 percent. I heard the same concerns from women in Latvia and the Republic of Georgia.

In many countries victims of domestic violence confront laws, or the absence of laws, that make it difficult or even dangerous to pursue justice. Many countries do not explicitly criminalize domestic violence, and even where they do, police and judges often treat it as a private or family matter and penalties are not enforced.

The United States funds education of law enforcement officers, judges, and medical personnel on the problem, trains attorneys in domestic violence prosecutions, and contributes funds for shelters and crisis centers for victims of domestic violence in many countries.

Attacking HIV, Mutilation

Inequality and violence against women contribute to women's vulnerability to many things--including HIV/AIDS. Women who suffer at the hands of an intimate partner, who are raped during times of armed conflict and political instability, or are trafficked for sexual purposes are at high risk of contracting HIV. Women known or suspected to be HIV positive are especially vulnerable. They may be abused, abandoned, or even killed. Even when women are not living with HIV themselves, they bear the brunt of caring for those with the disease.

Over half of the 42 million people living with HIV/AIDS today are women. Worse, among young people living with AIDS, nearly two-thirds are female. Over 2 million infected women give birth each year, transmitting HIV to newborns. Nearly 2,000 babies a day become infected with HIV during pregnancy, birth, or breastfeeding. Most of these children will die before their fifth birthday.

Because reducing mother-to-child transmission is a major U.S. priority, President Bush announced his $500 million International Mother and Child HIV Transmission Initiative, which dedicates funding specifically to prevent transmission of HIV from mothers to their newborns.

The United States' five-year, $15 billion program known as the President's Emergency Plan for AIDS Relief is working to prevent millions of new HIV infections, provide antiretroviral therapies to millions living with HIV/AIDS, and care for millions of HIV-infected individuals and AIDS orphans. The plan supports HIV/AIDS programs in 123 countries with a special focus on 15 countries in Africa, the Caribbean, and Southeast Asia representing more that half the world's infections. It also encompasses bilateral programs in nearly 100 other countries.

Women's health receives too little attention in the developing world. Each year more than 500,000 women (99 percent in developing countries) lose their lives to easily preventable complications of pregnancy and childbirth. Childbirth is the leading cause of death of women in Afghanistan, where the lifetime risk of maternal mortality is 1 in 15. The majority of maternal deaths are preventable through increased access to skilled birth attendants, antibiotics, and other currently available technology.

Last year I chaired a panel discussion at the U.N. aimed at increasing the political will so sorely needed to address this issue.

The United States has launched a $5 million initiative (REACH) to provide health-related accelerated learning and basic literacy training for women and girls in Afghanistan, including the training of midwives.

Worldwide, over the last four years, USAID has provided more than $475 million for maternal health, family planning, and reproductive health programs.

A harmful traditional practice that also threatens the health and violates the human rights of women is female genital mutilation or female circumcision, believed to prevent daughters from being unfaithful to their future husbands. Medically unqualified persons usually perform the practice--without anesthetic--on infants and girls. It may cause massive and fatal bleeding, and lead to chronic infections, sterility, and other complications.

USAID has supported activities to eliminate female genital mutilation in a number of countries. This includes training health care providers about the long-term implications of female genital mutilation and educating local communities to abandon this cultural practice.

Valuing Women's Education

Education is essential to addressing or averting every aspect of exploitation and despair, from reducing vulnerability to disease, maternal mortality, and violence to enhancing economic opportunity.

The ability to read and write is fundamental for life in today's world. Some one-sixth of the world's population is illiterate; two-thirds of the illiterate are women. Female education is strongly linked to economic development and health. For example, maternal and infant mortality is much higher--sometimes two to three times higher--among children of uneducated women compared with women with at least some secondary education.

President Bush has said, "Literacy and learning are the foundation of democracy and development. Indeed, educating women and girls raises every index of development."

When you educate a man you educate an individual; when you educate a woman you educate a whole family.

Many cultures do not place value on education for women. Her value to her family is her "bride price." Parents contract a future marriage relationship for their very young daughters. A man, often much older, may pay a bride price to the family of a girl 5 to 7 years old, with a commitment to marry when she becomes "of age"--puberty.

The high dropout rate of girls in primary grades is partly explained by this practice of early marriage and pregnancy. It also encourages seeing the girl as property. Like human trafficking, treating women and girls as commodities is dehumanizing.

Some 120 million children, most of them girls, do not attend school, in part because of hunger or malnourishment. They are expected to stay at home, care for their siblings, and do household chores. Often the distance to a school poses a threat to girls' safety.

The United States leverages food aid to do more than reduce hunger. The 2003 McGovern-Dole International Food for Education and Child Nutrition Program provides children with nutritious meals as part of their education. In 38 countries around the world, this program feeds 7 million children at school. In countries where education for girls is not inherently valued, when schools provide nutritious meals, parents have more incentive to allow their daughters to be educated.

Some of the greatest education needs are found in post-conflict societies like Afghanistan and Iraq. Today, it is so hopeful to see young girls--who were forbidden by the Taliban to leave their homes unless accompanied by a male relative; who had to hide their books under their burkas--now studying math and science. With U.S. support and the efforts of the Afghan people themselves, nearly 5 million Afghan children are enrolled in school. Of those schoolchildren, about 40 percent are girls--many more than at any point in Afghanistan's history. A new Women's Teacher Training Institute/Afghan Literacy Program, announced by our First Lady, opened in Kabul in September 2004. The Institute trains cadres of Afghan women to teach literacy throughout Afghanistan.

Similar progress is being made in Iraq, where the U.S. has renovated thousands of schools. Female attendance now exceeds pre-war rates, with girls making up some 45 percent of all primary students. U.S. programs are training teachers, and training Iraqi women in media, entrepreneurial, and democratic skills.

In 2002 President Bush launched the five-year Africa Education Initiative--to increase support for Africa's education programs by $200 million to provide 250,000 girls with scholarships and to offer teacher training.

The importance of education to securing women's rights was very evident during my recent visit to Côte d'Ivoire in West Africa. I went to train members of the recently formed Women Leaders Caucus of Côte d'Ivoire in leadership skills and the nuts and bolts of political campaigning. The women participating were well-educated professionals--professors, scientists, lawyers, pharmacists, etc., living in the capital city. They were highly motivated to run for political office and have an impact on the kind of society they live in.

By contrast, in what seemed like a time warp, we visited rural villages where the promise of education is an elusive dream. Women in these villages have little if any schooling, are married at 12 and 13, and live as little more than chattel.

There, we found illiterate women hoeing fields, gathering firewood, and hunting clean water for their children.

Picture women, babies on their backs, struggling under heavy loads of pineapples, water jugs, or baskets of firewood carried on their heads. Picture the dispossessed homeless widow with several small children in a culture that denies her the right to inherit her husband's property. These women--lacking education, ownership of property, or access to credit--can never be secure.

POLITICAL AND ECONOMIC RIGHTS

When women are educated, they are far less likely to fall victim to violence, poverty, or the scourge of AIDS. Women who have control over their economic assets are better able to avoid risky sexual and abusive relationships.

One key element in U.S. efforts to reduce women's vulnerability is promoting property and inheritance rights for women, which we do on the ground in many countries and in U.N. deliberations.

In many ways we support entrepreneurship and women's integration into the mainstream of economic life. One of our greatest commitments is to micro-finance programs. Over the last few years our investment in these small loan and technical assistance programs--about three-quarters of which go to women--has topped $130 million.

This simple tool--which may be a $100 loan to stock a stall in a market or acquire a sewing machine--gives millions of women the means to better their own lives, the lives of their families, and the economy of their countries. Huge gains for women can come from tiny investments.

To have an impact on the legal and social structures of any country, women must be a part of the political process. My own greatest accomplishment has been developing and leading negotiations at the U.N. General Assembly for a U.S. resolution urging countries to expand opportunities for women to participate in the political process. The resolution, passed by consensus with 110 co-sponsors, offers concrete steps countries and civil society can take to help reach this goal. Now I am helping to implement it in many countries.

President Bush has said, "respect for women is both a non-negotiable demand of human dignity and a foreign policy imperative of the United States."

In my work, I have seen things that have shocked and saddened me. I have met women who have energized and inspired me. And I am very proud of the work that the United States is doing to increase hope, human rights, and fundamental freedoms for women and their families.

MAKING THE HARM VISIBLE

At the end of the twentieth century, local and international forces have merged to escalate the sexual exploitation of women and girls. Policies, practices and crises are combining to increase both the supply of women and girls vulnerable to exploitation and the demand by men for women and girls to be used for their profit and sexual gratification.

Sexual exploitation takes many forms, such as sexual harassment, incest, rape, child marriages, temporary marriages, female genital mutilation, pornography, bride trafficking, battering, sexual torture and prostitution. All of these practices violate women's dignity and autonomy.

Globally, one form of sexual exploitation, prostitution, is becoming more normalized and industrialized, with some powerful agents and institutions advocating for its widespread legitimization and legalization. As prostitution has increased, the demand for women and girls has resulted in widespread recruitment and trafficking to fill the brothels, bars and street corners.

In July 1997, a group of survivors, activists and service providers came together from Asia, Africa, Europe, South America, the Caribbean, North America and the Middle East to report on the situation for women and girls in their region and discuss efforts to combat sexual exploitation and provide services to victims. Participants in "Working With Women and Girls in Prostitution: Programs and Policies" focused on how sexual exploitation affects the physical health and mental well being of women and girls, and what obstacles prevent women and girls from escaping prostitution. Making the Harm Visible has its roots in that international meeting in New York City organized by the Coalition Against Trafficking in Women.

Making the Harm Visible is a collection of writings from women who are working to make the harm of sexual violence and exploitation visible. They speak out about their experiences, provide services to survivors, and create policies that force governments and communities to protect the rights of girls and women, not profit from their exploitation.

Women from every world region report that the sexual exploitation of women and girls is increasing. All over the world, brothels and prostitution rings exist underground on a small scale, and on an increasingly larger scale, entire sections of cities are informally zoned into brothels, bars and clubs that house, and often enslave, women for the purposes of prostitution. The magnitude and violence of these practices of sexual exploitation constitutes an international human rights crisis of contemporary slavery. In "Prostitution: A Form of Modern Slavery," Dorchen Leidholdt, the Co-executive Director of the Coalition Against Trafficking in Women, examines the definitions of slavery and shows how prostitution, and related forms of sexual exploitation, fit into defined forms of slavery.

In some parts of the world, such as the Philippines, prostitution is illegal, but well entrenched from providing "recreational services" to military personnel. In "Blazing Trails, Confronting Challenges: The Sexual Exploitation of Women and Girls in the Philippines," Aida F. Santos describes the harmful conditions for women and girls in prostitution in the Philippines, with problems related to health, violence, the legal system, and services. In other regions, such as northern Norway, organized prostitution is a more recent problem, stemming from the economic crisis in Russia. In "Russian Women in Norway," Asta Beate Håland describes how an entire community is being transformed by the trafficking of women for prostitution from Russia to campgrounds and villages across the border in Norway.

Political changes combined with economic crises have devastated entire world regions, increasing the supply of vulnerable women willing to risk their lives to earn money for themselves and their families. Aurora Javate de Dios, President of the Coalition Against Trafficking in Women, discusses the impact of the Southeast Asian economic crisis on women's lives in "Confronting Trafficking, Prostitution and Sexual Exploitation: The Struggle for Survival and Dignity." Economic globalization controlled by a handful of multi-national corporations located in a few industrialized countries continues to shift wealth from poorer to richer countries. In her paper "Globalization, Human Rights and Sexual Exploitation," Aida F. Santos shows us the connection between global economics and the commodification and sexual exploitation of women and girls, especially in the Philippines. Structural adjustment programs implemented by international financial institutions impose loan repayment plans on poor countries, which sacrifice social and educational programs in order to service their debt to rich nations and banks. Fatoumata Sire Diakite points to structural adjustment programs as one of the factors contributing to poverty and sexual exploitation in her paper "Prostitution in Mali." Zoraida Ramirez Rodriguez writes in "Report on Latin America" that the foreign debt and policies of the International Monetary Fund (IMF) are primary factors in creating poverty for women and children. These forces leave women with few options, increasing the supply of women vulnerable to recruitment into bride trafficking and the prostitution industry.

Social problems such as sexual and physical abuse within families force girls and women to leave in search of safety and a better life, but often they find more exploitation and violence. Physical and sexual abuse of girls and women in their families and by intimate partners destroys girls' and women's sense of self and resiliency, making them easy targets for pimps and traffickers who prey on those who have few options left to them. These factors are evident in many of the papers from all world regions in this volume, such as Jill Leighton and Katherine DePasquale's, "A Commitment to Living" and Martha Daguno's, "Support Groups for Survivors of the Prostitution Industry in Manila."

Government policies and practices also fuel the demand for prostitution, as they legalize prostitution or refuse to enforce laws against pimps, traffickers and male buyers. In Making the Harm Visible, we see how countries with governmental structures and ideological foundations as different as the Netherlands and Iran, both promote and legalize sexual violence and exploitation of girls and women. In "Legalizing Pimping, Dutch Style," Marie-Victoire Louis exposes the liberal laws and policies that legalize prostitution and tolerate brothels in the Netherlands. On the other extreme, religious fundamentalists in Iran have legalized the sexual exploitation of girls and women in child and temporary marriages and the sexual torture of women in prison. Sarvnaz Chitsaz and

Soona Samsami document this harm and violation of human rights in "Iranian Women and Girls: Victims of Exploitation and Violence."

Global media and communication tools, such as the Internet, make access to pornography, catalogs of mail order brides, advertisements for prostitution tours, and information on where and how to buy women and girls in prostitution widely available. This open advertisement normalizes and increases the demand by men for women and girls to use in these different forms of exploitation. Donna M. Hughes describes her findings on how the Internet is being used to promote the sexual exploitation of women and children in "The Internet and the Global Prostitution Industry." In this milieu, women and girls become commodities-bought and sold locally and trafficked from one part of the world to another.

How do we make the harm of sexual exploitation visible? In a world where sexual exploitation is increasingly normalized and industrialized what is needed to make people see the harm and act to stop it? The women in Making the Harm Visible recommend four ways to make the harm of sexual exploitation visible: listen to the experiences of survivors, expose the ideological constructions that hide the harm, expose the agents that profit from the sexual exploitation of women and children, and document harm and conduct research that reveals the harm and offers findings that can be used for policy initiatives.

First, listen to the experiences of survivors. The contributors to this volume speak eloquently, passionately and urgently for the voices of survivors to be heard and used as the basis for a global movement against sexual exploitation. The power of survivors' testimony and their visible participation in political struggle is emphasized. The survivor testimonies of Jill Leighton, Alexia, Christine Grussendorf and Jenny speak clearly about the violence perpetrated against women and children in prostitution. In her poem, "They Are Showing Your Face," Victoria Marinelli shows us the harm of media sensationalization, which further exploits the victims of sexual abuse and exploitation. The sexual abuse, exploitation and torture of women political prisoners is recounted by Ladan Pardeshenas in "Women's Activism for Freedom in Iran" and by Aida F. Santos in the Philippines in "Memories."

Malka Marcovich, in "The Violence of Silence: Survivor Testimony in Political Struggle," calls upon her experience in interviewing the survivors of Nazi Germany's "final solution" to argue the importance of survivor testimony in a movement against violence. Angel Cassidy strongly and succinctly states the need to speak out about the violence and exploitation in "Never Be Quiet." And in "Not Sex Work," Victoria Marinelli gives us her manifesto against redefining sexual exploitation as "sex work."

Second, expose the ideological constructions that hide and excuse the violence, exploitation and harm. We are bombarded with misinformation and ideological constructions of prostitution and other forms of sexual exploitation that make the harm invisible, benefit the sex industry and provide cover for the men who buy and exploit women and girls. We need to expose the explicit and implicit rationales used to justify the sexual exploitation of women and girls. Contributors to Making the Harm Visible challenge the excuses men use for exploiting women and children, and call for everyone to do the same. The oldest excuse is the biological determinist one that men have to have sex. If they don't have a wife or available partner, then buying a woman or using a child is the only alternative. Men often escape accountability for the harm they inflict by this simple, but false, assumption. The same underlying thinking applies to men in the military, who supposedly need to buy women as part of "rest and relaxation." In the papers from the Philippines and Cambodia, the presence of military personnel is sited as resulting in increased sexual exploitation of indigenous women. In "Corregidor Tales," Aida F. Santos describes the underground remnants of cells where "comfort women" were kept in sexual slavery for Japanese military personnel during World War II.

Historically, patriarchal religious ideologies have justified the sexual abuse and exploitation of women and girls in many forms, including child marriages, temporary marriages, and women's lack of sexual autonomy. In the paper on Iran, several forms of sexual exploitation of women and girls have been legally instated under fundamentalist rule. In "Trafficking and Prostitution in Bangladesh: Contradictions in Law and Practice," Sigma Huda describes the no-win situation that girls and women face after being trafficked or prostituted. In countries to which Bangladeshi girls are trafficked, such as Pakistan, the victims face long prison sentences for illegal entry into the country, or under harsh Islamic law, can be stoned to death for fornication.

Liberal ideologies about sexuality also overlook the harm of exploitation by uncritically viewing all sexual activity, including prostitution, as forms of sexual expression that should be permitted and protected as individual choices and rights. This sexual liberal philosophy merges with the neoliberal economic policies and practices to rename prostitution as "sex work." This reconfiguration of sexual exploitation is condemned by numerous contributors to Making the Harm Visible.

The contributors to this volume also ask us to critically examine explanations of prostitution that search for the cause of "self-destructive behaviors" in girls or women's personal deficits and defects. Although women in prostitution often suffer from drug and alcohol addiction, several of the authors urge us to see this as a symptom of the harm of prostitution, not as the root cause. Although, several authors discuss poverty and economic crisis as factors in compelling women and girls into prostitution, they remind us that this is what is fueling the supply, but equally important is men's demand for women and girls they can buy.

Third, expose the agents that advocate for and profit from the normalization and legalization of sexual exploitation, whether they be individual men who buy women in prostitution, or governments and United Nations bodies that advocate for legalization of prostitution or the recognition of the prostitution industry as a legitimate economic sector. The Dutch government has legalized prostitution, legalized brothels and is putting into place a system of taxation to profit from the prostitution industry. The Netherlands is the leading advocate for the legalization of prostitution and redefinition of trafficking of women to include only those women who can prove they were coerced or deceived into prostitution. In "Human Rights: A European Challenge?" Malka Marcovich describes efforts to set new standards that will deprive women of their human rights in Europe as the European Union is being constructed. Mary Sullivan, in "Marketing Women in Australia" describes how Australia is incorporating legalized prostitution into its economic and tourism plan. In "Legalizing Prostitution: Legitimating Abuse," Donna M. Hughes argues against the legalization of prostitution in Eastern and Central Europe as a way to combat the trafficking of women from that region.

Fourth, document the harm and conduct research on sexual exploitation. The harm of sexual exploitation often remains invisible until someone focuses their attention on it and documents their findings. Often issues need to be theoretically reframed and different questions posed. Several women, Jill Leighton, Jenny, and Norma Hotaling, point out that even when there are visible signs of trauma in women's and girls' lives, no one asks the simple question: "What has happened to you in your life?" The contributors use their findings to describe and analyze the forces that compel women and girls into conditions of exploitation and, often, slavery. In "Strip Clubs According to Strippers," Kelly Holsopple systematically asks women about the verbal, physical and sexual violence that they were subjected to while working as strippers. Norma Hotaling reports on research she and others have done on violence against women in prostitution in "Women in Prostitution in the United States."

In "The Health Effects of Prostitution," Janice G. Raymond surveys previous research and reports on the multiple physical and mental health problems suffered by women in prostitution, many of which lead to shortened lives or death. The contributors to Making the Harm Visible urge us to ask different research questions about the demand from men to sexually exploit women and girls and the rationales that are used to justify this violence. The Research Project on Men and Prostitution in Japan provides us with a strong quantitative base and framework on which to examine men's use of women in prostitution. In "Why Men Buy Women in Prostitution," the findings from a survey of 2000 men on their use and attitudes towards prostitution are reported.

One of the most glaring problems in combating sexual exploitation is the lack of assistance for its victims. The need for services is poignantly evident in Minerva Kalenandi's testimony, "You Need Some Place to Escape To," in which she describes being turned away from a domestic violence shelter even though she had sustained serious injuries from a pimp. Compared to services for other victims of violence, there a few services for prostituted women, resulting in women receiving little or inappropriate treatment. Since prostituted women are viewed with prejudice, they are often treated disrespectfully in treatment programs. Also, since few mainstream service providers recognize the harm in prostitution, the trauma the women have suffered is not addressed.

Innovative programs for women escaping sexual exploitation that address the harm caused to victims, though few in number, have been created in many world regions. Numerous contributors to this volume report on the services they are providing to victims of sexual exploitation. They describe innovative work and share ideas on programs and projects to assist women and girls. The founders of these programs bring a feminist analysis to the multiple problems faced by women and girls in situations of sexual exploitation. The women and girls are treated with respect and care to restore their dignity.

In "She Let Me Talk and She Listened," Jill Leighton describes how the simple act of listening can save a life. The workers and volunteers in these agencies reach out to women and girls on the street and in jails. In "Phoenix Rising," Kathleen Mitchell relates how the plan for Dignity House was conceived while she herself was in jail after being arrested for prostitution. Many of the service providers in this volume were themselves prostituted women who know first hand the lack of services for women trying to escape prostitution. In Phnom Phen, Cambodia, girls who have escaped brutality and slavery in brothels can find services at the Cambodian Women's Crisis Center. A representative from this newly found center writes about "The Sale of Women and Girls to Brothels in Cambodia."

The contributors describe model programs that provide services to women and girl victims of sexual exploitation and create a space for survivors to come to together to heal and find their voices to speak out and organize. In "Support Group for Survivors of the Prostitution Industry in Manila," Martha Daguno describes the first survivor's group to be set-up in the Philippines. Other agencies and organizations, such as BUKAL (meaning spring), and Women's Education, Development, Productivity and

Research Organization (WEDPRO) are pioneers in developing services for sexually exploited women in the Philippines. Their efforts are chronicled by Aida F. Santos in "Blazing Trails, Confronting Challenges."

The involvement and leadership by survivors is emphasized in many programs. Working on an empowerment model these organizations work through peer educators. In "Casa de Passagem in Brazil," Ana Vasconcelos describes the empowerment and peer education model she uses with homeless street girls in Brazil. Norma Hotaling, in "First Offender Prostitution Program in San Francisco," describes their survivor run peer support program.

Women and girls trying to escape prostitution face fearsome odds. In "Breaking Free," Vednita Carter describes many of the obstacles the women face and their Afrocentric approach to providing services in Minnesota, USA. Pimps and perpetrators prey on the most vulnerable women and girls. Girls with disabilities are often targeted for exploitation because of their vulnerability. Claudia Vigil describes the work of the Homahi Foundation and its programs for mothers with special needs in "Prostitution and Mothers with Special Needs in Argentina." Services for victims of sexual exploitation receive little attention or support in most communities. Marlene Sandoval started the Psycho-Social Rehabilitation Center in Chile in one room in a house with no running water. She reports on the work of the center in this volume.

Some services to women escaping prostitution are combined with community education and programs that confront men's harm to women. SAGE (Standing Against Global Exploitation) in San Francisco is the 1998 winner of the Harvard University Kennedy School of Government's Award for Innovations in Government for their cooperative work with the District Attorney's office to create a program commonly referred to as "the John's School." Norma Hotaling describes their original and successful work to reeducate men about the harm they cause in "The First Offender Prostitution Program in San Francisco."

Another important aspect to ending the sexual exploitation of women and girls is prevention. Zoraida Ramirez Rodriguez describes her education and prevention programs for schools and community organizations in "Preventative Act on Against Prostitution in Venezuela."

Although the women in this volume come from all regions of the world, they share common goals and attitudes. They are survivors and visionaries who are not afraid to confront overwhelming problems and remain steadfast in their work. Most of them know that their goal of ending the sexual exploitation of women and girls is nothing less than revolutionary.

In "Surviving Sexual Slavery: Women in Search of Freedom," Chris Grussendorf writes graphically, with a searing analysis, about what is done to women in situations of torturous sexual abuse and exploitation in prostitution rings. She also forcefully proclaims the sustenance and aspiration of the women in resistance to sexual exploitation, "We stay alive because we are women in search of our lives; we are women in search of freedom. I stayed alive because my belief in something better than what they offered was greater than their hatred and destruction. I stayed alive because I wanted to be free, more than anything, I wanted to be free. I wanted to live in a world of respect."

Organization and activism by women is essential to create change and end violence against women and sexual exploitation. In "Women United Can Make a Difference: The Situation in Spain and the European Union," Asuncion Miura describes how women working together changed public attitudes about violence against women and created services to assist victims of battering.

Sarvnaz Chitsaz and Soona Samsami relate the importance of women's leadership in political and social activism to end of women's oppression and usher in true equality for women and girls in the world. Women must undertake the work of organization and advocacy for women because it is not in the interests of men to do this work, although there are a few men willing to stand against the oppression of women.

These writers understand that when the deepest forms of exploitation, violence and oppression are named, challenged and ended and all the victims healed, there will be a true social, economic and political revolution for women.

WOMAN'S CONSCIOUSNESS, MAN'S WORLD

The capitalist mode of production has penetrated farther and deeper than any other form of production. Geographically it has extended its technology in search of markets; politically it has devised the most ingenious methods of control in its own interests; economically it has created means of production, which are wonderful in their productive capacity and terrifying in their devastation. Its industry has devoured human labor power and human intelligence. In its search for raw materials it has laid waste the land and is beginning to exhaust even the sea. Worse, its version of itself has entered the souls and spirits of millions of men and women, so we no longer know what is our own and what is alienated to capital.

The antagonisms it generates produce the shifts and fissures that make the growth of new movements possible. In quiet times the hope of liberation grows lichenlike on inhospitable rock. In times of upheaval new growths can take root. In order to change capitalism we have to understand how it is made, how it moves, and how it came into being. We have to see how it is different from, or related to, other forms of production, how it is hinged together. It is a foxy old thing, wily at dealing with the opposition it brings into being, whether its opponent is the working class or movements for black or women's liberation.

The predicament of being born a woman in capitalism is specific. The social situation of women and the way in which we learn to be feminine is peculiar to us. Men do not share it, consequently we cannot be simply included under the general heading of "mankind." The only claim that this word has to be general comes from the dominance of men in society. As the rulers they presume to define others by their own criteria.

Women are not the same as other oppressed groups. Unlike the working class which has no need for the capitalist under socialism, the liberation of women does not mean that men will be eliminated. Sex and class are not the same. Similarly people from oppressed races have a memory of a cultural alternative somewhere in the past. Women have only myths made by men. We have to recognize our biological distinctness but this does not mean that we should become involved in an illusory hunt for our lost "nature."

The oppression of women differs too from class and race because it has not come out of capitalism and imperialism. The sexual division of labor and the possession of women by men predates capitalism. Patriarchal authority is based on male control over the woman's productive capacity, and over her person. This control existed before the development of capitalist commodity production. It belonged to a society in which the persons of human beings were owned by others. Patriarchy, however, is contradicted by the dominant mode of production in capitalism because in capitalism the owner of capital owns and controls the labor power but not the persons of his laborers.

In order to act effectively we have to try to work out the precise relationship between the patriarchal dominance of men over women, and the property relations which come from this, to class exploitation and racism. In order to understand the traces of patriarchy which have persisted into the present, it is essential to see what part patriarchy played in pre-capitalist society. The dominance of men over women in the past was more clearly a property relation than it is now. When a man married in a society in which production was only marginally beyond subsistence, he married a "yoke-fellow" whose labor was crucial if he were to prosper. Her procreative capacity was important not only because of the high infant mortality rate but also because children meant more hands to labor.

The family was a collective working group. The father was its head, but for survival the labor of wife and children was necessary. The introduction of individual wages and the end of the ownership of people in serfdom did not dissolve the economic and social control of men over women. The man remained the head of the family unit of production and he retained control over the ownership of property through primogeniture. Both his wife's capacity to labor and her capacity to bear his children were still part of his stock in the world. Moreover, the notion that this was part of the order of things was firmly embedded in all political, religious, and educational institutions.

Although capitalism temporarily strengthened the control over women by middleand upper-class men in the nineteenth century by removing them from production, it has tended to whittle away at the economic and ideological basis of patriarchy. As wage labor became general and the idea spread in society that it was unjust to own other people, although the exploitation of their labor power was considered perfectly fair, the position of the daughter and the wife appeared increasingly anomalous. Ironically, middle-class women came to the conviction that their dependence on men and the protection of patriarchal authority were intolerable precisely at a time when the separation of work from home was shattering the economic basis of patriarchy among the working class.

The factories meant that the economic hold of men over women in the working-class family was weakened. Machinery meant that tasks formerly done by men could be done by women. The woman's wage packet gave her some independence. Ideologically, however, men's hold persisted among workers and was nurtured by the male ruling class.

Subsequently by continually reducing the scope of production, by developing the separation between home and work, and by reducing the time spent in procreation, a great army of women workers has been "freed" for exploitation in the commodity system. This integration of married women into the labor market has been especially noticeable in the advanced capitalist countries since the Second World War.... The result in terms of women's consciousness at work is only now beginning to be felt. While the dissolution of the extended kinship networks has produced in the nuclear family a streamlined unit suitable for modern capitalism, it has forced an examination of the relationships of man to woman and parent to child.

The struggle of the early feminist movement for legal and political equality and the assumptions it has bequeathed to women now, despite the degeneration of its radical impulse, have strained the hold of patriarchy in the capitalist state, though without dislodging it. The power of the working class within capitalism and the growth of new kinds of political movements recently, particularly for black liberation, have touched the consciousness of women and brought many of us to question the domination of men over women. This has taken a political shape, in the new feminism of women's liberation.

The development of contraceptive technology in capitalism means that ideas of sexual liberation can begin to be realized. The fact that sexual pleasure now need not necessarily result in procreation means a new dimension of liberation in the relation of men and women is possible. It also removes some of patriarchy's most important sanctions against rebellion. The right to determine our own sexuality, to control when or if we want to give birth, and to choose who and how we want to love are central in both women's liberation and in gay liberation. All these are most subversive to patriarchy.

However, although capitalism has itself eroded patriarchy and has brought into being movements and ideas which are both anti-capitalist and anti-patriarchal, it still maintains the subordination of women as a group. Patriarchy has continued in capitalism as an ever present prop in time of need. Although women are not literally the property of men, the continuation of female production in the family means that women have not yet even won the right to be exploited equally. The wage system in capitalism has continued to be structured according to the assumption that women's labor is worth half that of men on the market. Behind this is the idea that women are somehow owned by men who should support them. Women are thus seen as economic attachments to men, not quite as free laborers. Their wage is still seen as supplementary. If a woman has no man she is seen as a sexual failure and the inference is often that she is a slut as well. She also has to struggle to bring up a family alone, on half a man's income. This very simple economic fact about the position of women in capitalism acts as a bribe to keep women with men: it has no regard for feeling or suffering and makes a mockery of any notion of choice or control over how we live. It also means that women make up a convenient reserve army which will work at half pay and can be reabsorbed back into the family if there is unemployment.

Equal pay is obviously only the beginning of an answer to this. The inequality of women at work is built into the structure of capitalist production and the division of labor in industry and in the family. The equality of women to men, even the equal exploitation of women in capitalism, would require such fundamental changes in work and at home that it is very hard to imagine how they could be effected while capitalism survives. Our labor in the family goes unrecognized except as an excuse to keep us out of the better jobs in industry and accuse us of absenteeism and unreliability. This separation between home and work, together with the responsibility of women for housework and child care, serves to perpetuate inequality. Women, as a group in the labor force, are badly paid and underprivileged. This is not only economically profitable to capitalism, it has proved a useful political safety valve. It is quite handy for capitalism if wives can be persuaded to oppose their husbands on strike or if men console themselves for their lack of control at work with the right to be master in their own home.

Because production in the family differs from commodity production we learn to feel that it is not quite work. This undermines our resentment and makes it harder to stress that it should be eliminated as much as possible not only by technology, but by new styles of living, new buildings, and new forms of social care for the young, the sick, and the old.

In capitalism housework and child care are lumped together. In fact they are completely different. Housework is drudgery, which is best reduced by mechanizing and socializing it, except for cooking, which can be shared. Caring for small children is important and absorbing work, which does not mean that one person should have to do it all the time. But we are taught to think there is something wrong with us if we seek any alternative. The lack of facilities for children and the rigid structuring of work and the division of labor between the sexes again makes choice impossible.

Propaganda about our feminine role helps to make us accept this state of affairs. Values linger on after the social structures which conceived them. Our ideas of what is "feminine" are a strange bundle of assumptions, some of which belong to the Victorian middle class and others which simply rationalize the form patriarchy assumes in capitalism. Either way the notion of "femininity" is a convenient means of making us believe submission is somehow natural. When we get angry we are called hysterical.

Thus, although capitalism has eroded the forms of production and property ownership which were the basis of patriarchy, it has still retained the domination of men over women in society. This domination continues to pervade economic, legal, social, and sexual life.

It is not enough to struggle for particular reforms, important as these are. Unless we understand the relationship of the various elements within the structure of male-dominated capitalism, we will find the improvements we achieve are twisted against us or serve one group at the expense of the rest. For example, the wider dissemination of contraceptive information and the weakening of guilt about our sexuality have meant a major improvement in the lives of many women. However, the removal of fear alone is not enough because relations between the sexes are based on the ownership of property—property consisting not only of the woman's labor in procreation, but also of her body. Therefore, while class, race, and sex domination remain a constituent element of relations between men and women, women and women, and men and men, these relations will continue to be distorted. Sexual liberation in capitalism can thus continue to be defined by men and also continue to be competitive. The only difference between this and the old set-up is that when patriarchy was secure, men measured their virility by the number of children they produced. Now they can apply more "suitable" means of assessing masculinity in a use-and-throw-away society and simply notch up sexual conquests.

There are other examples of feminist reforms being distorted by the structure of capitalist society. We are far from the situation of baby farms and state-controlled breeding, but these are the lines along which pure capitalism, shorn of the remnants of earlier forms of production, would develop. Similarly, one group of women can be bought off at the expense of another, young women against old, middle class against working class. If we are ready to settle for a slightly bigger bite of the existing cake for a privileged section, we will merely create gradations among the underprivileged. We will not change the context in which women are inferior. For instance, in Britain there has been some discussion about giving women better jobs in management and promoting secretaries because they will work harder for less pay. Capitalism is not based on the organization of production for people, but simply on the need to secure maximum profit. It is naive to expect that it will make exceptions of women.

It is impossible now to predict whether capitalism could accommodate itself to the complete elimination of all earlier forms of property and production and specifically to the abolition of patriarchy. But it is certain that the kind of accommodation it could make would provide no real solution for women when we are unable to labor in commodity production because we are pregnant: socially helpless people protected in capitalism are not only treated as parasites who are expected to show gratitude, but are under the direct power of the state. Also class and race cut across sexual oppression. A feminist movement that is confined to the specific oppression of women cannot, in isolation, end exploitation and imperialism.

We have to keep struggling to go beyond our own situation. This means recognizing that the emphases that have come out of women's liberation are important not only to ourselves. The capacity to bring into conscious combination the unorganizable, those who distrust one another, who have been taught to despise themselves, and the connection that comes out of our practice between work and home, personal and political, are of vital significance to other movements in advanced capitalism. Similarly, the comprehension in women's liberation of the delicate mechanism of communication between the structures of capitalist society and the most hidden part of our secret selves is too important not to become part of the general theory and practice of the Left. Women's liberation has mounted an attack on precisely those areas where socialists have been slow to resist capitalism: authoritarian social relationships, sexuality and the family. We have to struggle for control not merely over the means of production but over the conditions of reproduction.

The problem about how a revolutionary theory can come out of a day-to-day practice defined by the existence of capitalism has long bedeviled revolutionary socialism. The concept of the Leninist party as the conscious embodiment of an alternative has become dubious because the party in reality will still express the viewpoint of sections which are the stronger within capitalism, most obviously men, for example. Moreover, the party itself can become absorbed in the immediate problem of surviving within capitalism rather than in the task of exposing contradictions and seeking revolutionary transformation. The mobilization of new groups within capitalism against a specific form of oppression is thus very important, but more important still is the means of translating the experience of one group to another without merely annexing the weaker to the stronger.

Thus it is not just groups that have a position of power at the point of production in the advanced sectors of the capitalist economy, but the organization of groups whose consciousness spans several dimensions of oppression that becomes crucial in a revolutionary movement. This is not an idealization of weakness. Women as a group are extremely vulnerable within capitalism, but because of our social situation we are forced to find the means of going beyond our own specific oppression. The blocks against us are very real; male domination permeates every organization within capitalism including trade unions and revolutionary groups, and the problem of how to safeguard our autonomy while making a strategy of organizing with men is a persistent dilemma in the women's movement.

Nor is this an evasion of the urgent problem of making an offensive organization which is capable of overcoming the tremendous resources of the advanced capitalist state. The substitution of the women's movement for such an organization would be most evidently absurd. Although we have the capacity to go beyond our own predicament, and although alternatives must be continually drawn out of our day-to-day struggle to defend women against capitalism, neither our structure, nor our politics, are the same as those of a revolutionary organization. We come into women's liberation out of our specific predicament as women, not as people who necessarily are committed to the creation of socialism. We are, moreover, essentially a partial organization representing a specific group. There are no short-cuts. The making of a revolutionary socialist organization that is capable of taking the offensive without being either absorbed or smashed, which can at once safeguard the interests of the groups within it and not simply reproduce the structures of authority and domination that belong to capitalism, is a gigantic task. Autonomy and cohesive organization in the face of repression go uncomfortably together. The models of the past can help us, but do not fit the special problems of the modern capitalist state. However, the political process of making an effective movement for the liberation of women-which means a movement in which workingclass women are in the majority-is an essential part of this task.

FORCING MILLIONS OF WOMEN INTO THE SEX TRADE

A short play staged by a Filipino theatre group has become a popular feature on the international conference circuit, given the powerful message it conveys-women are abused when they are lured into the international sex trade by criminal gangs.

Written by Maria Paulin-Ballesteros, the play draws a parallel between women subjected to sexual exploitation and a chicken dish that is a favourite in the Philippines, 'lechon manok'. And Paulin-Ballesteros describes her work, titled We're Syndicated, Ma'am, as a 'fowl play'.

This Filipino human rights activist was inspired to write the play after attending an international forum, where three Filipino women narrated their plight after being forced into the sex trade in Nigeria. And the response the play has received-through its live performance or a videotaped account, in Asia, Europe and North America-has satisfied Paulin-Ballesteros.

'While Filipino consumers crave the lechon manok, male customers around the world are going crazy over their young women,' she told a Filipino newspaper in an interview. Paulin-Ballesteros' concern has been echoed by other human rights activists, who are equally worried about the rapid rise of women being transported around the world for the sex industry. Currently, according to available reports, close to two million women have been forced into 'sex slavery'. In February, Regan Ralph, the executive director of the women's rights division of the United

States-based Human Rights Watch (HRW), underscored the urgency for an international response to such abuse during his testimony before the US Senate's committee on foreign relations. HRW has been involved in documenting and monitoring this 'serious human rights violation' for many years, Ralph revealed. 'We have reported on the trafficking of women and girls from Bangladesh to Pakistan, from Burma to Thailand and from Nepal to India.'

In his view, the current trafficking in women is 'a slavery-like practice that must be eliminated', since it involves the 'illegal and highly profitable transport and sale of human beings for the purpose of exploiting their labour'.

He even exposed its prevalence in the United States. In August 1999, for instance, a trafficking ring was broken up in the southern state of Georgia that transported up to 1,000 women from several Asian countries into the United States and '(forced) them to work in brothels across the country'.

Similar evidence was presented in late February at a public hearing before the European Parliament. Close to 500,000 women are smuggled into Western Europe every year, experts said. According to researchers, nearly 60% of the women forced into the sex industry in some Western European countries are controlled by Russian and Albanian criminal networks.

No Control

The situation in Britain illustrates this scenario. According to research conducted by the University of North London's Child and Women Abuse Studies Unit, six out of 10 women in London's brothels have been 'trafficked' from countries such as the Ukraine. The study added that the 'criminal gangs trafficking prostitutes are not confining their activities to major cities'.

And once the women arrive in Britain, they are informed by the gangs responsible for their journey that they owe the gangs 'thousands of pounds for accommodation, fees to the brothel and advertising'.

In most cases, the manner in which women have been trapped into the sex industry hardly differs, say rights activists. The woman is approached with the promise of a good job in another country, 'and lacking better options at home, she agrees to migrate'.

Once overseas, however, she is delivered to her employer. In these new surroundings, the woman has 'no control over the nature or place of work, or the terms or conditions of her employment'.

What is more, when the woman learns she has 'been deceived about the nature of the work', she finds escape 'both difficult and dangerous', given the coercive and abusive situations in the brothels.

Kevin Bales, a lecturer in sociology at the University of Surrey, in Britain, sees this explosion of 'modern slavery' as a result of many factors, among which are 'corruption' in governments and the 'silence' that has encouraged it.

In his book, Disposable People: New Slavery in the Global Economy, Bales argues that the international community needs to perceive the difference between modern slavery and slavery as it was known before the Atlantic slave trade of 200 years ago.

'If you insist on defining slavery as 'the legal ownership of one person by another' then slavery has pretty much disappeared. But the key to slavery is not ownership, but control through violence...(or its threat). Couple that with economic exploitation in which someone is paid nothing and you have a good working definition of the new slavery that encompasses about 27 million people around the world,' he says.

Human rights groups, too, have brought to light that aspect of the sex industry. The United Nations Office of the High Commissioner for Human Rights (UNHCR), for instance, defines trafficking as a situation where someone is persuaded, tricked or forced into leaving their country for the promise of a 'better life', only to end up in forced or slavery-like conditions.

But to guarantee the rights of these women, most rights groups feel that new international standards are required, including a broadening of the definition of 'trafficking', harsher punishment for those involved in the international trafficking of women, and guaranteeing that the victims have an opportunity to seek 'remedies and redress for the human rights violations they have suffered'. And rights activists have stepped up their efforts to achieve such guarantees from the international community, given a projected UN convention that is due to be taken up this year-the UN Convention on Transnational Organised Crime. To end this cycle of human trafficking, they add, the language of this convention should not be watered down. For that would be 'extremely detrimental to women'.

Marwaan Macan-Markar is a correspondent for the Inter Press Service, with whose permission the above article is reprinted.

OLDER WOMEN'S HEALTH: FACING THE CHALLENGES

The health concerns of older women require special attention, especially in a changing social milieu in which there are fewer people around to care for them.

In a region where women continue to be valued less than men, older women's health reflects their life-long experience of discrimination, deprivation and neglect. The older women of Asia-Pacific today faced similar situations of poverty, malnutrition, poor health care, physical overwork and unhealthy work environments in their younger years. Along with high infant mortality rates, they faced high maternal mortality, maternal morbidity and reproductive tract infections. To add to all these, few of them received immunisation as children or benefited from the public health interventions that have developed since. Consequently, the diseases of the older years such as maturity onset diabetes, Alzheimer's disease, osteoporosis, stroke, heart disease, arthritis and cancer are superimposed on an already compromised state of health. These are acute issues facing the societies of the Asia-Pacific region. As life expectancy increases and fertility rates continue to decline, the region would see in the coming years more older persons, particularly older women, needing care and fewer people available to care for them.

Recognising this growing trend, the 1995 Beijing Platform for Action emphasised that older women's '...health concerns require particular attention. The long-term health prospects of women are influenced by changes at menopause, which, in combination with life-long conditions and other factors, such as poor nutrition and lack of physical activity, may increase the risk of cardiovascular disease and osteoporosis. Other diseases of ageing and the interrelationships of ageing and disability among women also need particular attention.' In an effort to call for the non-marginalisation of older people, which includes older women, the United Nations declared 1999 as the International Year of Older Persons, with the theme, 'Towards a Society for All Ages'.

Diverse Realities, Common Problems

Traditionally, women gained value, status and authority within their family and community as they became older, for their wisdom and nurturing role as grandmothers. With modernisation and urbanisation, traditional families are giving way to nuclear families-a single set of parents, their children and a grandparent or two. In this setting and with the growing need for families to have multiple incomes to survive, grandparents, especially grandmothers, have become convenient babysitters whose medical needs are addressed within the economic constraints of the family. Such a responsibility comes at a time when these women expect to have the freedom to focus on their own needs and begin to experience a range of health issues related to ageing. Caring for young children is a demanding task that can isolate women, particularly women who lack financial and social resources to create a support network to maintain their physical and emotional well-being. These burdens would be particularly felt by older migrant women who do not speak the local language of the host country (e.g. older women sponsored by their children to enter and stay in a foreign country).

Longer lives coupled with the tradition of marrying older men means that more women will face the loneliness and vulnerability of widowhood. With a spouse's death, older women face a significant loss of economic security. Discriminatory inheritance laws regarding parental and spousal property greatly contribute to their vulnerable economic situation. Thus, widows bcome financially dependent on their children, while single older women may have no one to turn to but the state. In several South-East Asian countries, older women who came as migrants from other parts of Asia worked in the informal sector to support their families back home. Few of them had access to state pension schemes. Today, they have practically no savings and are financially helpless.

Older women are vulnerable to violence from both their families and society. The risk increases with their loss of independence. The violence is physical and emotional. Glorification of youth in the modern culture has created negative stereotypes of the elderly, particularly older women, and they are subjected to much abuse as a result of ageism. Widows may suffer from violence by their own children or by relatives. For married older women, they may have suffered a history of violence since their younger years.

Addressing the Health Needs of Older Women

Clearly, the lack of health policies, programmes and services that address women's health needs from a life-cycle and holistic approach greatly affects their lives as they age. Special attention should be given to adequately meeting the specific physical, emotional and mental health needs of women aged 50 to 60, 70 to 80 and over 80. The views of older women are therefore important for any health policy and service development to be effective in addressing older women's realities. Mechanisms need to be put in place which would allow these women to be actively involved in the planning, design and implementation of health policies and programmes which concern their own health and that of their community. Care for older women must consider their pre-existing state of health and address their overall health-care needs instead of merely treating the immediate medical problem.

Due to their increased vulnerability in their later years, the issues of cost, quality and mobility or location of healthcare services would have to be considered carefully. Policies which promote parental care and support by the children need to be supplemented by appropriate support mechanisms (such as state-supported income security schemes), and high-quality affordable health and residential care for those older women who are unable to rely on family support. It is also imperative that boys and men are socialised into caring and nurturing roles so that the burden of caring for elders does not fall on women alone. Governments need to be committed to their social responsibility in the area of health and be ready to support effective community-based initiatives in meeting older women's health needs.

It is important to recognise that the ageing process, for some women, may be about declining health, frailty, emotional vulnerability and even senility. For other women, the ageing process may be a very positive experience. Nevertheless, decision-makers who plan policies and programmes for older women must recognise that active ageing will not circumvent the need for adequate care-giving, which can sometimes be intensive in nature. While it is true that older women have many contributions to make, their right to finally take a break from commitments and responsibilities in their old age should not be overlooked. Older women are not only survivors-they have made their contributions to society. In return, society should give them space to seek self-fulfillment.

8

Women's Role in Modernization

"The important thing for a country is that the men should be manly, the women womanly." This comment of Chesterton's embodies a fundamental principle of social order. In society, as in any organism, unity and order are achieved through the cooperation of very different members, each fulfilling his own functions and contributing his special qualities to the common good.

The deepest difference among human beings--far more fundamental than any difference of intelligence or ability, nation or race--is the difference of sex. "And God created man to His own image: to the image of God He created him; male and female He created them." This basic difference is not merely physical but also psychological, coloring the total personality. In the whole range of her being--her mind, her senses, her emotions, her will, her interests and reactions--woman differs profoundly from man.

It is obviously of the greatest importance that this difference find its proper expression in the social functions of the two sexes. Each has unique qualities to contribute to the enrichment of human life. It is essential for the full and harmonious development of society, and especially for a Christian society, that "the men should be manly, the women womanly." Man and woman are made to complement each other at every point. Man's capacity for theory, for forming an abstract and comprehensive view, is matched by woman's practical sense and her gift for detail. Man's ambition and self-assertion which spur him on to great achievement must be balanced by the creative power of woman's spirit of sacrifice and self-surrender. Man's ability for leadership and desire for power must be tempered by woman's spirit of love and selfless devotion.

The undue predominance of either masculine or feminine qualities creates profound disturbances which reverberate throughout the entire social structure, as we can see in our own culture. Western European civilization under the influence of Protestantism, rationalism, liberalism, and other secularizing trends, has become progressively more masculine in the last four centuries. Ours is a culture of the self-assertion of man: of man's reason and scientific method in the intellectual sphere; of man's will to power and conquest in business and world affairs; of man's independence of God in all aspects of life. In our time we need women with a vision of their great task as women who will help to restore the social equilibrium by creating a vital current of the great womanly virtues: the spirit of love, compassion for the suffering, generous self-sacrifice. As women our fundamental contribution to the new order lies in finding our proper role in society. Our most urgent task in the work of reconstruction is to face this problem: What is the function of woman in the social order?

The Universal Mission of Woman

Woman's essential mission in the world is to be for mankind a living example of the spirit of total dedication to God. To love God with her whole heart, her whole mind, her whole strength, and to radiate that love to the world--this is the universal task of woman. It is true that every human being is made for the love of God and is meant to be totally consecrated to His praise. In what sense, then, can we say that it is the particular mission of woman to be both an example and guide of man along the way of dedication?

There are two poles, two principles in human nature. Father Gerald Vann, O. P., in his recent book, "The Heart of Man," distinguishes these two basic tendencies as "man the maker" and "man the lover." Both principles are present to some extent in every human being, but man the maker is realized most perfectly in man; man the lover in woman. It is the maker who asserts, who imposes his idea and his will on the surroundings. The race takes its forward motion along the way of organization and invention from him. It is man the lover who gives, who yields his own will and gladly surrenders not only his will but his very self to the beloved.

Mankind has always recognized that love plays a far greater role in woman's life than in man's. Every woman when she looks into her own heart finds there the deep desire to surrender herself completely in love. Woman is by nature total in her giving; love absorbs her whole being. Byron was expressing the common experience of mankind when he wrote:

"Man's love is of man's life a thing apart

'Tis Woman's whole existence."

In relation to God, we must all fulfill the role of the lover, awaiting the divine initiative, surrendering completely to the divine will. As C. S. Lewis writes so beautifully, "Our role must be always that of patient to agent, female to male, mirror to light, echo to voice. Our highest activity must be response, not initiative. To experience the love of God in a true and not an illusory form is therefore to experience it as our surrender to His demand, our conformity to His desire." Christian tradition has often expressed man's relation to God in the beautiful phrase: the soul is the bride of Christ. But woman's nature has the greater innate affinity for the bridal role, for the act of loving surrender. That is why woman has been throughout Christian history a symbol and example of the spirit of complete consecration to God. Woman's natural capacity for wholehearted giving of herself in love is the basis for her glorious supernatural vocation. It is her function to help to lead mankind to God by becoming herself a radiant example of total dedication to His will.

The lover's surrender opens the way for the action of God's grace in the world. "The world can be moved by the strength of man, but it can be blessed in the real sense of the word only in the sign of woman," writes Gertrude von Le Fort. It is first of all to Our Lady that these words apply. In her, the universal mission of woman, the lover, was fulfilled most completely. Her "fiat" is the perfect expression of the creature's wholesouled surrender to the creator, and through her surrender the fullness of blessing entered into the world. These words may be applied, too, to the universal task of womankind, for it is the function of every woman to re-echo the "fiat" of Mary and thus to become a source of blessing to humanity.

Woman as Mother of Mankind

Woman helps to lead society Godward by her direct service of mankind as well as by her example. Total dedication to God implies wholehearted service of man. A loving care for one's neighbor is but the necessary practical expression of a genuine love of God.

In woman, the care for one's neighbor has the character of maternal love, with its warm personal devotion and generous sacrifice of self. Spiritually as well as physically, woman is the mother of mankind, the fountain and nurturer of life.

Through her relation to "man the maker" woman exercises a strong spiritual influence on the whole of a culture. Man leaves the imprint of his personality in the creations of his mind--works of science and art, monumental buildings and commercial empires. But woman's masterpiece is life itself. She is not interested in abstract or technical achievements but in persons, and in bringing persons to God. She stays in the background, the great inspirer, whose warm sympathy and encouragement spur man on.

Intuitively she perceives what is best and noblest in his proposals and helps to develop it. With her deep awareness of the sacramentality of life, she helps man to see matter as the image of spirit, inspiring him with her vision of the divine poetry of creation and the symbolism of human action.

In the life of every great man one finds this vital influence of a noble woman-Monica and Augustine, Paula and Jerome, Scholastica and Benedict, Clare and Francis, Blanche of Castile and King Louis, Clothilde and Clovis, Beatrice and Dante. Woman's influence is subtle and hard to define but nonetheless real. When she no longer fulfills her role as spiritual mother, culture becomes gross, materialistic, brutal, and loses grace and beauty.

The Three Spheres of Woman's Dedication

Woman must needs fulfill her universal mission of dedication to God and loving service of mankind in some concrete set of circumstances. There are three spheres in which she can carry out her primary task: religious life, marriage, and single life in the world. In the designs of God's

Providence, some women in every generation, the "first fruits," are meant to consecrate themselves to God in religion; most women are called to dedicate themselves to Him in marriage; and very few are intended for the life of the unmarried woman in the world. But whether she becomes a nun, a mother of a family, or a single woman in the world, her essential function remains the same: to be a living example of the spirit of surrender and love, the spiritual mother of mankind.

The virgin consecrated to God by her vow of chastity has always been regarded with highest honor in Christian civilization. Consecrated virginity diffuses a fragrant atmosphere of purity and spiritual integrity throughout society, which contributes to preserve the sanctity of marriage and the dignity of womanhood. The greater the respect and esteem shown to virginity in a society, the higher the position of all women will be. It is significant that the Protestant revolt which has had so many unfortunate consequences for the position of woman began with Luther's attacks on virginity and his liquidation of convents and monasteries.

The topic of woman's contribution to society through the religious life, however, demands a separate article for adequate treatment. The present discussion will be confined to the role of woman in marriage and in the single life in the world.

Woman in Marriage

Woman's nature is admirably adapted to her functions as wife and mother. The responsibilities of the family develop her powers and mature her spiritually, mentally. and physically.

Spiritually, a woman becomes mature through surrender, through finding the particular role in which she can accomplish her total dedication to God. The young woman who has found her vocation in life in marriage and is wholly given to her task of bringing her family to God is a mature person whatever her age. She will have that air of serenity and peace which are the sign of the basic fulfillment of her being.

The woman who has never surrendered wholeheartedly to any purpose outside herself remains immature all her life, like a bud which never unfolds itself. In marriage, woman can develop a spirit of selflessness which makes her dedication deeper and richer with the years. Her service to her family both expresses her love of God and increases her power of loving. The woman who has no outlet for her love, no one for whom she can spend herself, is apt to become hard, bitter, selfish, because she has no one but herself to consider. The woman who is constantly concerned with the needs of her family can unfold the qualities of love, tenderness, and unselfish devotion which make her truly great and truly happy.

Mentally, a woman's mind matures under the stimulus of the varied practical activities she performs for those she loves. In the concrete, living experience of the family, she can develop sound judgment and a keen insight into human nature. Lombroso's observation can readily be verified.

"The mother of a large family who has had no time to study, having been occupied with her children and her household, has more life, more breadth of ideas, than the old maid of the same age who has done nothing else than to potter about at universities and libraries." The responsibilities of her family life exercise all woman's mental powers. Her intuition and powers of observation are called into play constantly to discover the unexpressed desires of her family, particularly the needs of the helpless child. She has need of her intuition, too, as well as her tact, to help her solve the hundred problems of human relations and practical affairs that arise in the course of her day. Providing for the family helps to develop woman's natural ingenuity and inventiveness.

It is to the ingenuity of women intent on meeting the needs of their families that we owe the discovery of many of the most important arts: horticulture, for example; the creative arts of weaving, pottery, basketry; the domestic arts of food preparation and preservation; the uses of medicinal herbs in healing. Physically, too, marriage and child bearing represent a development and completion for the normal woman, giving her new beauty and vitality. The mother of a large family experiences a physical fulfillment with the birth of each child which gives her fresh vigor and health.

Dr. Alexis Carrell observes that women attain their full development as a rule only after the birth of several children. He writes in "Man The Unknown": "Women who have no children are not so well balanced and become more nervous than the others. The importance to woman of the generative function has not been sufficiently recognized. Such function is indispensable to her optimum development. It is therefore absurd to turn women against maternity.

The Gigantic Task

In a well balanced society, where the family performs all its proper functions, the home is a society in microcosm, presenting all the problems of human relations, all the variety of human activities. The home is at once an economic and industrial center, preparing goods for family use; a school in which the young are introduced to the universe; a sanctuary for rest and relaxation; a temple dedicated to the praise of God. It is woman's function to organize and direct this complex undertaking, a role which demands intelligence talents and spiritual qualities of a high order. Chesterton describes the vastness of woman's task in the family in the following passage from "What's Wrong With the World":

"To be Queen Elizabeth within a definite area, deciding sales, banquets, labors, and holidays; to be Whiteley within a certain area, providing toys, boots, sheets, cakes and books; to be Aristotle within a certain area, teaching morals, manners, theology and hygiene: I can understand how this might exhaust the mind, but I cannot imagine how it could narrow it. How can it be a large career to tell other people's children about the Rule of Three and a small career to tell one's own children about the universe? How can it be broad to be the same thing to everyone, and narrow to be everything to someone? No; a woman's function is laborious but because it is gigantic, not because it is minute."

One of the greatest of woman's responsibilities is her task as educator, transmitting the fundamental heritage of civilization, the traditions of culture and religion, to the new generation. The child receives his first introduction to civilization from his mother. The first formation of his mind and character belong almost entirely to her. She gives the child his first concepts of reality, his basic acquaintance with his mother tongue.

The child's ideas of God, of right and wrong, of repentance for faults, his first meeting with God in prayer--all come through the mother's teaching. She socializes the young human being, training him to honesty, courage, generosity, developing self-control, responsibility, and all those other virtues without which society cannot exist. She molds the men and women of the future. No other influence is as strong as the mother's in forming and preparing human beings for life.

Woman not only transmits the foundation of culture to the child; she is the great keeper of tradition in society, the custodian of manners and morals, conserving the gracious customs and fundamental standards of the race. She inspires and enforces the code of social behavior as, for example, the great chatelaines of the middle ages upheld the noble code of chivalry, and the hostesses of the seventeenth century salons cultivated the refinement of taste and manner. She keeps alive those religious customs and traditions in the home and community which link the daily life of man to God by so many intimate bonds. She is the guardian of the moral standard, especially in all that concerns the family. In this respect, as in so many others, the modern woman has abrogated her traditional role with tragic consequences for society.

It is impossible to exaggerate the importance for society of woman's achievement in the family. The family is the foundation of all the larger social structures, the basic cell on which all other agencies depend for the very existence and first formation of their members. A nation can flourish only to the extent that it is composed of healthy, flourishing families. But the family can endure only if the woman spends herself wholeheartedly to create a real home. If the woman looks down upon her function and neglects her task in the family, nothing can take her place; the family will disintegrate and with it the whole society. This should be abundantly clear to us when we see how powerless the most elaborate schools and the most advanced methods of social work are in the face of the rising tide of juvenile delinquents from neglected and broken homes.

It is superficial to think as women that we must be in the forefront of public affairs, politics, or business to influence the course of the world. "Not in the branches of a tree but in its roots do force and power reside," writes Gertrude von Le Fort. Woman is at the very roots of social life. If she keeps the sources of life pure and healthy, the entire social order will be renewed and reinvigorated by her effort.

Woman in Single Life

The other sphere through which woman can carry out her mission is the state of single life in the world. In normal times, only a few women are called to this vocation. But in our time, due to the war and to other abnormal social conditions, many women will remain unmarried. We should realize that this circumstance falls within God's Providence, and that He has destined the single woman to fulfill an important role in the modern world.

The task of the unmarried woman is, by her whole hearted surrender to God, to make virginity spiritually fruitful in the world. In embracing virginity, she should radiate purity and nobility of soul. Her very existence, like that of the virgin consecrated in religion, should be a strong positive influence upholding the dignity of womanhood and the sanctity of marriage.

By developing her capacity for spiritual motherhood, she should become a source of strength and comfort and inspiration to mankind. Never has the world been so full of misery, so desperately in need of the healing influence of woman's love. The mission of the unmarried woman in this time is to give the full riches of her maternal love and devotion to alleviate the sufferings and renew the hope of mankind.

In order to accomplish her vocation, the single woman must find an appropriate sphere in which she can carry out her dedication to God through loving service of human beings. She must strike out on new paths, searching for types of work in which she can use her womanly talents and develop her woman's nature. In the education and formation of the young; in agriculture, tending growing plants and animals; in the care of the sick, the weak, the poor, the helpless, woman finds fields of activity appropriate to her capacities as nurturer of life.

Unfortunately, work as it is carried on in these fields today often affords small opportunity for the use of woman's characteristic talents. In medicine, in education, in social work, we suffer from depersonalization, from too much large scale organization and mechanical routine, from too much concern with the physical aspects of the process. We need women to pioneer in these fields again, bringing with them their gift for warmly personal service and creating truly womanly occupations. We need women who will help to restore the emphasis on the spiritual, and who will make the work of healing, of teaching, of relieving the distressed a full expression of living charity between human persons.

How did We Lose the Concept of True Womanhood?

As we look over the modern world we may be tempted to echo King Solomon's cry: Who shall find a valiant woman? On every hand we see modern women turning away from this type of the greathearted woman. How does it happen that we have lost the concept of the woman of love and sacrifice and have accepted the ideal of the professional woman in its place?

Three major factors have contributed to the destruction of the womanly ideal: the Reformation, and the consequent secularization of western culture; the Industrial Revolution; the Feminist Movement. The Reformation was an ultra-masculine movement with small regard for woman's qualities and woman's functions. As society lost its Catholic sense, it lost also the concept of total dedication, the understanding of the sacramentality of life, the regard for the sanctity of marriage--all principles intimately connected with woman's mission and dignity. At the same time, "the masculine desire to dominate the woman found expression in the law." Public opinion looked down upon woman's sphere. "Kirche, kuche, and kinderstube" ("Church, kitchen, and nursery") were linked together and treated with scant respect as fit only for women. Along with the intellectual devaluation of woman's activities came the profound economic and social changes created by the Industrial Revolution. Seventy-five years ago the woman in the home was still the center of a variety of economic enterprises of unquestioned value and importance. But one by one almost all the activities through which a woman served her family, developed herself, and earned the esteem of society, have been lifted out of her hands and transferred to the factory. The sphere in which most women had found their means of dedication was severely curtailed. At the same time, economic necessity forced many women into the labor market to help support their families and thus led them further away from a womanly pattern.

The third influence which has contributed to the loss of a true concept of woman's function is the feminist fallacy. Feminism was born of woman's natural reaction against the depressed condition in which she found herself in a secularized, masculine, industrial culture. The feminists vociferously demanded equality, but unfortunately they conceived equality on a masculine pattern. Their whole struggle for woman's rights has simply helped to destroy the difference between the sexes and has worked to make the woman a slavish imitation of the man. Feminism is an abject surrender to the masculine ideal as the only ideal. The feminist has completely lost faith in herself as a woman. Her effort to prove herself "just as good as a man" betrays her insecurity and is a tacit admission of inferiority.

Woman's struggle for freedom has led her deeper and deeper into a morass of conditions which frustrate her nature and her mission. Chesterton's bon mot is more than a witty pun: "Twenty million women rose to their feet with the cry: 'We will not be dictated to' and proceeded to become stenographers." It is a summary of woman's situation in the modern world. Women rebelled against the confinement of the home; they find themselves now confined to the mechanical routine of the typewriter and the assembly line, rendered all the more monotonous for a woman because of its exceedingly impersonal character. Woman is made for marriage and motherhood; the modern woman in the name of freedom urges easy divorce and artificial sterility. Woman is well adapted to the universal activity of the home; her demand for freedom leads her to a narrowly specialized education and still more narrowly specialized career. Woman is made for love, for the giving of herself in personal, devoted service. In the modern world she has found her way to a position of lonely and selfish independence.

Towards a Solution

The problem of woman's role is fundamental and no simple, facile solution will meet it. It is not surprising that a society which has lost its sense for divine things and for man's own nature should have lost also the true concept of woman. The unnatural position of woman in our society is but one aspect of the disintegration of modern culture. Nothing short of an intensive and all-embracing renewal of the modern world in the Christian spirit will restore woman to her proper functions. What can we do as women to restore a true concept of womanhood?

(1) *Know Thyself*: As women, our first task is to regain our self-respect in the light of a clear concept of our nature and our role. We must grasp the full splendor of the divine idea of woman as it is revealed to us in the sacred writings, climaxing in the figure of Our Lady. If we have the courage to be ourselves and to follow our spiritual mission, then the world will once again recognize and reverence the immeasurable dignity of womanhood.

(2) *Restore the Christian Family*: We must strive in all ways to restore the family to its rightful dignity and full vigor as the basic cell of the social organism. The family must regain the entire range of its functions, the full scope of its gigantic task--religious, educational, cultural, economic. As women it is our particular responsibility to develop a new pattern of integral Christian life in the family, in which common prayer, work, study and recreation will build the bonds of unity and draw the family heavenwards.

(3) *Create Womanly Work*: If woman is to give the full benefit of her special qualities to society, it is of the utmost importance that we create, especially for the unmarried woman, many types of womanly work. We need pioneers of vision and imagination to take the lead in developing

occupations which give woman the opportunity to mature and use her distinctive gifts. We must be alert to discover appropriate spheres of activity in which woman may realize her dedication to God in loving service of humankind.

(4) *Become Radiant Examples of the Spirit of Total Dedication*: Most important of all we must fulfill our primary mission to radiate the spirit of dedication in the world. Never has there been a period in the history of the race when the need for woman's spiritual mission was so great. At the root of all the disorders of our sad, sick world lies man's attempt to assert his independence of God. To bring tranquillity and joy into the chaos of modern society, the first necessity is a profound renewal of spirit, a wholehearted surrender of man to God, a humble and joyful acknowledgment of our complete dependence on Him. To light the way to this surrender is the spiritual mission of the women of the twentieth century, the task of woman in the modern world.

FAITH AND FREEDOM

Muslim women around the world see their future in democracy-and in Islam. To veil or not to veil is hardly the question. The fate of women's rights throughout the Islamic world today hinges on matters of far greater substance, from reforms of family and penal codes to new understandings of Islamic law and teaching. In these best and worst of times for Muslim women, it is perhaps not surprising that every promising bit of news seems to come with a disturbing counterpoint.

Take Shirin Ebadi, an Iranian lawyer and former judge, who in mid-October won the Nobel Peace Prize for her unceasing efforts to promote women's rights and democracy in her native land. In response to the jubilant reaction of Iranians throughout the Islamic republic, President Mohammad Khatami--a reformist, no less--dismissed it as "not worth all that fuss!" Several days after the Nobel was announced, Morocco's King Mohammed VI, who claims descent from the prophet Mohammed, proposed reforms in family law that stand to improve the lot of women throughout the North African kingdom. But long before he presented the reforms to the national parliament, Islamists had taken to the streets to denounce them, dwarfing a pro-reform demonstration by roughly 3 to 1. Also in mid-October, in an unusual instance of Bedouin perestroika, authorities in Saudi Arabia announced that the kingdom would permit the holding of municipal elections within a year--though it's still unclear whether women will be able to run for office or even vote. And at the end of September, in one of a dozen Nigerian states that have adopted sharia (Islamic law), a religious appeals court overturned the death sentence of Amina Lawal, 32, a Muslim woman accused of adultery. Yet while Lawal was spared the gruesome fate of death by stoning, at least five other women in Nigeria still face the same sentence.

Women's rights face an uncertain future throughout much of the Islamic world--though nowhere more pointedly than in the constitution-making efforts now underway in both Afghanistan and Iraq. In two nations widely viewed as test cases of the compatibility of Islamic and universal values, it remains to be seen whether and how the principles of sharia, or even the more general spirit of Islamic traditions, will inform their future laws. And behind those uncertainties loom even broader questions facing Muslim women everywhere. In particular, rights activists wonder, are the foundations of Islamic law and theology compatible with international standards of human rights in general and women's right in particular? And if so, what must be done to surmount the practical hurdles--including the crucial matter of who interprets the law--that stand in the way of reconciling Islam with universal principles of women's rights?

Muslim women themselves are already actively engaged with these issues. "When I talk with educated women from Morocco to Pakistan," says Ann Mayer, a professor of legal studies at the University of Pennsylvania's Wharton School and author of Islam and Human Rights: Tradition and Politics, "I find that they are much more inclined to evaluate their condition in relation to international standards of human rights. And they say that international standards only reinforce Islamic standards."

Confidence. That underscores one notable development of the past decade: a new confidence among Muslim feminists and human-rights activists that Islamic teachings and sources can support their efforts. This represents a sea change, says Amina Wadud, professor of Islamic studies at Virginia Commonwealth University and author of Qu'ran and Woman: Rereading the Sacred Text From a Woman's Perspective. As late as 1995, at the Global Women's Conference in Beijing, many feminists from Islamic countries insisted women's equality could be attained only by jettisoning religion, including the outward trappings of the faith, such as the veil.

Since then, though, an expanding reform movement within Islam, driven largely by increased literacy and an explosion of new media outlets, has led more Muslims to explore the sacred writings on their own. While this has often reinforced the patriarchal viewpoint of militant Islamists, it has also supported progressive and feminist interpretations. Wadud insists that it is unnecessary and even constraining to argue only on the basis of historical precedent, but she finds there is more in the sacred texts and traditions to support notions of gender equality than there is to deny them. She notes, for example, that in the period after Mohammed's death, women, including the Prophet's favorite wife, Aisha, played "key roles in preserving traditions, disseminating knowledge, and challenging authority when it went against their understanding of the Koran or the prophetic legacy."

Referring to the decision of Iran's mullahs to remove Nobel winner Ebadi from her judgeship on religious grounds, Wadud notes, "Nowhere is it said that women cannot interpret the law." Ebadi herself, in a recent interview with Iranian emigre author Amir Taheri, makes the same point in her words of advice to Muslim women: "Don't believe that you are decreed to have an inferior position. Study the Koran carefully, so that the oppressors cannot impress you with citations and interpretations. Don't let individuals masquerading as theologians claim they have a monopoly on understanding Islam."

Fine words, but have they yet had any practical consequences? The answer, many activists say, is a qualified yes. In that widely followed adultery case in Nigeria, for example, Amina Lawal's attorney, Hauwa Ibrahim, got her client exonerated, but on several technicalities that may not work for other women. The real problem, says Mayer, is that Nigeria's version of sharia involves a "folkloric version" of Islamic adultery law. First of all, the rules of evidence spelled out in the Koran require either a freely gained confession from the accused or four eyewitnesses to the act of sexual penetration, neither of which was obtained in Nawal's case. Just as important, the maximum punishment for the crime is supposed to be 100 lashes, not stoning.

Illegal. Of course, even if the Nawal case and others did not involve a corrupted use of sharia, the punishments that Nawal faced would be in violation of both the spirit and letter of the U.N. Convention on the Elimination of All Forms of Discrimination Against Women (CEDAW), which Nigeria has signed and ratified. But appeals to international agreements have only limited effectiveness in advancing women's rights in the Islamic world. (Saudi Arabia is one of 50 out of the 57 Organization of Islamic Conference nations to sign and ratify CEDAW, but it explicitly stipulates that it will not observe any terms that contradict "norms of Islamic law.") In some cases, appeals might even backfire. According to Wadud, the defense attorneys involved in another Nigerian adultery case had to send out word that any additional international pressure might actually sway the jurists on a religious appeals court not to overturn the verdict.

In a more general way, says New York University law Prof. Noah Feldman, the former U.S. adviser to the Iraqi Governing Council on constitutional matters, the United States faces a similar challenge in its efforts to guide Afghanistan and Iraq toward becoming democratic and rights-respecting regimes. Feldman points out that as long as America is an occupying power, it can accomplish much "just by suggesting"--though, he promptly adds, the U.S.-led Coalition Provisional Authority had to insist on the appointment of several women to the 25-person Governing Council. "But at a certain point," Feldman cautions, "you cross the line to coercing people on how to run their lives."

Feldman prefers to stop short of that line, having disagreed openly with Sen. Sam Brownback and Rep. Frank Wolf's proposal for requiring explicit religious-freedom language in the Iraqi constitution. "Senator Brownback says if we allow the constitution to mention the word `Islam,' we'll have problems down the road, but I say if we don't, we'll have troubles immediately," Feldman explains. That does not mean that he has little hope for women's rights. To the contrary, says the author of After Jihad, an argument for the future of Islamic democracy, "I am for promoting women's rights by saying they are compatible with Islam."

In Iraq, there are good reasons for thinking that Islam and women's rights can go together. Before the U.S. invasion, says Khaled Abou el Fadl, a visiting professor at Yale Law School, Iraq was one of the most progressive of Muslim nations in relation to women. Not only were there female jurists and lawyers, but there was a civil code that blended the best of French and Islamic laws. Among the latter, he points out, was a law allowing a woman the right to divorce her husband and sue for alimony and child support if he decided to take another wife. (A similar expansion of women's prerogatives is one of the reforms that Morocco's king has just proposed.) Like Feldman, Abou el Fadl worries that attempts to expunge Islam from Iraq's laws will only trigger a stronger urge on the part of many Iraqis to put more of Islam in--and that might mean the most sexist and partriarchal versions of Islam.

Which raises the most important issue: How can Muslim feminists and rights activists win the interpretive struggle against those mullahs and muftis who confuse partriarchal codes and customs with the core principles of the faith? That is a major concern for Irshad Manji, a Canadian author and journalist. Like many other Muslim feminists, she sees the real problem of interpretation as one of overturning Arab traditions of honor that accompanied the spread of Islam and are now being recirculated throughout the world via the Saudi-funded Wahhabi religious establishment. As Manji explains, within the Arab honor code, individual rights are secondary to one's status within the family or tribe. Women are reduced to "communal or tribal property." In Pakistan or Nigeria, she says, a man from one tribe or family may rape a woman from another as an act of communal retribution. For Manji, who develops her argument in her forthcoming book The Trouble With Islam, one of the best solutions lies in women's growing participation in trade, commerce, and capitalism, all of which have been valued since Islam's founding. (Mohammed's first wife, Khadija, was an astute businessperson.) And the economic empowerment of women in the Islamic world is not merely theoretical. It is already underway even in the most Arab of states, Saudi Arabia. In Jidda and Riyadh, respectively, women own a quarter and a third of all businesses. And it is no secret among foreigners working in Saudi Arabia that women are the most educated, able, and productive employees in the kingdom.

By consolidating and advancing their economic position, Manji says, and by becoming tax-paying citizens, women can assert their standing as individuals. This emerging reality is hard to ignore, whether in Saudi Arabia or Iran. Already in Malaysia, Amina Wadud notes, women working through Sisters in Islam and other groups have helped reform domestic violence law by promoting what she calls a "nice blend of sharia and civil law."

Still, it is one of the sad ironies of Islam, Manji says, that a religion originally intended to transcend tribalism has, at least in many parts of the world, allowed the tribalist codes to reassert themselves. But Manji refuses to accept that irony as the last word on women's fate within Islam. And she is far from alone.

•

9

Women's Empowerment: Myth or Reality

Wives are lonelier now than they ever used to be. In older, gentler times, when age still had its privileges, the old folks never harbored any guilt feelings about being a drag on the young. They either moved in, reasoning that it was high time they were supported for a change, or else they lived nearby. People moved less, and families stuck closer together. Grandma, never having become emancipated, was always around for advice and help. (Today grandma is likely to be off fund raising or taking courses at Columbia.) I know a Polish area in Chicago where everyone in the family lives within a few blocks of the others, and there are usually two generations in each house. They may have other problems, but loneliness isn't one of them.

The young college-educated mother with a medium amount of money is the one who reflects all the problems at once. In spite of her hopes for fulfillment through her children and contentment with woman's great career, she vaguely feels that she is frittering away her days and that a half-defined but important part of her ability is lying about unused; she is guilty about her feeling of futility because of her belief in the magic medicine of love. This is the housewife's syndrome, the vicious circle, the feeling of emptiness in the gap between what she thought marriage was going to be like and what it is really like.

Let's take a look at a fairly typical young mother. She married her husband because she loved him, and she still does. She has two children and is pregnant with a third. Whether in city or country, she is more or less surrounded by gadgets which free her from drudgery. If she is lucky, she has a cleaning woman once a week. She and her husband have enough money for a fairly comfortable life, but for time alone together are dependent on baby sitters and possibly a grandma who will help out in a pinch. If the young mother is in the country, the children play in the yard, and she watches them from the window; if she is in the city, she takes them out once or twice a day, pushing a carriage and pulling a tricycle. Talking to her friends on these outings is her solution to loneliness. Her day is full of a thousand pressures, some miniature, some large. Two of the main worries are illness and money. If everyone in the family is healthy for two weeks at a stretch, she counts herself fortunate. Every cold goes the rounds of the family, and she sometimes feels that she supports the pediatrician singlehandedly.

During the healthy periods she strives to improve her home, cook a new dish, do something about her looks, give a dinner party and a children's birthday party, go to the theater with her husband, catch up on her reading, have coffee with a friend. Her life vacillates between being very organized and completely disorganized, because she has the struggle of all women: to keep the house clean and in repair without being a shrew about people's messing it up. Because children are natural makers of havoc, she constantly strives to maintain the delicate line of balance. Usually, when the first child starts school, she is drawn into community or P.T.A. work of some kind. If she is normally conscientious, she feels she should do something, but if she is normally realistic, she knows she doesn't have time. So she does it anyway. Joining things as a virtue is a hangover from college, where well-roundedness and abundant interests were considered rungs on the ladder to heaven.

The demands of her family and community cause her to feel, as one woman put it, like a pie with not enough pieces to go around. Depending on whether or not she is gregarious, she longs for time to talk to her friends or time to be alone; I should say, the busier she is, the greater her urge to be by herself, to feel unique and separate again. Great numbers of friends are a luxury she can no longer afford; old friends often diminish in importance, which she is sorry about. But there is a limit to her capacity for giving affection, and maintaining old friendships at their original intensity requires an effort she hardly has the energy for. Besides, she is often forced into unwanted and demanding friendships with the next-door neighbor, the boss's wife, or the ladies' club chairman, and she must learn to cover up her real feelings. (To her surprise, she often ends by liking these women.) Another group of demanding relationships is required with her in-laws, and if she gets along well with them, she is lucky. If her husband now lacks the mystery and fascination of the wedding night, he is now more loved and appreciated. The occasions when they have time alone together are among her precious jewels.

In spite of this full life, the old illusions of what life was supposed to hold, the restless remnants, the undefined dreams do not die as they were supposed to. Probably every educated wife has found herself staring at a mountain of dirty diapers and asking herself desperately, "Is this all there is?" And at the same time she is embarrassed by her dissatisfaction; she, of all people, with her intelligence and realistic view of life, should be able to rise above it. But the paradox is that it is she who is least able to. She lives for a better day. Things will be easier when this baby is born, or that one toilet-trained, or the children are all in school; and she will have time to be pretty and intelligent and young again. The mistake is in thinking that everything is going to solve itself by magic. What our girl must do, as she stares at the diapers, is to accept some of the truths about marriage and motherhood that her education and society conspired to keep from her, and go on from there. And if she would appreciate what she has, she must do it now, not next year or five years from now.

The first truth is that marriage does not automatically equal security and contentment. An unmarried friend of mine told me once that she did not see how any problem in marriage could be as bad as one outside of it, because if you had your man, anything else could be easily straightened out. We had a long argument about whether the heart sank more over a sick child or a departed boy friend, and neither of us won. She is one of a good many girls who think that three dates a week, secretarial jobs, and the responsibility of keeping themselves clothed are a nerve-shattering, frantic business, and who look forward to marriage and motherhood as a long, relaxing rest cure. "Getting married and settling down" is a valid notion for men, as it has been throughout history, but not for potential mothers. The day the doctor confirms one's pregnancy is the day to start bracing oneself for the really hard work. (I cannot convince my unmarried friends of this, but, of course, that is as it should be, or many babies might never be born.)

The truth is that, with the birth of the first child, marvelous changes take place. From that moment on, mama is no longer the center of attention; the baby is. Mama and papa will give-and willingly-and the baby will take. They will assume responsibility, earn money, employ their energy, change their lives, if necessary-all for the baby. This is no light undertaking, but the business of life is starting now, and every day of mama's life proves it to be so. And here her struggle starts. She wants to give everything to the baby; she wants equally to hold on to herself, her intelligence and uniqueness, while the baby con-stantly tries her patience, her strength, her nerves, and roots out of her the deepest emotions she has ever known in her life.

This is a whole new process, and not one that provides built-in security. It is a mistake to assume that marriage is a cure-all, a miraculous bit of psychiatry that is going to banish all the old problems overnight and, like phenobarbital, put disturbingly violent instincts to sleep. The benediction of church and state is not enough to still the quality of excitement that comes from strangeness and the idealization of a still-unknown experience. These things, after all, were part and parcel of sex before marriage, and half its value. Sex in marriage makes up in intimacy what it loses in mystery, but this does not mean that mystery is no longer attractive. The most embarrassing lust for the least likely person can exist in the best-adjusted P.T.A. member in town. Whether or not anything is done about it is another story, but probably most of the time nothing is. We take marriage very seriously; our Puritan heritage is still very much with us; and we fear the wages of sin. Besides, the communities of young married couples are built for decency and togetherness, and the woman who considers taking a lover simply has no place to go.

All of the notions about peace being intrinsic in the state of marriage have to do with the happiness-togetherness cult, the great American dream, the return to the hearth. The peak of all earthly satisfaction is said to be found in the family, popping corn together in matching pajamas, not in hard work and self-denial, or even in the self-knowledge that came with the Freudian age. In our unending search for panaceas, we believe that happiness and "success"-which, loosely translated, means money-are the things to strive for. People are constantly surprised that, even though they have acquired material things, discontent still gnaws.

An Englishman said to me recently, "You Americans live on a much higher plane of expectancy than we do. You constantly work toward some impossible goal of happiness and perfection, and you unfortunately don't have our ability just to give up. Really, it's much easier to accept the fact that some things can't be solved." He is right; we never accept it, and we kill ourselves trying. The feeling of futility of the housewife is based on a history of high expectancy, a faith in external things, and an inability to see that the rewards are found within oneself. It is a paradox that the achievement of a home and family is so often regarded by women as the consummate solution for human ills, when actually the responsibilities it entails are enough to reduce some people to nervous wrecks. Marriage, entered upon maturely, is the only life for most women. But it is a way of life, not a magic bag of goodies at the end of the road.

The fact is that marriage and motherhood bring forth deeper and more staggering emotions than any experience before marriage. There is nothing soothing or secure about the feeling, familiar to all mothers, of wanting to murder one's child and really feeling capable of it, and then the next moment dissolving into the deepest love and repentance. There is nothing soothing about the insane annoyance that one can feel at some irritating habit of a loved one, or at loathing the knowledge of what he or she is going to say; one feels trapped by a total ability to see-mystery gone forever. It can be painful to find oneself isolated, in marriage, with problems that have always been shared with mother or girl friends, and to realize that there are some things that even one's husband cannot be told. This is the hard lesson of discretion. And there is nothing soothing to participants or onlookers about the spine-chilling habit of some couples who goad each other to a fever pitch of irritation, with repeated fingernail rasps on each other's well-known sensitive spots-all in the name of playful affection. It is frightening to see how close emotions are to the surface and how little it takes to make destruction.

And it is equally frightening to know suddenly how complete love is and how much one gives to it, to see how little one can really stand when someone in the family is sick, and to know how quickly one can be torn apart by nothing at all. A young mother said the other day, speaking of young mothers in general, "It always amazes me how vulnerable we are and how we, who are supposed to be so responsible, are such preys of our own feelings." In a family of love, one must become infinitely flexible to withstand the continuous jounce of emotion. This is the muscle that develops, not superefficiency or physical strength, and it is the weariness of this muscle that causes young mothers to want to run away and hide in a solitary place where nothing can jar the heart. The second truth is that a girl does not need a college education to take care of babies and keep house. I recall a lot of talk at college among engaged girls that bringing up children is a vastly complicated business which makes full use of a mother's brains and energy, and that no man on earth has a position as responsible and delicate as that of being totally in charge of the education of minds, souls, and bodies of two or three important human beings.

Well, for one thing, mother is not totally in charge, though she may like to think so. The influences of father, school, doctor, friends, neighborhood, city, or country are equally important. Besides, mother is not really in charge of herself enough to be in charge of her children. What the children learn is what mother is, not what she thinks she is. For another thing, the job is hardly complicated and delicate, at least at first. It is the simple, nerve-wracking, mindless, battering-ram process of trying to teach a savage to use a fork. It requires bloodless patience, a deadly will, enormous physical stamina, and a stable disposition, but no precision instruments. It takes strength and determination. For the fact is that motherhood makes the heaviest demands in what might be called the areas of least experience. I would be surprised if there were a single college-educated mother who has not been struck by the total uselessness of her liberal education when it comes to housewifery.

Instead of distilling pearls of knowledge from a large body of facts, she must now master a whole new set of domestic facts: how to roast a chicken, remove gum from the rug, take a child's temperature, keep the shine on the Sheraton table, iron a blouse, or even change a tire or build a bookcase. Some of these necessities are positively shocking. The care of dirty diapers and the job of keeping the oven clean call for a strong-minded unfastidiousness; even more does the whole process of having a baby, which is certainly nature at its rawest. Learning all of these things calls for a day-to-day resourcefulness and is a new and rather frightening responsibility.

Choosing a house and everything that goes into it, and a school, and a competent doctor are decisions that the young mother makes without adequate knowledge, and she can ill afford mistakes. If her husband is sympathetic, he helps her with these decisions. If not, she gropes her way along and takes the blame when that lovely color for the living-room walls turns out to be bilious salmon pink in the sunlight. And this calls for a brand-new virtue, too; the ability to adapt oneself completely, in about thirty seconds flat, to an entirely new viewpoint. Around a house, no achievement is very permanent, and the day can turn inside out before one's eyes. The salmon-pink walls must suddenly be repainted, the baby sitter suddenly fails, the clean living room is no longer clean, the elevator in the apartment building breaks down, and mother and baby carriage are trapped for the day on the seventh floor.

BACKGROUND

The National Commission on Population which was set up to review, monitor and give directions for the implementation of the National Population Policy with a view to meeting the goals set out in the Policy constituted eight Working Groups on the following subjects related to population stabilization in the country:

I. Strategies to Meet Unmet Needs;

II. Primary and Secondary Education in relation to Population and Civilization;

III. Registration of Births, Deaths and Marriages;

IV. Media for Information, Education and Communication and Motivation;

V. Role of Panchayati Raj Institutions and Self-Help Groups;

VI. Mainstreaming of Indian System of Medicine and Homeopathy into the Health System;

VII. Task Force on Monitoring;

VIII. Advisory Group on Tribal Communities.

Four Sub-Groups have been constituted under the first Working Group on Strategies to meet the following specific unmet needs:

a) Sub-Group on Strategies to Address Unmet Needs of Contraception;

b) Sub-Group on Unmet Needs on Maternal and Child Health;

c) Sub-Group on Strategies for Unmet Needs for Public Health, Drinking Water, Sanitation and Nutrition; and

d) Sub-Group on Empowerment of Women, Development of Children and issues for Adolescents.

The Sub-Group met twice under the Chairpersonship of Smt. Margaret Alva, Member of Parliament and Chairperson of Parliamentary Standing Committee on Empowerment of Women. During the course of the deliberations of the Sub Group, two important developments took place-first, the provisional results of Census 2001 were published and National Policy for Empowerment of Women was approved by the Government. The Sub Group considered both the developments and deliberated on various issues of empowerment of women and development of children and adolescents in the context of the National population Policy.

The Sub-Group felt that the 'unmet needs' of empowerment of women and development of children and adolescents cover a whole gamut of issues which cut through the terms of references of all the Sub Groups and of the Working Groups and, therefore, there is bound to be considerable degree of overlapping in the terms of reference and deliberations of this Sub-Group. The issue of empowerment of women and development of children and adolescents is not a side or peripheral but a core issue for stabilizing the population growth of the country.

DEMOGRAPHIC TRANSITION

The demographic transition of the country in the recent years has brought the issues of women and children into the forefront of the country's development strategy. From a "high birth rate-high death rate" country of the pre Independence era, which provided fodder for the theory of Malthus, India had reached the stage of " high birth rate-low death rate" in the early fifties, which contributed to the high rate of growth of population. This continued till the beginning of the eighties, with a decadal growth rising to 21.51% in the fifties, from 13.31% in the previous decade, followed by 24.80% in the sixties and 24.66% in the seventies, despite all the national efforts made to contain this growth. The transition to the phase of "low birth rate-low death rate" has started at a very slow pace, with population growth sliding to 23.85% in the eighties and 21.34% in the nineties. If the goal of National population Policy of bringing TFR to the replacement level has to be achieved by 2010, the growth rate of population has to be brought down to 10.7% during the current decade, which is a very tall order and can not be achieved unless the issues of women, adolescents and children are brought to the centre stage of our development planning.

The changing demographic profile of the country indicate a few important trends which will have significant bearing on the position of women and children of the country. First, although the percentage of child population below the age of 14 has declined from 37.76% in 1991 to 34.33% in 2001, the absolute numbers of children are still on the rise. The population of children in the age group of 0-6 has increased from 150.42 million in 1991 to 157.86 million in 2001. Likewise the population in the age group of 7-14 is projected to be 170.34 million today as compared to 161.94 million in 1991. Together they constitute 31.9% of the country's population-a huge 328.20 million out of 1.02 billion-the largest number of children in any country anywhere in the world. The adolescents in the age group of 15 to 19 constitute another nearly 10% of the population. Together they constitute the most important potential human resource and it is the health, nutrition, education and well being of these children and adolescents that will determine the future of the country.

The second trend in the country's demography is the declining sex ratio. The overall sex ratio has declined almost consistently over the years-from 972 females per 1000 males in 1901 to 933 in 2001-although the numbers had improved marginally by 1 point in 1951, 3 points in 1981 and 6 points in 2001, but sliding by 5 points in 1961, 9 points in 1971 and 7 points in 1991. The decline of sex ratio have been particularly striking in the age group of 0 to 6 years in recent years. Census 2001 has registered this decline by 18 points-from 927 in 1991 to 945. This decline has been registered in all the States and Union Territories except Kerala, Mizoram, Sikkim, Tripura and Lakshadeep. The decline has been very sharp in prosperous States like Punjab, Haryana, Maharastra and Gujrat. In Punjab the gap in the sex ratio has widened to more than 200 per 1000 children. Unfortunately, the trend could not be arrested by rising female literacy during the decade. This is reflective of a deep seated prejudice against the girl child in the country. Countering this trend should be one of the priorities in the National Socio Economic Goals of the country.

While the female sex ratio among the children is declining, it is increasing among the aged, due to increased life expectancy among the females, leading to a strange gender asymmetry in the population pyramid of the country. With the gradual weakening of family based social security and absence of any strong alternate system, the care of the aged and particularly of the widows, is increasingly assuming the shape of a national problem to be reckoned with in the coming years.

The age pyramid of Indian population will swell in the centre in the years to come. At present 58% of Indians are in the age group of 15-59 years. This will increase to nearly 64% during the next ten years-from 596 million at present to 708 million by 2010, even if TFR reaches its replacement level. The implication of this transition in terms of additional needs of food, water, energy, health care, education and employment will be enormous. At the same time, the gradual increase in literacy particularly among the females on the one hand and the rise in the mean age of marriage of girls on the other, would mean that more and more girls will demand employment, particularly in the organized sector. New types of demands will be placed on the country's educational and training institutions for building capacity and skill of the workers and particularly of the female workers and of those who will be employed in the self employed and informal sectors.

The national demographic features often conceal substantial differences between States and between regions and sub regions within the same State in the achievement of basic demographic indices. These differences are conditioned by factors such as illiteracy, poverty, inadequate access to health and family welfare services etc, which often coexist and reinforce each other. At one end of the spectrum is Kerala with IMR and TFR comparable to many developed countries, but there are districts within the same State like ldukki and Malappuram where IMR and CBR are higher than the national average. At the other end are the States like Bihar and Uttar Pradesh (including newly created Uttaranchal an Jharkhand) which have the worst HDI indices in the world, but with districts like Almora and Ranchi with IMR and CBR much lower than the national level.

The co-relationship between various indices have also been conditioned by a complex web of 'other' factors which need to be studied in depth. Kerala and Tamil Nadu, for example, have achieved replacement level of fertility well before CPR of 60% was reached, whereas, in spite of a developed health infrastructure and CPR much above 60% Punjab is yet to reach that level. Inspite of low female literacy, Andhra Pradesh will be achieving replacement level of fertility much ahead of States with higher literacy rates. Maharastra, Haryana and Punjab have higher SDP than Kerala and Tamil Nadu, but are much behind the southern States in the rates of female literacy, infant mortality and fertility. These suggest that different strategic interventions are required in different States and in different regions and sub regions within the same States for reaching the desired goals of population stabilization. The Sub Group felt that concerted attention should be paid on 5 BIMARU States (Bihar, Madhya Pradesh, Rajasthan and Uttar Pradesh) plus Orissa which account for nearly 44% of the total population of India and which are anticipated to contribute 55% of the population growth in the next decade. Here again district and sub-district specific strategies and action plan should be worked out.

CONCEPTUAL ISSUES

National Population Policy has rightly looked at the issue of population stabilization not as a technical issue that has a technical fix. Population stabilization cannot be achieved by mere physical provisioning of contraception mix or emergency obstetric care. It is critical to involve people-and enable women in particular-to have a say in decisions relating to reproduction and livelihood. This brings in the issues of reproductive rights of women and of the larger conceptual issues of gender equality and of empowerment of women within and outside the household.

The linking of the issue of reproductive health with women's empowerment recognizes that underlying the issue of good health and nutrition for women, we need to examine the issue of power and the nature of gender relations between men and women within the family and community. Here the following conceptual issues need to be highlighted.

Defining Women's Health and Meeting Women's Health Needs: While there have been intense debates attempting to distinguish "women's health" as a more holistic concept than "reproductive health", the issue perhaps is to clearly define what is meant, for our purposes, by women's health and to locate the discourse within a framework of rights. While decision making linked to reproduction and regulation of fertility is important, meeting health needs of women through a system that is sensitive to the differential needs of men and women and their differential access to health care also needs to be taken into account. There are some aspects regarding organizational issues of health delivery which need to be specifically addressed. The division of the health delivery system in terms of two structures-family welfare and health-is not very conducive to a holistic approach to women's health.

Enhanced Awareness and Information: Linked to women's empowerment is the issue of raising awareness about rights-legal literacy, rights to education and health and enhancing information sharing about basic issues. Various studies have indicated that the knowledge of women and adolescent girls about their bodies, and reproductive functions is very limited. Substantial systematic efforts need to be made for enhancing women's and adolescent girls understanding and awareness about various issues.

Linking Health and Reproductive Rights to Other Issues Related to Human Rights: It is essential to recognize the connection between women's health and food security and other economic and environmental conditions. For example, lack of access to water impacts on hygiene, heavy load bearing leads to occupational diseases, lack of nutrition impairs productivity and so on. Therefore the issue of access to safe contraception cannot be delinked from the larger issue of access to food, water, shelter and the issues of sustainable livelihood and a safe environment.

Involvement of Men and Changing Power Relations in Family and Society: In view of the fact that we are laying emphasis on reproductive rights, informed choice and autonomy, it is important that attention is given to underlying social issues which relate to decision making and lack of choices at the level of the family.

This involves the social conditioning of roles and responsibilities which one learns from one's 'culture'. It also means trying to address the structural/fundamental inequalities that exist and give rise to certain situations. For example, it is important that solution to anemia etc. is not viewed as a problem, which can be solved by distributing folic acid, but also as an issue of inadequate nutrition, which also has socio-cultural determinants.

Women's Participation: For an empowerment approach to be well integrated into health programmes it is important that women's participation is incorporated at each stage of the programme and issues regarding power structures are also dealt with. The entire conceptual shift from targeted family planning to reproductive health, which is based on informed choice, is to allow women to voice their preference and needs. However, for women to be able to speak out within the family and community social factors have to be taken into account and conditions create for an enabling environment which would allow this to happen.

STATUS OF WOMEN'S HEALTH

The experience of economic progress, political developments and social transformation of the last 50 years, indicate that although women of India have made major gains in terms of decline in maternal mortality and rise in life expectancy, increase in female literacy and employment, mobilization through self help groups and representation at the grassroots level democracy etc., large gender gaps still exist in almost every sphere of life, which do not empower women to have informed choices on their health and nutrition. India accounts for nearly 25% of the world's maternal deaths. Every year about 1,25,000 Indian women die from pregnancy-related causes many of which are preventable. Poor maternal health results in low birth weight and premature babies. More than 7% of the new born babies perish every year. Nearly 2.3% of the babies who survive the first year perish before they complete five years. The number is more in case of female babies.

The mean age of marriage at the national level is 19.5 years, but about 17.4 percent of girls are married below the age of 18 years. Corresponding rates show marked rural (20.3%) and urban (7.4%) difference. 8.3% of fertility in India is contributed by mothers below 19 years of age and this is also linked with pregnancy wastages ranging form premature death, still birth, neonatal deaths, low birth weight babies and maternal morbidity.

Micro Studies have indicated that women do not get adequate nutrition during pregnancy and lactation. The dietary intake of women in the lower economic group is deficient by 500 to 600 calories. In the above 7 years age group there are gender differences in consumption of cereals, pulses, and milk products. In the above 18 years groups, gender difference is quite prominent in the intake of energy rich food. According to an assessment of underweight and stunted growth of children (1997), in the age group of 1-5 years, almost half (49.1 %) of the girls were underweight and 20.3 per cent were severely underweight. Stunting was observed in 56 % percent of girls. The Body Mass Index (BMI) indicates that more women (36.1 %) than male (28.6%) are affected by various stages of Chronic Energy Deficiency.

Research has provided enough information on women's morbidity linked with the environment like indoor air pollution, iodine deficiency of soil/water, flurosis and arsenic related disorder, use of fossil fuels etc. The spread of Tetanus, Pneumonia, Dysentery, Typhoid, Cholera, Plague do not need any further research to prove their relationship with environment and sanitation. The brunt of all these fall disproportionately on women. Several domestic chores as also occupational work of many kinds affects the women and leads to an incurable state of health. This is true both at household level and at the work place specially in the unorganised industry sector where maximum number of women earn their livelihood. Chronic Mental depression and neurosis in girls and adult females is quite wide spread, but the present health care delivery system and social attitude are ill equipped to tackle them especially in rural areas.

Studies have indicated that women are biologically and epidemiologically more vulnerable to AIDS. Male to female transmission of HIV is twice as efficient than female to male. Moreover, majority of Indian women being anemic, transfusion of blood during child birth is quite common making the women more susceptible to the contact. Besides social factors like lack of control over their own body, early marriage and repeated pregnancies, lack of information, poverty induced/forced prostitution, promiscuity of husbands etc. make them more vulnerable to this disease. The impact of HIV and Aids on women is also much more severe and critical. First, inter-generational transmission of the disease takes place through women. Secondly, the rejection and ostracisation of women and girls are much more than for males. Further, women and girls suffer disproportionately from the burden of the disease. The traditional gender role of women in caring for the sick make them more susceptible to the disease. Girls of AIDS affected families often have to leave the school to care for the sick.

Women are the victims of a whole plethora of violence committed against them-infanticide, torture, rape, molestation, battering, trafficking, prostitution, forced marriage, dowry death, custodial violence and so on. This is a reflection of the deep rooted 'gender ideology' of society. Often the crimes are committed by people who are close to the victims and are traditionally supposed to be their protectors. But the victims, especially the sexually abused girls and women, face the brunt of the act more than the abuser. Only a miniscule of the acts of violence committed against women are covered under legal provisions and the bulk of them go unreported. Complex and lengthy legal procedures, often involving substantial expenditure, poor rate of conviction and lack of support from relatives and community are the important reasons for under reporting of crimes against women. Even then the crimes committed against women in relation to the total crimes, has increased from 11% in 1996 to 13.5% in 1998.

Poverty in general, and extreme poverty in particular, has a significant gender dimension. Studies has been revealed that (i) the percentage of adult women exceeds the percentage of adult men below the poverty line, both in rural and urban areas; (ii) the percentage of children in the 0-4 age group in poor households exceeds that of non-poor households, and (iii) in both urban and rural areas, disadvantaged groups of women from Scheduled Castes and Tribes constitute a high proportion of the poor. Incidence of poverty is positively co-related with IMR-a poor couple perceives an additional child to be an investment, both as security against probable mortality of the surviving child and as a potential wage earner. Significant co-relation between spread of female literacy and decline of fertility has been observed throughout the country although there are regions where fertility has declined despite prevalence of illiteracy. A lot of gains have been made in the recent years in female illiteracy. For the first time the number of absolute illiterates has declined and rate of growth of female literacy has outpaced that of males. But still 45.84% of females in the age group of 6 to 50 are illiterates. The gap between male and female literacy is still as wide as 22 percentage points.

THE STATE OF INDIAN CHILDREN

India is to home the largest number of children in the world. Nearly one third of its population-328.20 million in absolute terms-is children below the age of 15 years. About 45% of its population are minors i.e, below the age of 18 years. The country had formulated a National Policy for Children in 1974 and ratified the United Nations Convention on the Rights of the Child in 1992. A National Plan of Action for Children (NPAC) was also drawn up in 1992, which had set goals for various indicators to be achieved by the year 2000. But most of these goals have remained unfulfilled, although significant improvements have taken place in all the crucial indicators like infant and child mortality rates, school enrolment ratios, drop-out rates, levels of mal-nutrition etc.

Infant mortality has remained around 72 per 1000 live births with no significant improvement in the nineties unlike in the eighties. This is much below the average of 6 in developed countries, 64 in developing countries and the world average of 59. There are significant disparities across States, within the States and among castes, communities and other ethnic groups. Kerala for instance, has IMR of 13 per 1000 live births against 94 in Madhya Pradesh: The Infant mortality rate among Scheduled Castes is 24% higher than the national average. Like-wise, the rural and urban differentials also continue to be very high-46 in urban areas as compared to 78 in rural areas. The underlying reasons of high infant mortality are early marriage and childbearing, lack of birth spacing, inadequate maternal nutrition, inadequate antenatal care, and large proportion of deliveries lacking supervision by trained birth attendants.

The Child Mortality Rate (CMR) of India is also very high 25 children out of every 1000 who survive the first year die before they complete 5 years. India ranks 49 out of 189 countries in CMR i.e, if the worst is ranked 1, India is 49th. This reflects the inability of families to look after their young children. Despite efforts being made under the Integrated Child Development Services programme, malnutrition continues to remain a principal underlying cause of morbidity and mortality in under-5 children. This is because intrauterine growth retardation caused by inadequate nutrition during pregnancy cannot be corrected later on. It is an alarming fact that one out of three children are born in India with low birth weight (<2500 g). Coupled with unsupervised delivery and delayed complementary feeding, unhygienic sanitary practices and lack of access to safe drinking water, the average child succumbs to acute respiratory infections and diarrhea.

Malnutrition constitutes a major threat to the development potential of young children. Although surveys conducted by the National Nutrition Monitoring Bureau, Hyderabad have confirmed that there has been a declining trend in severe and moderate degrees of malnutrition amongst children, the micro-nutrient deficiencies, viz. Vitamin A, iron and iodine have been affecting children in various degrees.

The national data indicates that although the proportion of nutritional blindness has reduced drastically, yet the sub-clinical deficiency of vitamin A still continues. Other health concerns of the children are vaccine preventable diseases, birth asphyxia, injury and disability, Mother to Child Transmission (MTCT) of HIV and iodine deficiency disorders. While India has achieved great success with the Pulse Polio Campaign, reports indicate that this has affected routine immunization under the Universal Immunization Programme where the coverage has slipped in recent times. Birth asphyxia is linked to lack of resuscitation facilities during delivery. Many cases of congenital birth defects and mental retardation are caused due to neglect at the time of birth, which are preventable.

A growing incidence of HIV positive mothers in the general population suggests that problem of HIV infected children may soon emerge as a serious problem to be reckoned with. The rate of transmission from a HIV positive mother to her child varies between 15 to 40% with increased risk if the child is breastfed. A child infected at birth, unlike in the case of adults with HIV has a short window period of 3-5 years before the infection overwhelms the developing immune system of the child.

Education is a right of every child. The Directive Principles of State Policy enshrined in the Constitution of India require the State to provide free and compulsory elementary education to all children up to the age of 14 years. Although there has been a substantial increase in the enrolment of children at all levels of schooling, yet 100 million children are estimated to be out of school. Most of these children are vulnerable to neglect. The NSS survey of 1977 has indicated that child labour in the country has increased to 17 million as compared to 13.6 million in 1981 and 11.3 million in 1991. As many as 4.15 lakh children live on the streets in the mega cities of Bangalore, Mumbai, Calcutta, Delhi, Hyderabad and Chennai and are exposed to all types of exploitation.

ISSUES OF THE ADOLESCENTS

Adolescents comprise about a fifth of India's population, but they have so far not been recognized as a target of any strategy for development in the country. They are important human resource material, which can be effectively moulded and channelised for nation building. A bulk of population in this age group, particularly in the rural areas, are drop outs from schools and are vulnerable to exploitation of various sorts. The adolescent girls particularly are at high risk of anemia and mental and behavioral disorder. A three-fold strategy must be adopted for helping adolescents in the country. First, efforts should be made to retain them in the education system by progressively reducing the rate of dropouts from schools and colleges through improvement in educational facilities.

Secondly, vocational training and skill development for the drop outs should be organized in various traditional and non traditional trades, depending on their aptitudes and job opportunities, to prepare them to become self sufficient economically and responsible citizens of the country. Thirdly, the nutritional requirement of the adolescents, particularly of the adolescent girls, should be a matter of special concern, since they are the potential mothers and any investment in their health and nutrition shall not only empower them to be better women, but also be an insurance against the underweight and under nourished children of the future.

Improvement of health of the adolescent girl is a definite way of breaking the inter generational cycle of malnutrition in the population. The adolescent girls need also to be protected from unwanted pregnancies and sexually transmitted diseases. Reproductive health services for adolescent boys and girls is particularly needed in rural areas where adolescent marriages and pregnancies are widely prevalent.

STRATEGIES FOR INTERVENTION

The intervention strategy for empowering women to have informed and effective choices on their health and nutrition and for the development of children and adolescents has to be multi-pronged.

Convergence of Service Delivery at Village Levels

There are two main programmes in the Department of Women and Child Development, which aim at convergence of services delivery at the village level, namely, Integrated Child Development Scheme (ICDS) and Integrated Women.'s Empowennent Programme (IWEP). The ICDS network through Anganwadi Centres reaches 85% of the villages and hamlets in the country. The IWEP (erstwhile Indira Mahila Yojana) which extends to 650 blocks operates through the self help groups of women. Both these programmes can be effective vehicles for the implementation of the National Population Policy. It is therefore critical that both the schemes are universalized.

Nutrition

The Supplementary Nutrition provided under the ICDS Scheme is one of the most vital components under Basic Minimum Service Programme aimed at eradication of the menace of malnutrition of children and women. The success of the programme however depends largely on adequate provision of funds to the States and UTs. An Action plan needs to be drawn up for taking up nutrition in a mission mode to cover infants, adolescent girls, pregnant and lactating mothers-the three critical links in the inter-generational cycle of malnutrition. One intervention that has successfully worked in improving nutrition levels as well as impacting favourably on retention of children in schools is the mid-day meal scheme. This has shown positive results in programmes like TINP and needs to be replicated widely.

Formation of Self-Help Groups

The formation of self-help groups as a basis for the social and economic empowerment of deprived and disadvantaged women has been found to be a successful mechanism for the organization, mobilization and self development of women. This has been tested through the IMY and Swa Shakti projects of the Department of Women and Child Development and is being replicated in a number of programmes of other Departments. These groups can facilitate the process of economic empowerment through thrift and savings, training and skill upgradation and access to credit and other productive resources. They can also be instruments of social empowerment through awareness generation and convergence of delivery of schemes. With the feeling of ownership and management of their own resources and savings, poor women have been able to choose their priorities and have even been found to cover the cost of additional nutrition and health gaps. The success of this approach has resulted in universalization of this mode of organization in all the southern States. There is a need to replicate this mode throughout the country.

Access to Resources

The issue of improved health and nutrition is intimately linked to access to and control over local, social, and economic structures. For women to be empowered we need to ensure

(a) equitable access and distribution of resources like land, credit etc.

(b) access to education.

(c) access to health/nutrition

(d) access to water and sanitation

This implies that resources should flow into these areas to bridge the gender gap and that systems be developed to plan, implement and monitor the 'bridging' of the gap. Various studies have shown that ownership of land tends to reduce fertility by providing an alternate means of security.

Similarly education has its own impact on reproductive behaviour of both men and women. Improving the access of women/households in rural areas and urban slums to safe sources of drinking water will free them from the drudgery of fetching water and in decreasing the morbidity resulting from water-borne diseases such as diarrhoea and cholera. This will impact positively on the health and energy levels of women. Access to technologies which can reduce the drudgery of women on the various works performed by them both within and outside the household is also a very useful intervention for empowering the women.

Women's Component Plan

While the Planning Commission has already incorporated the concept of Women's Component Plan in the 9th Five Year Plan whereby 30% of funds/benefit on every women related sector actually flow to women, it is important that guidelines are finalized early so that this could be implemented effectively.

Development of Gender Disaggregated Data System

One of the constraints in the preparation, implementation and monitoring of plans for the development of women is the absence of gender segregated data on various indices of development at the State, district and sub district levels. This lacunae in our statistical system should be addressed on a priority basis.

Legislation

Laws should be gender sensitive and ensure equal provision and access to resources for men and women. Also there needs to be a much broader focus on implementation issues. Many of the existing statutes such as Indecent Representation of Women's Act, Minimum Wages Act, Equal Remuneration Act, and Pre-natal Diagnostic Act, Maternity Benefit Act, etc., are implemented more in their violation. A number of these Acts are under review in order to strengthen their provisions. The Maternity Benefit Act needs to be strictly implemented and expanded to cover women in the informal sector, along with provision of paid leave for a longer period.

Freedom from Violence

Women and girls face violence in various forms at various stages of their life cycle. This takes the form of female foeticide and infanticide, rape, dowry death and more indirect forms such as desertion or abandonment of older women. This calls for a multipronged strategy of implementation of laws, awareness, community sanctions etc.

Participation in Political Life

For empowerment, women need to have a voice in decision making and planning through adequate representation. Reservation of women in the rural and urban local bodies had enabled representation of nearly a million women at the grassroots who play a very important catalytic role in transforming the society. Similar representation in State Legislature and Parliament would further strengthen the process of empowerment of women.

Sustained Media Campaign

One of the most effective interventions that can take place to address the issues of attitude and mind sets of men and women, of the community and also of the functionaries of the government-the bureaucracy, police and judiciary is media campaigns. A sustained campaign through the print, electronic and folk media is necessary on various issues related to empowerment of women, health and nutrition, laws, value of the girl child, violence against women etc. As the Sub Group was deliberating on the issue of empowerment of women, the National Policy for Empowerment of Women (NPEW) was approved by the Government. The Policy makes a series of prescriptions for the economic and social empowerment of women and for mainstreaming the gender perspective in the development process. The policy has also enjoined upon all Central and State Ministries to draw up time bound Action Plan for translating the Policy into a set of concrete actions and measurable goals to be achieved by 2010.

The Policy has also talked about identification and commitment of resources and responsibilities for implementation of the action plans and of development of suitable structures and mechanisms to ensure efficient monitoring, review and gender impact assessment of plans and policies.

NATIONAL SOCIO ECONOMIC GOALS

The objectives of National Population Policy have been conceptualised into three stages:

(a) *Immediate*-to address the unmet needs for contraception, health care infrastructure, and health personnel, and to provide integrated service delivery for basic reproductive and child health care.

(b) *Medium-term*-to bring the TFR to replacement levels by 2010, through vigorous implementation of inter-sectoral operational strategies.

(c) *Long-term*-to achieve a stable population by 2045, at a level consistent with the requirements of sustainable economic growth, social development, and environmental protection.

In pursuance of these objectives, the NPP has fixed a set of fourteen National Socio Demographic Goals to be achieved in each case by 2010.

The NPEW has also urged that measurable goals to be achieved by 2010 have to be fixed in the Action Plan although these goals have not been stated in the Policy itself. Both the Action Plans of NPEW and of the medium term objectives of the NPP have taken the year 2010 as their time frame. There is urgent need therefore for operationalisation of the convergence of the two Policies through the Action Plans of the Governments at the national and State levels. In other words, the fourteen National Socio Demographic Goals should inform the preparation of the Action Plans under NPEW and to that extent guidelines should be issued by the Department of Women and Child Development to all the State Governments and Union Territories. These fourteen National Socio Demographic Goals of NPP are:

(a) Address the unmet needs for basic reproductive and child health services, supplies and infrastructure.

(b) Make school education up to age 14 free and compulsory, and reduce drop outs at primary and secondary school levels to below 20 percent for both boys and girls.

(c) Reduce infant mortality rate to below 30 per 1000 live births.

(d) Reduce maternal mortality ratio to below 100 per 100,000 live births.

(e) Achieve universal immunization of children against all vaccine preventable diseases.

(f) Promote delayed marriage for girls, not earlier than age 18 and preferably after 20 years of age.

(g) Achieve 80 percent institutional deliveries and 100 percent deliveries by trained persons.

(h) Achieve universal access to information/counseling, and services for fertility regulation and contraception with a wide basket of choices.

(i) Achieve 100 per cent registration of births, deaths, marriage and pregnancy.

(j) Contain the spread of Acquired Immunodeficiency Syndrome (AIDS), and promote greater integration between the management of reproductive tract infections (RTI) and sexually transmitted infections (STI) and the National AIDS Control Organisation.

(k) Prevent and control communicable diseases.

(l) Integrate Indian Systems of Medicine (ISM) in the provision of reproductive and child health services, and in reaching out to households.

(m) Promote vigorously the small family norm to achieve replacement levels of TFR.

(n) Bring about convergence in implementation of related social sector programs so that family welfare becomes a people centred programme.

It may be seen that out of these fourteen goals the first seven relate directly to the women and children and the remaining seven concern them indirectly, although vitally. The Sub Group deliberated on each of these goals. Judging by the pace of progress achieved in the social sectors in the last fifty years, the Sub group felt that implementation of these goals during the course of a decade may become extremely difficult and challenging unless there is commitment of adequate resources by the Central and State Governments on the social sector, particularly in the fields of health, education and nutrition and unless there is strong and effective convergence of services at the grassroot level involving all the stakeholders and the functionaries of all the related Government agencies.

Reduction of IMR to below 30 per 1000 and of MMR to below 100 per 100,000 live births from 72 and 408 at present would require identification of the blocks (i) where IMR has already reached below 30 level, (ii) where it has reached a threshold level, (iii) where it would reach the mark during the decade given the normal rate of progress already achieved, (iv) where it would need additional input and (v) where it would require substantially additional input of both child and maternal care services. At present no scientific system of continuous grading and monitoring of ICDS services, according to the level of achievements of IMR and MMR, exists at the national level. Uniform guidelines and criteria are applied to all the ICDS blocks throughout the country, irrespective of the levels of achievement. This must be replaced by a block specific flexible approach with additional anganwadi centers and additional supplementary nutrition wherever required. This should be put in place immediately in consultation with the State Governments and other stakeholders.

Although there are marked differences in the level of IMR/ MMR between ICDS and non-ICDS blocks, such differences are very marginal in many blocks. In Uttar Pradesh, for example, average IMR in ICDS blocks is 86 per 1000 live births against 86.5 in non-ICDS blocks. This strongly suggests that the programme has not been properly implemented in certain States of the country. There is an urgent need for analyzing the causes of poor performance in some blocks and to take effective remedial steps for improving the level of performance in a time bound manner.

It is unfortunate that in the division of responsibilities between the Central and State Governments, Government of India have chosen the 'easy to manage' task of providing the cost administrative services and of medicines and learning materials, while entrusting the job of funding and arranging the nutrition items to the State Governments. Given the critical resource position of most of the State Governments, nutrition always remains a neglected priority for them.

There are reports that the supplementary feeding programme in the States was not taken up for months together. Even the Additional Plan Assistance under Prime Minister's Gramodaya Yojana (PMGY) was not utilized for supplementary nutrition in many States. It is unfortunate that when the country is facing the problem of storage of surplus food grains procured by the Food

Corporation of India, there are large number of infants and mothers who die every year due to lack of nutrition.

The country's achievement in food security must be converted into nutritional security by effectively distributing the surplus food grains at least to infants and mothers through the network of ICDS centers. This should be taken up in a mission mode, if the targets of IMR/MMR are to be achieved within the given time frame.

It is also unfortunate that the most backward areas of Bihar, Jharkhand and Uttar Pradesh, which have the highest incidence of infant and maternal mortality, have not yet been covered under the ICDS. These 450 blocks, which should have been the first charge on the programme, have been kept last in the priorities of the Government. The ICDS must immediately be extended to all the remaining blocks of the country and the unusual time lag between the sanctioning of the projects and the actual operationalisation must be reduced to a minimum. It is seen that the time lag is sometimes as high as two years, which cannot be justified by any means whatsoever.

The ICDS programme must also be effectively converged with the grassroot level programmes and infrastructure of Health and Family Welfare Departments, if the desired goals of IMR/MMR and of universal immunization of children against all vaccine preventable diseases are to be achieved. The States like Orissa and Gujrat, where such convergence has taken place, have done remarkably well, in a relatively short period of time. In most of the States the programmes suffer due to the lack of effective co ordination between the Department of Women and Child development and the Department of Health and Family Welfare. The village Panchayats and the community should also be involved more effectively with the functioning of the ICDS centers.

It is a matter of national shame that despite the Constitutional directive to the State to endeavour to provide within a period of ten years from the commencement of the Constitution, free and compulsory education for all children until they complete the age of fourteen years, more than 100 million Indian children either do not get admitted to schools or drop out.

It is high time that the Directive Principle is converted into justifiable Fundamental Right of citizens and a comprehensive package of incentives and disincentives are built into our national education system to make it a reality. The Balika Samriddhi Yojana, which links payment of scholarship to girls to duration of school attendance should be implemented more vigorously and provided with adequate funds.

The average age of marriage at the national level has already reached 19.5 years and therefore achieving the target of 20 years by 2010 would seem to be an easily achievable task. But the average conceals significant regional differences. Child marriage is still a practice in many States.

About 20.3% percent of girls in the rural areas are married before 18 years. 8.3% percent of fertility in India is contributed by mothers below 19 years of age and this is closely linked with pregnancy wastages ranging form pre-mature death, stillbirth, neonatal deaths, low birth weight and maternal morbidity. Therefore, region specific strategies and action plans need to be worked out to achieve this national goal.

OPERATIONAL STRATEGIES

The Action Plan under NPP 2000 has outlined operational strategies for (i) empowering women for health and nutrition, (ii) child health and survival and (iii) adolescents. The Sub Group considered these strategies, but while broadly agreeing with them felt that the overwhelming emphasis placed on maternity and childcare services can not be taken as 'stand alone strategies'. Rather these should be effectively integrated with the overall perspectives, strategies and programmes for empowerment of women and of development of children and adolescents, as outlined in this report.

Recommendations

The Sub Group makes the following recommendations for the consideration of the National Commission on Population: The task of stabilization of population is not simply a question of birth control or contraceptives. It is intrinsically connected with the larger issues of alleviation of poverty, empowerment of women, changing mind set of men, women and community and of creation of opportunities and enabling environment of all round development of women, children and adolescents. There is a tendency to marginalize these 'strategic' issues in the belief that 'practical' needs are in some sense more immediate, urgent and easier to manage. Unless these practical needs of women are conceived within a long run and 'strategic' framework, there is a danger of losing sight of the essential inter connections between the two. In principle a long-run goal may well be achieved through a series of co-ordinated short-term strategies, but in practice these may turn out to be stand-alone pieces, which could be symptoms of a long run structural malaise. Defining 'short term' goals simply in terms of combating such symptoms would be tantamount to treating the symptom of the disease rather than treating the disease itself. Therefore, it is extremely important to design strategies for empowerment of women and for development of children and adolescents, keeping this disease in mind.

The long awaited approval of National Policy for Empowerment of Women which has closely followed the National Population Policy is a welcome development. It is understood that a new National Policy on Health and a National Policy on Youth are under consideration. The Government is also seized with the idea of declaring basic education as a Fundamental Right of citizens and formulating a Charter of Rights of Children. All these efforts should be integrated and the National and State Action Plans to be framed under each of these Policies should be effectively converged for the effective delivery of services at the grassroot level. The broad National Socio Economic Goals of NPP should inform the process of preparation of the Action Plans under NPEW.

The Planning Commission should make a commitment of adequate resources for the effective implementation of Plans to achieve the National Socio Economic Goals. At present less than 10% of the Annual Budget is spent on the social sector. There is a strong need and justification to substantially step up allocation to all these sectors, such as health, education, women and child development, rural development, social welfare etc.

Both the programmes on Integrated Child Development Services (ICDS) and Integrated Women's Empowerment

Programme (IWEP) should be universalized covering all the development blocks of the country, but the design, content and guidelines of the projects under both the programmes should be flexible enough to meet the specific requirement of the blocks so that they are in a position to achieve the National Socio Economic Goals within the time frame prescribed in the NPP.

Larger number of creches/day care centers should be opened to encourage female participation in the economy and also to create a positive impact on enrolment and drop out rates of girl children.

The Kishori Shakti Yojana as a component of ICDS, which has been taken up in 2000 blocks needs to be reworked and restructured to have a developmental approach rather sectoral approach. It should have a gender centred adolescent nutrition and development programme and should aim at a high level of adolescent participation. It should meet the requirements of nutrition, training and education of the adolescent girls so that they can gain the knowledge and self-confidence to be informed and capable members of society. The restructured programme should be universalized to cover all the blocks in the country.

A strong focus on the adolescents should be built in various programmes and schemes to address their concerns related to health, nutrition, sexual activity and behivour, vulnerability to HIV/AIDS etc. Sex education is an area which needs to be specifically addressed.

The gains made by the country in food security should be converted into nutritional security of children and the mothers below the poverty line to completely eliminate nutrition related deaths within a given time frame. Here again block specific strategies need to be worked out in consultation with all the stakeholders.

The constitutionally mandated country wide Panchayat Raj Institutions with one third of its Members and Chairpersons from among the women, has the potential to co-ordinate various programmes of the government on women and children according to the needs and requirements of the micro level realities and to monitor the services to the community. If properly constituted and adequately empowered, they have the potential to ensure the highest degree of transparency and accountability at the grassroot level. Panchayats can also be used for initiating popular movements, as has been done in the context of the National Literacy Mission in a number of States. A nation wide movement on informed fertility control through the Panchayats can very well be initiated under the auspices of the National Commission on Population. Village Panchayats can become regular forums for discussions on village health issues, including issues of reproductive health and fertility control.

Capacity of elected representatives at the grass roots should be developed so that they will be in a position to design projects on health and related areas as appropriate to the needs and requirements of local areas.

Given the size and heterogeneity of our population and the power structure within the Panchayats, even the Gram Panchayats may still be far away from the community. Some NGOs have found it expedient to create intermediate structures between the Panchatyats and the village communities for more efficient processes of information and dissemination and better service delivery. But these local elected bodies are by and large the best instruments for implementing community programmes.

The self help groups of women have been found very effective in organizing and sensitizing women to various issues and empowering them socially and economically. The collaboration of Panchayats, NGOs and Self Help Groups at the grassroots level could become very effective for implementation of grassroot level initiatives in the social sectors. Depending on the strength of the stakeholders at the field level, different models of collaboration can be worked out for effective synergy of these initiatives, to transform the situation at the ground level.

The districts and blocks should be graded according to the level of achievements in the social sectors and block specific action plans should be framed for achieving the National Socio Economic Goals within the given time frame. Instead of uniform allocation of resources to blocks as is currently the practice in almost all the programmes, a more flexible and need-based approach should be taken. The segment of population and areas which have lagged behind in national development efforts, should be positively discriminated, so that they can be helped as quickly as possible to reach the minimum desired levels of standards and goals. But care should be taken to ensure that those blocks which have shown results do not feel discriminated against.

In order that district or block specific plans and projects can be prepared, implemented and monitored it is necessary to develop a system of gender segregated data on various indices of development at the district and sub district level at regular intervals. The absence of such data constraints the preparation of sound Women Development Plans at the field level.

The Medium Term perspective of 10 years should be adopted for the empowerment of women and development of children and adolescents. To that extent the National Socio Economic Goals of NPP should be accepted in the Action Plans for the Empowerment of Women and Development of Children and Adolescents. The achievement of these goals should be monitored on a quarterly basis and appraised on a bi-annual basis.

Involving the male is equally important for the empowerment of women and for stabilization of population. Reproductive decisions are typically taken within the family and hence promoting gender equality within the family has to be based on partnership and not on relationship of domination or subordination within the family. To achieve better understanding, every effort must be made to involve men in the promotion of reproductive rights. This is vital in order to change the societal perceptions about the contribution of women. This can happen only when women are seen by men-and by society-not as 'better halves' but as 'equal halves'. There is a large unmet need for contraceptives and comprehensive information regarding their efficacy and usage. There has to be greater focus on male contraceptives as they are safer and easier to use. New contraceptives for women need to be carefully introduced with the fully informed participation of women.

A system of incentives/disincentive for the functionaries as also the beneficiaries of various programmes should be developed to convey clear messages about the priorities of the Government regarding population stabilization of the country. However, in order to ensure that disincentives do not become a tool for harassing the disadvantaged, it is necessary to create an environment enabling the women to have self-determination in terms of their reproductive life.

The target of achieving 80% institutional deliveries by 2010 is a tall order, considering that more than half of the deliveries still take place at home at present. The idea of maternity hut in each village to be used as the village delivery room, with storage space for supplies and medicine, and equipped adequately with kits for midwifery, antenatal care and delivery and basic medicines, contraceptives and drugs and medicines for common ailments, is conceptually very sound but may be difficult to implement within the given time frame. A more realistic and practical alternative is to train and equip the village midwives to ensure 100% safe deliveries. This must be taken up immediately as a time bound national programme, to upgrade their skills.

In view of the shortage of trained medical personnel at the PHCs and dispensaries, it should be made mandatory for medical students in both Government and private medical colleges to go to designated rural areas for service for a period of 12 months after they complete one year of residency but before their final degree is awarded. Posting to rural areas for a minimum period of two years at a time should be legally binding for medical officers. Similar arrangements should also be made mandatory for nurses, pharmacists and other paramedical staff.

A Core Group of Women Functionaries at the village level such as ANM, AWW, lady school teacher and elected women Panchayat members could co-ordinate the various programmes on women and children at the village or hamlet level. They should meet once in a fortnight at a fixed place and date to discuss among themselves the progress of the implementation of the programmes and to sort out the problems and difficulties at the purely local level. Coordinating and an integrated approach rather than competition among the local functionaries is essential to ensure positive results. Common training and parity in salaries could ensure this.

Training and capacity building of field level functionaries, NGOs, SHG workers and PRI members are extremely important if they are to perform their desired roles for the achievement of National Socio Economic Goals. Role of Angan Wadi Workers (AWW) is very crucial for the success of the various grassroot level initiatives of the Government. Today the contribution of AWW is not limited to the ICDS only. Her services are required in other programmes also. But she is paid very little-even less than the minimum wage prescribed by the Government itself. Therefore, the honorarium of the AWWs should be enhanced suitably with incentives for results shown. But the AWW must be a local person who stays in the villages.

In view of unacceptable high neonatal and perinatal mortality a comprehensive package needs to be developed at block level concentrating on improving home based care through trained personnel, with adequate referral linkages.

Every infant and maternal death must be compulsorily audited, to have better understanding of the underlying factors for such deaths. Simultaneously, a system of accountability of every functionary must be put in place to fix responsibility for every action or inaction for causing or precipitating such deaths.

Certain clinical and medical interventions can result in immediate and significant improvement in the maternal mortality. Such interventions can also be very cost effective. For example, Tetanus Toxoid injections can prevent a significant percentage of maternal deaths. Such interventions can be taken as a campaign on fixed dates throughout the country, for which nation wide publicity can be given. The same occasion can also be utilized for the health check up of pregnant mothers.

The provisions of Pre-natal Diagnostic Act is not at all be effective in checking the practice of female foeticide, which have become rampant in many States. The requirement of prior permission of 'competent authority' before a case for violation of the provisions of the Act can be challaned before the court, has been found to be a hindrance for booking the offenders, since most of the States have designated the Director of Health Services as the competent authority and they have been found to be reluctant to take action against their colleague doctors. The Act needs to be reviewed thoroughly. More than that a concerted public opinion involving religious leaders and opinion makers from every field should be built up against this highly undesirable social practice.

A sustained, systematic, concerted and pervasive campaign in the print, electronic and folk media should be built up in support of the National Socio Economic Goals of NPP and on various issues related to empowerment of women, health related issues, value of girl child, rights of women, violence against women etc. Village melas and festivals, which bring people together, should be used to popularize these messages. The media budget of the entire social sector Ministries / departments should be pooled together for this campaign.

10

Future Prospects for Women Development

To be strictly logical one should not treat of woman apart from the rest of the human race, for this is in a manner to admit that women are a distinct class, not affected by conditions, environment, etc., as men are. But we find a "woman question" actually existing. A great deal of discussion has been going on as to what is proper for woman, what her real nature is, and how many of the duties and privileges of man she should be admitted to. Women do not occupy the same position, socially, politically, economically, or intellectually that men do, and her powers are not equal to her brother's. She is daily reproached for trying to be other than she is, and reminded that her very nature forbids her presuming to climb out of the subserviency and inferiority which are now undeniably her portion. Thus a "woman question" is forced upon us whether we will or not. It is to discover, if possible, whether she may ever become equal to and like man without perverting her inherent nature, that this inquiry is made.

It is impossible to ascertain whether there ever was a time when woman stood an equally strong intellectual and physical being, on an equal footing with man, or not. If it ever existed, its memory is now very hazy. Yet there are writers who refer to it as a fact. August Bébel, in "Woman: Past, Present, and Future," refers to it thus: "We have no grounds for assuming that in this primitive state men were physically or mentally superior to women.... Certain savage tribes were governed by women instead of men owing to the superior strength of the former.... Primeval woman, although the equal of man in bodily and mental power, nevertheless became his inferior when periods of pregnancy, birth, and lactation forced her to look to him for assistance, support, and protection."

And in a more mystical sense Olive Schreiner refers to the time: "And he answered: 'Listen and I will tell you. Ages and ages long she has lain here, and the wind has blown over her. The oldest, oldest man living has never seen her move; the oldest book records that she lay here then as she lays here now. But listen! Older than the oldest book, older than the oldest recorded memory of man, on the rocks of language, on the hard baked clay of ancient custom, are found the marks of her footsteps. Side by side with him who stands beside her, you may trace them, and you may know that she who now lies here once wandered free over the rocks with him.'"

Matilda Joslyn Gage, in her "Woman, Church, and State," lays great emphasis upon the days of matriarchy, when women, as mothers of the race, ruled the people. But we have no evidence that any such period ever existed. Letourneau shows that cases have been where inheritances descended and relationships were determined through the women of the tribe. Accompanying this usage, a certain importance adhered to the mothers of the tribe. It is true, women attained powerful and prominent positions in the old civilizations that have come and gone. The mythical lost Atlantis was peopled with great women of divine aspect. There were queens in the days of Solomon; and the Helens, Cleopatras, and Hypatias of history dot the dark pages with glints of a glory to come. A matriarchy never existed; cases of matriarchy have been known. Woman never stood beside man his equal in all things; women have ruled in isolated instances.

Be that as it may, woman's subordination came to be complete. She was first knocked down, dragged away senseless, and made a slave. She was bought and sold, or traded; she became a thing, a piece of property, a bond slave. Her degraded position among men became a custom, then an institution, then a tradition. There were centuries of "dark ages for her, into whose gloom no ray of light ever pierced, and from whose depths little has come down to us to tell the sombre story."

Slowly, very slowly man developed in intellect and acquired a rude knowledge of art. The woman in his tents could not remain very far behind him, and in time arose to some degree of companionship. That he treated her with a little kindness, and even appealed to her in times of weariness or perplexity for sympathy or counsel, was due, not to his traditions and creeds conceived in another grade of civilization, but to changed conditions and his own developed nature. There might even have arisen a "woman's rights question" in those old Mosaic days, had not the priests, who feared any loosening of their control over the people, issued a "Thus saith the Lord," and so riveted her chains for another three thousand years. "Thy desire shall be unto thy husband, and he shall rule over thee," settled the problem for the time.

"Economic dependence is the basis of all slavery," Bébel says; and he is right. All forms of slavery had their inception in some kind of economic dependence, but the slavery often exists long after the dependent condition has passed away. A thing, once established, once made an institution, is very apt to outlast the economic phase which determined its existence, and become a very troublesome matter. Institutions are crystallized ideas; they stand still: people grow--grow beyond and outside of them. Yet there they remain, unwieldy, mischief-breeding; to get rid of them at all is to tear them out by the roots at great cost of life and suffering. The bonds made ages ago, by economic conditions prevailing at the time, have become sacred; they bear another strength than that which they possessed when first formed. Though no longer with any economical basis for existing, they are even more effective in power than when first established.

Individually men are not to blame for the inferior position of women. They accepted a condition, a chain of customs, as they found them. Though long past the time when constant danger from without rendered it necessary that his whole family give him implicit obedience, the habit of expecting filial deference is fixed. Though the days of absolute property in wives have gone by, the sense of proprietorship in and responsibility for wives still prevails. That sentiment which played upon the superstitious fears of woman, setting a sort of mental watchdog to guard the master's property in his absence as well as when present, still exists in a modified form in the demand for perfect chastity in woman not expected man. The old feeling of ownership, which led men to seclude their women, has softened into that modern sentiment which would keep women guarded from the public gaze in every respect. The stern commands of old are toned down into "what is expected of womanly women," but that expectation is as binding as any chain or title deed to person could be.

Thus, through ages of subserviency, of which there were many grades, women have come to be what they are: emotional, since any prominent display of other faculties has been unnecessary in that "sphere to which it has pleased God to call her;" deceitful, since deceit has been her only weapon; illogical, since the encouragement of her reasoning powers would have often placed her in direct opposition to her master; vain, since her personal charms were long the only qualities for which she was considered; weak-minded, since strong brains were not desirable in that function to which man wished to limit her. So from long persisting conditions woman has come to be the creature she is.

But the change in woman's position and in the manner in which woman is considered during the last fifty years has been a remarkable one. We scarcely realize its greatness until we begin to compare the prominent women of today with women of the last century. It is perhaps correct to say that Mary Wollstonecraft began the modern woman's-rights movement. Her work, "The Rights of Women," written toward the close of the last century, is read more widely now than at the time of publication. It was many years before an organized effort was made to secure political equality for women. The movement, which has lasted through the lifetime of some of America's noblest women, though a little too narrow for modern sociological students, has been a great element in the remarkable change. Unconsciously it has builded better than it knew, and helped to widen the field and elevate the aspirations of women far more than the originators ever intended.

The introduction of machinery has been the most potent factor in the transition. When the work of the world was done in the home, when the spinning-wheel, the loom, the soap vat, the "pig-killing," the bake oven, and the slender needle were institutions in every household, naturally "woman's place" was at home. But spinning-wheel and loom turned into great cotton and woollen mills; the pork-barrel became the vast packing-houses of our large cities; the needle was reserved for mending, and great clothing establishments took its place; the old lye barrel gave way to immense soap factories; and family ovens were relegated to the past, for the bakeries that now supply the staff of life.

It was no longer profitable to make these things in the seclusion of the home; and women followed the machines and went in great crowds to the factories. The demand for women's work came at a time when a new restlessness was pervading the inner sanctum of the home. Secluded and protected, kindly treated though they might happen to be, women began to feel that they were not living full, true lives. They felt that all their faculties were not being developed, that all their powers for giving and receiving happiness were not being called out. Though the duties of motherhood might for the time being occupy all their time and energies, it was also true that not all women were mothers of children, nor were the mothers always mothers of young children. A woman's life stretches over many periods, as does man's. In a lifetime she is capable of being much more than a mother, as man is expected to be much more than a father.

The restlessness was natural. Women came out into the world and became acquainted with each other and with their working brothers; they took a broader view of life; and something of that feeling of fraternity to which men had attained in their clubs, lodges, and unions, began to take lodgment in their breasts. For the "old" woman had no conception of the brotherhood of the human race. She loved her own passionately, and she loved her immediate friends; she loved her church and believed in a vague way that she "loved all men," as a good Christian should. But of the real solidarity of the human race, of the truth that "an injury to one is the concern of all," she had no conception. The "new woman" has a very fair realizing sense of this great social truth today. And therefore, though she may be more of a slave in the factory than she was in the narrow confines of home, she has come up higher. She has reached greater opportunities for full, well-developed existence; and though she makes some mistakes, she is far advanced in her evolutionary progress. But as yet she is no happier, and men are not pleased. They think she has taken their places in the workshop, in the office, and at the business desk; they fear to lose the sweet, clinging, fragile, wheedling little creature they imagine they love; and they have not reached a conception of what the free, self-poised, capable, womanly woman of the future will be. They are not very well satisfied with the crude sample of the "new woman;" and they are in a manner drawing away from her in the consciousness of a lofty superiority which never needs a transitional stage.

Women themselves are not happy, because they are not yet accustomed to the new order--an order that is as yet chaotic and undefined. Just out from the unwholesome hothouse air of their old seclusion, the atmosphere of comparative freedom and independence strikes too harshly upon them, and they shiver. They cannot go back, and they cannot yet breathe easily. They can do wonders in adaptation, but they cannot find their equilibrium in half a generation of partial freedom. The adjusting process hurts; it always does.

What is it that woman wants? What is it she hopes to attain? What is it she lacks that men are not willing to give? It is no wonderful thing; nothing preposterous or presumptuous. She simply wants to be a human being, not a slave, not a toy, not a queen. She wants the equal personal liberty that every man demands in order to become a fully developed, well-balanced, happy, and useful being. Only this and nothing more.

With this emancipation--this "liberty to do whatsoever one wills so long as one [does not infringe] on the equal right of others to do as they will"--she needs not even the chivalry of old. Kindness, sympathy, love from equals she needs in common with man. She needs not that spirit of worship which some men who think they are "advanced" seem willing to pour out upon her; she needs not that undue devotion on account of her motherhood which many good people believe is right and just; she needs not that right which Robert Ingersoll declared she must possess when he said: "Women should have all the rights that men possess and one more--the right to be protected." The right to be a human being includes that right when necessary. If every individual in the world possesses an equal right to life, liberty, and the pursuit of happiness, the right of opportunity at nature's table, the right to develop to the highest she is capable of becoming, the rights of motherhood and womanhood are conceded. No better protection is needed than that which any enlightened human being will naturally give to another if circumstances make it imperative. A free woman will not choose to be "protected" in the old sense. Protection has ever been an implication of weakness and a willingness to occupy a subordinate position. Nations which call upon other nations for protection must needs give up for that protection some portion of their independence; and industries that can flourish only under "protection" create slaves in their turn.

A great fear seems to exist that if women were perfectly free to become whatever they see fit many dire calamities would happen. Woman would become "mannish;" she would lose her delicate sense of morality; and she might slight that one great duty to which she has been almost wholly consigned for so many ages. But why do we hesitate to trust woman free, when she has fulfilled so many precious trusts in bondage? I have no fear that motherhood and love is a great part of the sweetness of life, and free women are not likely to yield up any part of their happiness.

This one great fear seems to lie at the bottom of every objection to the full freedom and equality of woman--the fear that she will refuse to do her duty by the human race. It is the last prejudice, the last of the old traditions, that man is willing to let go. He will go so far as to admit the right of suffrage, to accept equal property rights, to grant equal opportunities in all the fields of human activity, but he cannot rid himself of that sacred old tenet: that a woman cannot be a good wife and mother if she have any other interest in life besides her home and children. Even very radical thinkers still at times declare that "woman's crowning glory is motherhood;" and only insist on equal opportunities and unequal consideration that she may be more fully and perfectly the mother. I am aware that I am proving myself a startling heretic to generally accepted ideas, but I most emphatically dissent.

I am aware that throughout the realm of nature the one blind impulse of every living thing is to reproduce itself. Everything else seems to be sacrificed to this one object. In the lowest living organisms individual identity is completely lost in the separation which creates two where one existed before. A little higher up in the scale extinction follows reproduction; and for many degrees in the ascending gamut the sole purpose of existence seems to be simply reproduction. But as the higher forms of life evolve, in both the animal and the vegetable kingdoms, more and more of life is utilized in other ways. Trees live to give shelter and shade, and they minister to our sense of beauty through many years; the higher animals have many uses, and many years of animal enjoyment, aside from the function of reproduction.

In the lower grades of human life the power of reproduction seems the most important part of existence. But as the race advances, develops, acquires knowledge, the existence of its members becomes rich and full with the wealth of life itself. The individual becomes an emphasized, distinct identity. It is something to the world that a bright, sound individual lives, acts, and thinks, even though it is never reproduced. The male portion of the race already feel as though fatherhood were a mere incident in their lives, and would be insulted were you to intimate that fatherhood should be the crowning glory of their lives. They know that they possess powers and capabilities that the world needs and appreciates, and that fatherhood, blessed though it be, is not the fullest and best manifestation of their existence. The idea is in every way as applicable to woman as to man. Why should all the faculties and energies of woman be turned to the fulfilment of this one function of her being?

It is flattering to man to think that it takes all of a woman's whole life to carry out her duty to him and his children. But if he only knew it, the entire devotion of her powers to this one purpose is the poorest preparation for wifehood and motherhood that can be made. Even the man himself feels a sort of undefined contempt for the woman who is nothing but wife and mother. A woman becomes morbid who simply retires within herself to brood over her fitness or unfitness for her "crowning glory." It is distorting, dwarfish, narrowing. Her child is unfavorably affected by this intensity of thought centred upon its embryonic existence. It is like that unwholesome "self-analysis" which has ever made up so great a part of the old religious creeds, and which still crops up in modified forms in the "new philosophies."

Let the woman live for herself, not for unborn children. Let her fill her life to the brim with happiness, knowledge, mental and physical activity; let lofty emotions and vigorous thoughts fill her being; let her whole existence expand to its fullest extent; let her forget her motherhood; she will be the better mother for first being a perfect woman. And to be this she must first be free. It will not do to ask what she will do with her freedom, to criticise, to judge; one must only wait. "The cure for the evils of liberty is more liberty."

Do not fear for the result. The trend of human evolution is upward and onward. The plant allowed to grow freely, in the sunlight, with warm rich soil and pure fresh air, will develop to its very highest possibilities. Cramp it, interfere with it, abstract either light or warmth, and it becomes a stunted, pale, sickly growth. Looking upon it, no one could tell what it might have become under proper conditions.

Do not fear that woman thus freed would become a poor mimicry of a poor sample of a man. To become "mannish" is in the eyes of conventional society worse than to commit a crime. But what do we mean by this term? If it is anything reprehensible, believe me, it is as bad in man as in woman. Does it apply to the manners, morals, or the intellect? It is very vague at best. For those qualities which we call "good" are as beautiful in man as in woman. We love bravery, self-poise, strength, honor, truthfulness in one as well as in the other. We love gentleness, kindness, sympathy, tact in both sexes. We see today timid men and brave women; weak-minded men and strong-minded women; deceitful men and truthful women; vain men and self-forgetful women. Under equal and similar conditions the virtues and vices would be diffused much more equally. For I hold another heresy: that there is no sex in intellect, sentiment, or morals. The same environment, the same treatment, the same teachings would result in a similarity of characteristics. There will never cease to be variety, but we should not find a greater tendency toward any particular group of faculties in one sex over the other.

True, some scientific scholars declare that it is a physical impossibility for woman under any condition to become man's equal in physical and mental strength, or to become free from her emotional disturbances and sensitiveness of nerves. The shape, size, and quality of the brain, they say, preclude this; her peculiar functions, the time and energy necessary to the bearing of children and the nourishing of them, prevent a change from her present nature. Nevertheless this is not a demonstrated truth; no one knows by actual experiment whether it is true or not. The fact that all human creatures are the subject of environment and of hereditary conditions signifies that woman is no exception. There is every reason to suppose that under like conditions with men, women would develop in a manner as men do. Woman's peculiar functions should not create the sharp distinctions now seen. Weakness, dependence, emotionalism, vanity, deceitfulness have been cultivated in woman; these traits have been considered her greatest attractions; tradition, custom, public opinion have fixed them upon her, and it will take long to eliminate them.

There is no reason why woman should devote more of her time and energies to motherhood than man does to fatherhood. Work, activity, interest in other things, both while carrying and nourishing children, are better than idleness. No special training, no particular occupation or exercise of one's faculties, or the cessation of activities, are necessary as a preparation for motherhood. The life which makes a woman all she is capable of being as a human being is the only one essential to the rearing of good children. So little is required of a mother that need interfere with ordinary duties and occupations, that it is difficult to see how motherhood should have, in itself, such a wonderful differentiating effect.

Woman has been considered too much as woman, and not enough as a human being. The constant reference to her sex has been neither ennobling, complimentary, nor agreeable. Either as slave, toy, pet, or queen, this ceaseless thinking of her sex instead of herself has been degrading. To finally arrive at her best she simply needs consideration as a fellow member of society.

Do not fear liberty. Just now the results of the beginnings of freedom do not seem very satisfactory. Woman seems to be an intruder; she cannot overcome at once the prejudices that had their inception in the time of her complete economic dependence. She herself is dissatisfied. She is not as lovable perhaps. She has lost some of the charm of clinging womanhood which at best man only heeded in his leisure moments, and has not yet gained the poise and individuality that will draw him to her as a companion. She is dissatisfied with the old gallantry, and has not yet attained the spontaneous recognition and respectful love she longs for. But this will come. There will be a time when men and women, equal human beings, clasping hands and looking each other in the eyes on a level--not leaning on each other, but upright--will feel a true fellowship; and mutual admiration and respect will exist between them. Then will love be sweeter, purer, more beautiful than the world has ever known.

11

Women's Law in India

Community organization is an essential component of Action India's multi-pronged approach to stop violence against women. We provide direct support to women experiencing abuse and injustice through our Women, Law and Social Change program, which has trained sixty-four paralegal workers from the community to take on case work; counsel women in need; and provide referrals to the police, lawyers, or the formal judicial system when necessary. Our program includes the following components:

- Organizes Mahila Panchayats at the grassroots level.
- Oversees the investigation, case registration, arbitration, judgment, and follow-up of domestic violence cases.
- Conducts legal literacy workshops for educating grassroots women.
- Builds the capacity of community based paralegal caseworkers.
- Provides legal aid and counseling to women in crisis situations.

The Mahila Panchayats provide an opportunity for women and men to speak openly and fearlessly when seeking interventions and arbitrations to resolve disputes. The panchayats do not replace the judicial system. Instead, they present a cost-effective, intermediary solution that is women-led, gender-sensitive, and in touch with the needs of the community.

Our goals for the coming year include enlisting the support of our panchayat networks toward the implementation of the recently passed Domestic Violence Act. We envision that the panchayats could serve as an intermediary link in the referral of domestic violence cases to 'protection officers' — officials designated by the act for the protection of women.

Innovation: Action India believes that any strategy toward systemic change and policy advocacy requires a mass demand from the grassroots. A woman seeking redress for injustice can come to the Mahila Panchayat to express her problems in a safe and welcoming environment. Our Mahila Panchayat network has mobilized women and community leaders to change their subordinate position in the family and move towards building more equal partnerships. As an example of how recognized and integrated the Mahila Panchayats are within their communities, in the year 2006 ten Mahila Panchayats in the four slums of Dakshinpuri, Jahangirpuri, Sundernagri and New Seemapuri saw 450 women.

In September 2000, the Delhi Commission for Women recognized the Mahila Panchayats as a critically important aspect of its Make Delhi Safe for Women campaign. The Commission asked Action India to replicate our program with twenty-nine NGOs and community-based organizations in Delhi. The structure of our Mahila Panchayat system now consists of fifteen partner organizations throughout the NCT Delhi, who collaborate closely with Action India to maintain thirty-eight Mahila Panchayats. Action India directly oversees eight Mahila Panchayats, and additionally supervises the remaining fifteen partner organizations in their oversight of thirty Mahila Panchayats. Each panchayat is equipped with two paralegals, trained by Action India. The remaining panchayat members are volunteers from the community.

The Mahila Panchayat system is unique in that it employs a collective structure to promote women's decision-making power. Social pressure is a powerful motivating force for the community. Both men and women listen to the judgments made by the Mahila Panchayat because to ignore the decisions can mean social embarrassment and ostracism. Women in the panchayat are known for their outspoken actions to bring attention to a case, including publicly shaming men who have abused their wives and demanding action from the police.

Delivery Model: The Mahila Panchayat, including two paralegals, holds hearings every Wednesday. The panchayat meets at a designated time and place to ensure that the communities have a regular mechanism to address violence against women. Parties come with their family or friends and place their arguments in a non-threatening atmosphere.

To develop a panchayat, paralegals must build relationships with the community and identify members who can strengthen their individual panchayats. Once a case is heard, a notice is served to call the other party to the panchayat. Both parties are encouraged to speak face-to-face and resolve conflict on their own terms. A compromise and/or settlement are written on letterhead paper in the presence of witnesses.

Once a case has been concluded, follow-up is crucially important. The paralegals visit the family as many times as necessary to determine that the family is upholding its responsibility to the compromise made in the panchayat.

When panchayat members are not arbitrating cases, Action India facilitates workshops on gender awareness and legal literacy to help sharpen their understanding of the social and political environment. Gender awareness is taught by Action India's case workers and other grassroots staff. Legal literacy is introduced by legal resource persons from numerous organizations. Action India hosts numerous legal awareness camps, trainings for paralegals and coordinators, and trainings for Mahila Panchayat members.

The Mahila Panchayats also serve as an important mobilization mechanism for the launching of grassroots campaigns on violence against women. The Mahila Panchayat network has taken up the issue of child marriage, India's declining sex ratio, and the domestic violence act. This year, the network will focus heavily on the implementation of the domestic violence act, the PNDT Act, and the elimination of gender-based violence through our participation in Oxfam's We Can Campaign.

Key Operational Partnerships: Action India has cultivated important partnerships at every level of the Mahila Panchayat network. Our primary partnerships are our relationships with the fifteen NGOs that we currently partner with to run the network, including Child Survival India, Navrishti, MYRADO, and Indicare. In addition, the Delhi Commission for Women has provided financial support and designated Action India the 'mother NGO' of the network.

The panchayat regularly refers cases to lawyers through a free legal aid cell established by the government, through NGOs that provide legal services, through the Delhi Commission for Women, the National Commission for Women, or to the police. Once or twice a year, Action India facilitates a meeting between the police and the members of the Mahila Panchayat. The police have also been known to refer cases back to the Mahila Panchayats—an example of how established the Mahila Panchayats have become within their communities.

Our trainings of paralegals and Mahila Panchayat volunteers also rely heavily on partnerships that we have developed with local NGOs, government authorities, and our own grassroots workers from other Action India programs. These partnerships ensure sustainability and play a central role in driving our initiatives. Financial Model: Action India's programs are entirely designed to support low-income and marginalized populations. Beneficiaries are not required to pay any money. If they are able to pay, Action India asks that those filing cases pay Rs.20 (approximately US .45). In addition, during the arbitration phase of the proceedings, those filing cases are required to pay Rs.50/ day (approximately US$1). This helps move along the arbitration process by ensuring that participants work to resolve the conflict, as opposed to getting mired in the conflict.

Mahila Panchayat members are volunteers from the community who volunteer their time and resource inputs. As a result of their efforts, the entire community benefits in its ability to access Mahila Panchayat courts. The Mahila Panchayat system itself is an extremely cost-effective mechanism by which women can access justice. Mahila Panchayats allow women to save money and time as India's formal court systems are notoriously backlogged and corrupt. This additionally provides a great service to women who feel that they have no where to turn. The panchayat system provides them most of all with a feeling of community support.

- What percentage, if any, of the total operating costs does earned income (from products, services, or other fees) represent?
- How is the initiative financed? Is it financially self-sustainable or profitable? How much do beneficiaries contribute? The initiative is currently financed by a grant from the Delhi Commission for Women, which is in its last phase. The project is neither financially self-sustainable or profitable. Beneficiaries contribute only through the services provided. They do not earn monetary compensation.

Effectiveness: Over time, we have seen tremendous success through our Mahila Panchayat network. Fourteen hundred women are accessing the courts, and the courts continue to provide an intermediary mechanism of redress that assists the community. In addition, the Mahila Panchayat is a women's space to share joys and sorrows, give and get information, and become a concerned and active citizen. We have seen that survivors of domestic violence realize that they are not alone. The feelings of collective strength offered by the support group allow women to move beyond their fears and recognize their struggle in the context of a patriarchal system that oppresses women.

Thus our ultimate success has been the growth of empowered women in the slums. These women learn to articulate their problems without feeling guilt or failure. With counseling, they learn to make decisions and find solutions to their problems. Often, they feel satisfied with the process and the resolution, and all parties work to cooperate following the outcome. This change reflects positively on children and family members, and works to enhance the quality of their lives. These aspects of personal development come through a process that is not always clear-cut. Though there are setbacks and failures, the encouragement of the support group enables women to continue their struggle to end the violence in their lives. In a supportive environment, the "victims" of violence can come forward to help other women.

How many people have benefited from your program over the last year? Which element of the program proved itself most effective? The full network of courts deals with approximately 1,400 cases per year. There are approximately 900 grassroots members in the network, all volunteers. In 2006, our 219 legal awareness camps were attended by nearly 10,000 people. These workshops were held for the women in the panchayats, and participating women's groups, and included information on women's rights and the opportunities and limitations of the laws. We also held trainings to build the capacity of members of the panchayats, to train women at the grassroots level in the areas of law, gender, leadership and conflict resolution. 1,140 people participated in these trainings last year. These number do not represent the thousands of additional people who benefit from the program second-hand: the families of those women who seek redress in panchayat courts, and the community-members who benefit from access to the panchayat network.

The most effective element of the program has been the strength of the community's participation toward building pressure to prevent violence against women. Women are willing to volunteer their time and energy to be a part of this functioning system.

Scaling up Strategy: Our priority for the coming years is to position the Mahila Panchayat network to act as service providers to facilitate the implementation of the Protection of Women from Domestic Violence Act.

The Mahila Panchayat network has been deeply engaged in advocacy around the PWDV Act, which is far more comprehensive and gender-sensitive than any other recognized legislation on gender-based violence. With the passage of the law in 2005, we must now turn our attention to its implementation—assuring that appropriate protection officers are appointed, and that an appropriate budget is allocated to fulfill the obligations of the bill. The success of this civil law is that it recognizes the widespread prevalence of violence in the home and lays out steps for victims of abuse to take action.

We envision that the Mahila Panchayat network can play an important role in ensuring that proper steps are taken, by working with women at the community level to educate them about the act, and referring victims of abuse to the appropriate authorities.

We intend to continue our regular Mahila Panchayat arbitration proceedings, but also serve as a direct conduit in the implementation of the act.

STAGE OF THE INITIATIVE: MATURE

Origin of the Initiative: At the height of the women's autonomous movement in India in the 1980s, Action India initiated forums that enabled women from the community to articulate discontent and recognize underlying patterns of discrimination in their lives. The forums introduced a safe space to share the reality of domestic violence, dowry burning, rape, and sexual harassment. As these collectives developed, they evolved into Mahila Panchayats in 1994, which formalized the role that women had begun to play in resolving marital disputes and conflict situations within the family. As an outgrowth of this work, we began to train paralegal workers from the community to assist in the arbitration of family disputes.

Main Obstacles to Scaling Up: 1. Lack of sustainable financial support. Lack of long-term support. We find ourselves scrambling periodically to renew funding, which severly exhausts our time and existing resources.

Main Partnership Challenges: Our biggest challenge with our partners is training them to adhere to our rights-based model, which we have developed over a long period of time. Individual NGOs may attempt to develop their Mahila Panchayats in their own way, and it is the responsibility of Action India to conduct trainings to ensure that the process is systematized and based on a human rights framework.

DOWRY LAW IN INDIA

Payment of a dowry, gift — often financial, has a long history in many parts of the world. In India, the payment of a dowry was prohibited in 1961 under Indian civil law and subsequently by Sections 304B and 498a of the Indian Penal Code were enacted to make it easier for the wife to seek redress from potential harassment by the husband's family. Dowry laws has come under criticism that they are misused by women and their families.

Dowries

Gifts given by the parents of the bride are considered "stri-dhan", i.e. property of the woman, traditionally representing her share of her parent's wealth.

The 1961 Dowry Prohibition Act

This act prohibits the request, payment or acceptance of a dowry, "as consideration for the marriage". where "dowry" is defined as a gift demanded or given as a precondition for a marriage. Gifts given without a precondition are not considered dowry, and are legal. Asking or giving of dowry can be punished by an imprisonment of up to six months, or a fine of up to Rs. 5000. It replaced several pieces of anti-dowry legislation that had been enacted by various Indian states.

IPC Section 304B

This Section of the Indian Penal Code was inserted by a 1986 amendment. The Dowry deaths law defines a 'dowry death' as the death of a woman caused by any burns or bodily injury or which does not occur under normal circumstances within seven years of her marriage. For a woman's death to be a dowry death, it must also be shown that soon before her death she was subjected to cruelty or harassment by her husband or any relative of her husband for, or in connection with, any demand for dowry. If this is proved, the woman's husband or relative is required to be deemed to have caused her death. Whoever commits dowry death is required to be punished with imprisonment for a term which shall not be less than seven years but which may extend to imprisonment for life.

IPC Section 498A

Section 498A was inserted into the penal code in 1983 it reads:

Whoever, being the husband or the relative of the husband of a woman, subjects such woman to cruelty shall be punished with imprisonment for a term which may extend to three years and shall also be liable to fine. In practice, cruelty is taken to include the demanding of a dowry. This section is non-bailable, non-compoundable (i.e. it cannot be privately resolved between the parties concerned) and cognizable (i.e. the police can arrest the accused without investigation or warrants) on a report from a woman or close relative. Another examples of a cognizable law in India was the Prevention of Terrorist Activities Act.

Police often file charges against the husband, his parents and other relatives (whoever being named on the complaint by the wife or her close relatives) and put them in jail. There is no penalty (even a fine) for filing a false case. Many individuals have claimed this is being abused by the wife or her close relatives.

In urban India, the majority of families have adequate knowledge regarding section 498A of the Indian Penal Code, 1860. The Malimath committee in 2003 proposed making amendments to this section although such amendments have been opposed by women's groups. The Centre for Social Research India has released a research report opposing amendments to section 498A. According to this report, in the studied cases there were no convictions based solely on section 498A. Although the report states that 60.5 percent of the studied cases were falsified. They also state that many people believe the law has been abused by "educated and independent minded women." A police official asserted that in his district one-third of dowry murder cases were found totally false by the police.

However, on December 17, 2003, the then Minister of State for Home Affairs, Mr. I.D Swami said: "There is no information available with the Government to come to the conclusion that many families in India are suffering due to exaggerated allegations of harassment and dowry cases made by women against their husbands and other family members involving them in criminal misappropriation and cruelty."

On 20 July 2005, Justices Arijit Pasayat and H.K. Seema of the Indian Supreme Court declared Section 498A to be constitutional."The object is to strike at the root of dowry menace. But by misuse of the provision a new legal terrorism can be unleashed. The provision is intended to be used as a shield and not an assassin's weapon. If [the] cry of "wolf" is made too often as a prank, assistance and protection may not be available when the actual wolf appears," the Bench said.

Several reports of the abuse of Section 498A have involved couples based outside India especially in the US. The United States Department of State has published the following travel warning: A number of U.S. citizen men who have come to India to marry Indian nationals have been arrested and charged with crimes related to dowry extraction. Many of the charges stem from the U.S. citizen's inability to provide an immigrant visa for his prospective spouse to travel immediately to the United States.

The courts sometimes order the U.S. citizen to pay large sums of money to his spouse in exchange for the dismissal of charges. The courts normally confiscate the American's passport, and he must remain in India until the case has been settled.

In a well publicized case, Dr. Balamurali Ambati, who earned his MD at age 17, and his family were detained in India for over 3 years in a suit related to alleged dowry demands by the family for his brother's wife Archana, which delayed Dr. Ambati's entry to the ophthalmology program for 2 years, leaving him to begin his residency in 1998. All charges against him were dismissed in October of 1996 and all his family members were acquitted in June 1999 . During the course of the trial the Ambatis produced a tape in which the father of Archana, demanded US $500,000 to drop all the charges although the details of this particular case are still debated in India. Section 498A in itself is, however, not meant to deal specifically with dowry — it is commonly considered to be a 'dowry law' because domestic violence against a wife related to dowry demands is considered to be within the scope of 'cruelty' envisaged by the Section.

DIVORCE IN INDIA

The Law

All major religions have their own laws which govern divorces within their own community, and separate regulations exist regarding divorce in interfaith marriages.

Hindus, including Buddhists, Sikhs and Jains, are governed by the Hindu Marriage Act, 1955; Christians by the Indian Divorce Act, 1869; Parsis by the Parsi Marriage and Divorce Act, 1936; and Muslims by the Dissolution of Muslim Marriages Act, 1939, which provides the grounds on which women can obtain a divorce, and the uncodified civil law. Civil marriages and inter-community marriages and divorces are governed by the Special Marriage Act, 1956 (Kapur and Cossman 101).

Other community specific legislation includes the Native Converts' Marriage Dissolution Act, 1866 that allows a Hindu to appeal for a divorce if a spouse converts to Christianity (Virdi 36-37).

Grounds for Divorce

In most Western nations, there are approximately 16 distinct reasons for which divorces are granted. In India, however, only five main reasons are generally accepted as sufficient grounds for divorce (Choudhary 90).

Adultery. While no formal definition of adultery exists, it does have "a fairly established meaning in matrimonial law" (Diwan 171), namely "the voluntary sexual intercourse of a married man or woman with a person other than the offender's wife or husband" (Choudhary 91). While the law considers it valid grounds for either sex, adulterous women are "judged more harshly" than men (Kapur and Cossman 102). The various religious regulations a e not unanimous on this issue. The law regarding Hindus allows divorce to be granted on the grounds of infidelity of either husband or wife. The Christian law, however, would traditionally not have granted a divorce to a woman solely on the grounds of adultery. She would have had to prove another violation, such as cruelty (Kapur and Cossman 102-4). A recent Bombay High Court decision "recognised cruelty and desertion as independent grounds for the dissolution of a Christian marriage," striking down a section of the law that allowed for an unconstitutional distinction between the sexes (Raiker-Mhatre 1).

Desertion. The three main components of desertion are the "disruption of cohabitation, absence of just or reasonable cause and their combination throughout three years" before the abandoned spouse may petition for a divorce (Virdi 71). There also must be an obvious intent on the part of the offending spouse to remain permanently apart from the other. This statute also applies to cases in which a spouse has been heard from for at least seven years (Choudhary 91). Cruelty. As with adultery, "the definition of the type of behavior that constitutes cruelty varies according to the gender of the petitioner" of the divorce. "Despite the fact that cruelty is often equally available to husbands and wives, the way in which the law is interpreted and applied suggests that women and men are evaluated by rather different standards" (Kapur and Cossman 105). This category includes both physical and mental abuse and neglect (Choudhary 91). A court decision made in early May 1997 made cruelty sufficient grounds for a Christian woman to obtain a; previously, the law required both adultery and cruelty to be proven. The national Indian Christian community seems to have embraced this judgment (Raikar-Mhatre 1-2.

Impotency. This refers to the physical inability of the couple to consummate the marriage (Choudhary 91) or the refusal by one spouse to do so (Diwan 136). Some cases have established that sterility can be construed to mean non-consummation if the other partner is not aware of the condition before the marriage (Diwan 139).

Chronic Disease. Both mental and physical illnesses are included in this category, as well as sexually transmitted diseases (Choudhary 92). Not all religions recognize identical diseases as grounds for divorce. Christians and Parsis do not allow divorce for a sexually transmitted disease or leprosy while the other communities do (Diwan 204-5).

Consequences of Divorce

Economic. There is great disparity between the economic ramifications of divorce between men and women. Men remain relatively unaffected while women, especially those with children, have difficulty "providing food, clothing and shelter for themselves and their children." The government in urban areas usually provides some form of public assistance to single mothers, but this service is not fully taken advantage of because most do not know of its existence (Amato 210). Often a woman is not able to rely on her family for support because many parents "feel they have discharged their obligations to a daughter by arranging her marriage and providing a dowry." Dowries are not returned after a divorce. Also, due to the social stigma of divorce, women find it difficult to remarry and usually attempt to establish an independent household (Amato 211).

Social. While India feels that one should have the right to divorce, it is still a highly stigmatizing action. Women are looked upon more harshly than men in this regard. There continue to be segments of Indian society that feel divorce is never an option, regardless of how abusive or adulterous the husband may be which adds to the greater disapproval for women. A divorced woman often will return to her family, but may not be wholeheartedly welcomed. She puts, especially if she has children, an economic burden on her family and is often given lowly household tasks to perform. There is also the risk that a divorced woman's presence would ward off possible marriages for other daughters within the household. Unavoidably, the overall status of the family and household are lowered by having a divorcee living with amongst them. A woman's class and caste are a major factor in her acceptance back into society. Women from higher classes tend to have an easier time than middle or lower class women in returning to the social order after a divorce. An exception to this model is the extreme bottom of the society who have experienced little rebuff from peers after a divorce. This results from their already atypical status in society (Amato 212-4).

Divorce in The God of Small Things

In Arundhati Roy's The God of Small Things, the marriage and quick divorce of Ammu has devastating consequences, reflecting the social and cultural stigma of divorce in India:

> "...Ammu left her husband and returned, unwelcomed, to her parents in Ayemenem. To everything she had fled from only a few years ago. Excpet now she had two children. And no more dreams" (42).

> "Baby Kochamma resented Ammu, because she saw her quarreling with a fate that she, Baby Kochamma herself, felt she had graciously accepted. The fate of the wretched Man-less woman" (44-5).

> "...the commonly held view that a married daughter had no position in her parents' home. As for a divorced

daughteræaccording to Baby Kochamma, she had no position anywhere at ali" (45).

Chacko "said that Ammu and Estha and Rahel were millstones around his neck" (82).

"Die-vorced?" His voice rose in such a high register that it cracked on the question mark. He even pronounced the word as though it was a form of death" (124).

"She was [Estha and Rahel's] Ammu and their Baba and she had loved them Double" (155).

Women's Rights and Wrongs

The All India Muslim Personal Law Board proclaims that triple talaq is a social evil, but it is equally assertive that this social evil should not be removed by legislative reform. There is no question of banning the practice. Maulana Sayed Rabey Al-Hasani Naqvi, the Board president, says: "Our laws are based on divine inspiration and triple talaq comes from the same inspiration, that is, Shariat. We have no powers to amend or abolish it. So the triple talaq is irrevocable." It is difficult to understand how what is divine can at the same time be evil.

The Hindu religion has also been replete with many social evils that Hindu women had to face. The practice of sati which forceda Hindu woman to sit on the funeral pyre of her husband was abolished by the Sati Regulation Act, 1829, itself the result of a social reform movement launched by Raja Rammohun Roy. The reform was taken to its logical conclusion with the Widows Remarriage Act of 1856.

Among Hindus, polygamy too was rampant. Yet it was abolished first in Bombay State by the Bombay Prevention of Hindu Bigamous Marriages Act, 1946. Later, the Hindu Marriage Act, 1955, put an end to polygamy throughout the country. Marriage among Hindus had been held to be sacrosanct, something that could not be dissolved — yet the Hindu Marriage Act, 1955, provides for dissolution of marriage both by husband and wife on the grounds stated in the Hindu Marriage Act. The Indian Divorce Act has also been recently amended to do away with inequality between women and men in matters of divorce among

Christians. Untouchability, yet another social evil, was outlawed by Article 17 of our Constitution.

Social and legal reforms must move together to ensure that all social evils are banished. It is often said that personal laws are outside the purview of challenge under Article 13 of the Constitution of India. But this has no constitutional or legal basis. The fact is that what is inhuman is both unconstitutional and illegal.

A very interesting answer to the argument of the Muslim Personal Law Board lies in the fact that in several Muslim countries triple talaq has been banned or restricted. There are several countries where there is a uniform law of divorce, for all citizens irrespective of their religion. The power to legislate on marriage and divorce is specifically conferred in entry 5, List III, Schedule VII of our Constitution.

In legal awareness camps for Muslim women which I attend and help organise regularly, women of all ages, young and old, ask me one question again and again: How can a Muslim marry four times when Hindu, Christian or Parsi men can marry only once? How is that there is a right of triple talaq for men and no right of divorce for us? I ask them to raise their voice against triple talaq, for a model Nikahnama that will secure them their rights.

Discrimination against women regardless of their religion is a matter of grave concern. The days of patriarchy are at an end. Today women are taking their rightful place in all walks of life. After the Second World War, we made a transition to a world of human rights. The United Nations Charter proclaims that all human beings are born free and equal. Contrast this with the American constitution, which proclaimed that all men are born free and equal. The Beijing Declaration also proclaims women's rights as human rights.

We cannot continue to dither on the enforcement of basic fundamental rights of women. The sooner the evil of polygamy and triple talaq in our country are banned and banished the better. The Women's Reservation Bill has still to be passed. In the Hindi belt of our country, Hindu women have been deprived of the right of inheritance and partition in a joint Hindu family. A daughter just cannot be a coparcener like a son. This discrimination has been removed in Kerala, Tamil Nadu, Karnataka, Maharashtra and Gujarat. The Law Commission report recommending equal rights to daughters and sons in HUF property is gathering dust.

The community and the state must work together to ensure that our sisters enjoy full rights equal to men. The Constitution is supreme. Liberty and equality are the pillars of our Constitution. Let us make India a country of equal rights and dignity for women and men.

Bibliography

Afkhami, Mahnaz: Faith and Freedom: Women's Human Rights in the Muslim World, Syracuse Univ. Press, 1996.

Alam, Bilquis: 1981, Women Members of Union Parishad, A Few Statistics, NILG, Dhaka.

Ali, Aruna Asaf: Resurgence of Indian Women, Strosius Inc./Advent Books Division, 1991.

Arvind, Sharma : Women in World Religion, New York Press, New York, 1990.

Ashrafi, Talat Ara: Muslim Women in Changing Perspective, Commonwealth Publishers, New Delhi, 1992.

Bagilhole, Barbara Sexual Harassment. Contemporary Feminist Perspective, Open University Press, 1997.

Barry, Kathleen: Female Sexual Slavery, New York, NYU Press, 1979.

Bhai, N.: Harijan Women in Independent India, Delhi, BR Publishing 1986

Bowie, Fiona: Women and Missions: Past and Present: Anthropological and Historical Perceptions, Providence, Rhode Island: Berg, 1993.

Bullough, Vern and Bonnie Bullough: Women and Prostitution: A Social History, Buffalo, Prometheus Books, 1987.

Calman, J.: Toward Empowerment: Women and Politics in India, Colorado, Westview Press, 1992.

Campbell-Johnson, Alan: Mission with Mountbatten, London, Hale, 1982.

Chakrapani, C.: Changing Status and Role of Women in Indian Society, South Asia Books, 1994.

Chandra, S.K.: Development of Women Entrepreneurship in India. A Study of Public Policies and Programmes, New Delhi, Mittal 1991

Chaudhuri, Nupur: Western Women and Imperialism: Complicity and Resistance, Bloomington, Indiana University Press, 1992.

Chilly Collective: Breaking Anonymity: The Chilly Climate for Women Faculty, Wilfrid Laurier University, 1995.

Choi, Chungmoo: The Comfort Women: Colonialism, War, and Sex, Durham N.C., Duke University Press, 1997.

Cynthia Fuchs Epstein: Women in Law, University of Illinois Press, 1993.

Dak, T.M.: Women and Work in Indian Society, Delhi, Discovery, 1988.

Datta, V.N.: Sati: Widow Burning in India, New Delhi, Manohar, 1990.

Dixon-Mueller, R.: Women's Work in Third World Agriculture, Geneva, ILO, 1985.

Dube, L. & Palriwala, R.: Structures and Strategies. Women, Work and Family, New Delhi, Sage 1990.

Feldhaus, Anne: Images of Women in Maharashtrian Literature and Religion, SUNY Press, 1996.

Gilligan, C.: In a Different Voice: Psychological Theory and Women's Development, Cambridge, Harvard University Press, 1993.

Grewal, Inderpal: Home and Harem: Nation, Gender, Empire, and the Cultures of Travel, Durham, Duke University Press, 1996.

Hogan, Anne: Women of Faith in Victorian Culture: Reassessing the Angel in the House, New York, St. Martin's Press, 1998.

Jain, D.: Women's Quest for Power, Sahibabad, Vikas, 1980.

Jamison, Stephanie: Sacrificed Wife/Sacrificer's Wife: Women, Ritual, and Hospitality in Ancient India, Oxford. 1996.

Jordan, J. V.: Women's Growth in Diversity, New York, Guilford Press, 1997.

Jumani, U.: Dealing with Poverty. Self-employment for Poor, Rural Women, London, Sage 1991.

Karl Marilee: 1995, Women and Empowerment: Participation and Decision-Making, Zed Books Limited, London.

Kaul, Rekha: Caste, Class and Education: Politics of the Capitation Fee Phenomenon in Karnataka, New Delhi, Sage Publications, 1993.

Kelles-Viitanen, A.: Invisible Hands. Women in Home-based Production, New Delhi, Sage, 1987.

Khan, N.S.: Against All Odds: Essays on Women, Religion and Development from India and Pakistan, Delhi, Isis International and Kali for Women 1994

Kwok, Pui-lan: Chinese Women and Christianity, 1860-1927, Atlanta, Scholars Press, 1992.

Lawes, Carolyn J.: Women and Reform in a New England Community, 1815-1860, Lexington, University Press of Kentucky, 2000.

Leslie, J.: Toward Empowerment: Women and Politics in India, Colorado, Westview Press, 1992.

Lois Benjamin: Black Women in the Academy: Promises and Perils, University Press of Florida, 1997.

Mathur, B.B.: Women and Depressed Class Population in India, Allahabad, Chugh, 1994.

Mueller, R.: Women's Work in Third World Agriculture, Geneva, ILO, 1985.

Nadya Aisenberg: Women of Academe: Outsiders in the Sacred Grove, University of Massachusetts Press, 1988.

Nanda, B.R.: Indian Women. From Purdah to Modernity, New Delhi, Vikas, 1976.

Palriwala, R.: Structures and Strategies. Women, Work and Family, New Delhi, Sage 1990.

Ray., Raka: Fields of Protest: Women's Movements in India, Univ. of Minnesota Press, 1999.

Roy, Manisha: Bengali Women, Univ. of Chicago Press, 1992.

Selliah, S.: The Self-Employed Women's Association, Ahmedabad, Geneva, ILO, 1989.

Singh, S.: Women's Studies in India. Information Sources, Services and Programmes, New Delhi, Sage, 1993.

Tinker, I.: Persistent Inequalities: Women and World Development, New York, OUP, 1990.

Viitanen, A.: Invisible Hands. Women in Home-based Production, New Delhi, Sage, 1987.

Visweswaran, Kamala: Fictions of Feminist Ethnography. Univ. of Minnesota Press, 1994.

Vyas, A. & Singh, S.: Women's Studies in India. Information Sources, Services and Programmes, New Delhi, Sage, 1993.

Yohn, Susan M: A Contest of Faiths: Missionary Women and Pluralism in the American Southwest. Ithaca, Cornell University Press, 1995.

Index

L

M

N

O

P

♦♦♦

Index

L

M

N

O

P

♦♦♦